From the Series Editor

In an era of educational reform where new labels often only substitute for truly new practices, Valerie Lee and Julia Smith in this volume take a hard look at school restructuring, a term used by too many to signify not enough. By framing their work in a thoughtful theoretical analysis of the social organization of schools, they provide a contextual understanding missing from much contemporary work on restructuring. By basing their work on careful empirical analyses, they guard against idle speculation. The combination of theory and data evident throughout the book provides a solid foundation to examine some of the most practical concerns confronting educators and educational policy makers. The authors address a host of concrete issues faced by those operating and working in middle schools and high schools. In addition, they deal directly with issues such as school size that raise questions for a wider community of policy makers, and ultimately the public. They draw on their research to offer a perspective on the difficulty of changing schools. Throughout this volume, the focus returns to a consideration of student learning. The treatment of context, organization, structure, and learning makes this book an important addition to the Sociology of Education Series.

Gary Natriello

Restructuring High Schools for Equity and Excellence

WHAT WORKS

Valerie E. Lee

with Julia B. Smith

Foreword by
Anthony S. Bryk

TEACHERS
COLLEGE
PRESS

Teachers College, Columbia University
New York and London

Published by Teachers College Press, 1234 Amsterdam Avenue, New York, NY 10027

Authors' note: the following chapters appeared in an earlier form. Their original titles are cited below, as well as the publication in which they appeared:
Chapter 3. Lee, V. E., & Smith, J. B. (1993). Effects of school restructuring on the achievement and engagement of middle-grade students. *Sociology of Education*, 66(3), 164–187. © 1993 the American Sociological Association. Adapted with permission.
Chapter 4. Lee, V. E., & Smith, J. B. (1995). Effects of high school restructuring and size on early gains in achievement and engagement. *Sociology of Education*, 68(3), 241–270. © 1995 the American Sociological Association. Adapted with permission.
Chapter 5. Lee, V. E., & Smith, J. B. (1996). Collective on gains in achievement for early secondary school students. *American Journal of Education*, 104, 103–147. © 1996 by the University of Chicago. Adapted with permission.
Chapter 6. Lee, V. E., Smith, J. B., & Croninger, R. G. (1997, April). How high school organization influences the equitable distribution of learning in mathematics and science. *Sociology of Education*, 70, 128–250. © 1997 the American Sociological Association. Adapted with permission.
Chapter 7. Lee, V. E., & Smith, J. B. (1997). High school size: Which works best and for whom? *Educational Evaluation and Policy Analysis*, 19(3), 205–227. © 1997 by the American Education Research Association. Adapted with permission.

Library of Congress Cataloging-in-Publication Data
Lee, Valerie E.
   Restructuring high schools for equity and excellence : what works / Valerie E. Lee with Julia B. Smith ; foreword by Anthony S. Bryk
     p. cm. — (Sociology of education series)
   Includes bibliographical references and index.
   ISBN 0-8077-4055-1 (cloth : alk. paper) — ISBN 0-8077-4054-3 (pbk. : alk. paper)
   1. High schools—United States—Administration.   2. Educational equalization—United States.   3. Educational change—United States.
I. Smith, Julia B., 1962–   . II. Title.   III. Sociology of education series (New York, N.Y.)
LB2822.2 .L44 2001
373.73—dc21   00-053273

ISBN 0-8077-4054-3 (paper)
ISBN 0-8077-4055-1 (cloth)

Printed on acid-free paper
Manufactured in the United States of America

08   07   06   05   04   03   02   01   8   7   6   5   4   3   2   1

for Maritza

Contents

Foreword

We live in interesting times. The current system of public education was formed over a hundred years ago in the cauldron of economic upheaval wrought by the industrial revolution and the rising social unrest associated with mass immigration of non-English speaking, non-Protestants at the turn of the century. We are now amidst a similar "revolution" that again is economic, technological, and social. Student populations have again become more diverse. Technology has changed virtually every workplace and is affecting schools as well. On the economic front, both business and civic leaders agree that improving the quality of education is a national priority. Indeed, schools are improving, but perhaps not fast enough to keep pace with these other forces. While the precise direction of change remains unclear, it seems quite possible that we will witness the emergence of a new paradigm for publicly supported schooling over the next 10 years.

Also, research has documented dramatic changes in the economic value of educational attainment over the last two decades. Many analysts worry that we are evolving into a two-tier economy where formal schooling becomes a strict gatekeeper to those who gain access to well paying jobs and those who do not. Serious academic work, which was only required for a few in the past, has now become a universal aim. Whereas just two decades ago we would have triumphed an increase in basic skill scores in reading and mathematics and a reduction of high school dropouts, reform rhetoric now emphasizes "World Class Standards" of academic attainment for all.

Equally compelling arguments for change arise as we consider the intellectual demands for effective political participation in an increasingly complex democratic society. It has been long recognized that the vitality of a democratic government depends on the social intelligence of its citizenry. Considerably more than a minimal level of skills in reading and mathematics are needed now if citizens are to engage meaningfully in public debates on issues such as reforming social security, global warming, or how best to improve our health care system. The modest academic aims of public schooling that served most citizens adequately in the past are unlikely to meet the needs of a critical-thinking public.

It is especially in times of great social upheaval such as the one now confronting us in public education that visionary ideas matter most. Unfortunately, we also now confront a cacophony of opinions about what should be done. Within the past decade, we have seen the emergence of efforts at comprehensive school redesign. States and districts are experimenting with various forms of decentralization, chartering, and contracting. Also ongoing are efforts to reorganize teachers' and students' work, intensive scrutiny of teachers' knowledge and skills, and efforts to introduce "best practices" into classrooms. An expansive array of policy initiatives intended to advance school improvement has emerged around accountability, professional development, and student assessment. Literally every aspect of the basic structure of public education has been seriously challenged, and new reforms seem to be introduced almost continuously somewhere across the national landscape.

Whatever direction public education takes in the years ahead—whether it be a systemic reform driven by high-stakes testing or a dramatic turn toward competition and choice—these developments need to be informed by the best possible research about the processes of teaching and learning, about the capacities to develop professionals and organize schools toward more ambitious aims, and about how to shape policy environments to promote such improvement. It is unfortunate that too little of today's school reform movement is actually informed by such evidence.

Much to Valerie Lee and Julia Smith's credit, the research presented in this volume pushes us strongly in that direction. An important conclusion stands out very clearly in their findings. Organizing schools to achieve high levels of academic attainment for all students is not a simple task. Lee and Smith remind us that, while individual school restructuring practices can help, no single practice or set of practices constitutes the "silver bullet." Yes, new instructional materials can make a difference. Better staff matters. New organizational structures and smaller schools are needed. But in the end, Lee and Smith demonstrate that advancing academic achievement for all students requires deep organizational changes, both structural and cultural, in the nature of schools as a workplace for students and adults alike. Absent such broad-based organizational improvement, Lee and Smith's findings demonstrate that school restructuring can be just one more version of a less than adequate educational reform déjà vu.

Anthony S. Bryk
Chicago, Illinois

Preface

How can schools work better than they do? Can schools simultaneously induce both excellence and equity, defined in terms of how much their students learn and which students learn what? If so, how might schools accomplish these very desirable aims? Answering these questions has occupied much of my professional activity for almost two decades. These same questions have also motivated the research described in this book. The book's focus narrows somewhat the scope of these very broad questions, in that it focuses on adolescents and their secondary school experiences. Moreover, the book's sights are set on a set of contemporary school reforms that are drawn together under the umbrella label, "school restructuring."

My interest in, and attention to, these questions has grown during my participation in two separate research projects. The more recent project, which is directly connected to the work described in this book, is the Center on Organization and Restructuring of Schools (CORS), in which I participated as a principal investigator. Beginning in 1990, CORS was a five-year program of research that was sponsored by the U.S. Department of Education, headquartered at the University of Wisconsin, and directed by Professor Fred M. Newmann.

Fred Newmann was an inspirational leader who worked hard to build a community of scholars that included Karen Seashore Louis, Adam Gamoran, Walter Secada, Anthony Bryk, and Helen Marks as regular members. Fred and this wonderful set of colleagues comprised a community that made my participation in CORS an exceptionally enriching experience. Even more important to me than the financial support from CORS for this work (although this was critical), membership in this team was something that any researcher is likely to experience only rarely but values greatly.

Although the CORS association is more directly and recently tied to the research described in this book, I have accrued more foundational and more enduring benefits from participating in an earlier research project. Beginning in 1981 as an older, nontraditional student in Administration, Planning, and Social Policy at the Harvard Graduate School of Education, I was associated with a project that studied U.S. Catholic high schools and compared them to counterpart public schools. The work is described in *Catholic Schools and the Common Good* (1993), which was co-authored by Anthony Bryk, Peter Holland, and me.

Tony Bryk, together with my doctoral colleague Peter Holland, had been commissioned by the National Catholic Educational Association to conduct a modestly-funded study of Catholic high schools. The study was to use field-work both in a modest number of "good" Catholic high schools and High School and Beyond (HS&B), a new, large, and nationally representative study of students in high school whose first wave became available in 1981. Tony asked me, based on my modest but developing research skills, to conduct the quantitative analyses for this project. Looking back, I am embarrassed to admit to my initial reluctance to accept this offer. I had little interest in Catholic education, I was not Catholic myself, I wasn't educating my children in Catholic schools, and I surely did not see these schools as the shining beacons of how public schools should be organized.

As they say, the rest is history. The Catholic schools project and my research collaboration with Tony Bryk represent seminal events in my life. Early in that work and in my doctoral program, I decided that I wanted to do with my life what Tony did—be an academic, do educational research, write about it, and guide a few fledging researchers along the way. Tony has been a serious mentor, a demanding taskmaster, an excellent guide, and a wonderful colleague. We have continued our work together, even after completion of the "Catholic school book"—first with CORS and more recently through the Chicago Annenberg Research Project and the Consortium for Chicago School Research. It is difficult for me to separate my experience on the Catholic school project from my work with Tony Bryk. But both have been absolutely foundational for me. Although words are a feeble means to express my gratitude, I'll say them anyway: "Thanks, Tony!"

What about the Catholic school work motivated this book? I learned first-hand that it is possible for schools to simultaneously induce both excellence and equity in their students, defined in terms of academic learning and its equitable distribution. My dissertation focused on this topic. Our research on Catholic schools also highlighted two important organizational dimensions of these schools that largely explain the positive outcomes that accrue to their students. The first dimension concerns how schools organize their academic curriculum: which courses they choose to offer and which they decide not to offer, and which students are mapped to which courses. The second important dimension focuses on school social organization, what we have called "communal school organization." Here, the focus is on how human beings (especially teachers and students) relate to one another in school. As will be clear in Part III of this book, these larger organizational dimensions of schools emerge as important, above and beyond the focus in Part II on school restructuring.

Although the two research projects described above (and the leaders of those projects) have been foundational for the research described in this book, equally important to the work is the enormous contribution of my colleague Julia Smith. Julia's work with me began with her entry as a doctoral student in the Foundations and Policy program at the University of Michigan's School of Education, where I served as her advisor. She has worked with me on several research projects, including the CORS-sponsored work, and our collaboration continues. In general, our research collaboration has involved a fundamental sharing of ideas that we develop in common and also embed into (and develop from) the existing literature. Based on our theorizing, our common understanding of the research base in which our work is located, we sketch out an analysis strategy to explore our research questions with data. Although Julia's skills in the areas of theory and review are very strong, her skills in analyzing data are exceptional. In the middle of a professional collaboration that has endured and that continues, I pause to say, "Thanks, Julie!"

A large group of people have helped enormously with this work, beyond the major contributions from Julia Smith, Anthony Bryk, and Fred Newmann. Dating back to the CORS project, I am grateful for Diane Randall's help with administrative details, as well as her sympathetic and supportive presence. Editors and anonymous reviewers from the several journals in which our restructuring studies have appeared helped to clarify our presentations, our writing, and our thinking. More important, they have allowed us to share our developing research about school restructuring with our academic colleagues. I am grateful to various publishers for permission to incorporate into this book material that appeared in slightly different form elsewhere. In the process of moving the ideas and work about school restructuring into a book, I am terribly grateful to Vickie Wellman, who produced almost all of the many graphs in the book. Vickie continues to provide much more than secretarial support for my work.

My associations with Teachers College Press have been both productive and positive. Susan Liddicoat, Acquisitions Editor, not only began conversations with me about the book, but she has shepherded me through virtually every stage of the process. Together with Gary Natriello, the Sociology of Education series editor for Teachers College Press, Susan has helped me to refine what began as a rough idea into the book you hold in your hands. Aureliano Vazquez, the Production Editor at the press, was extremely helpful and gracious in the final editorial stages, asking just the right questions to make sure that the small details came out right.

Beginning a totally new career as I did in my 40s has required psychic and physical support from my children. Although they were both away at school when I started graduate work (my daughter Allison in college and my son Matthew in boarding school), their graceful transition from expecting their mother to take care of their needs to partnership with me in our educational and professional journeys together is lovingly appreciated. Especially exciting were the two years when Matthew and I were students together at Harvard, he as a freshman and sophomore living in a dorm in the Harvard yard and I as a doctoral student spending long nights at the computer center. Our casual encounters at the same university were wonderful, as were his occasional raids of my refrigerator and drop-in invitations to "do lunch." As Allison and Matthew have moved into and through their own careers as professionals and parents, their support and, perhaps, pride in their mother's accomplishments mean very much to me. My grandchildren Henry Cole, Celestina Lee, and Joey Ramos know what an academic life is all about. Hopefully they value a grandmother who works hard, loves them very much, but doesn't see them as often as she would like.

Many people have provided me with enormous help and support as I have conducted the research and written up the findings that comprise this book, many more than I have mentioned here. Although they may rightfully take credit for all that is good about this work, the responsibility for any mistakes therein rests squarely on my shoulders.

Valerie E. Lee
Ann Arbor, Michigan

PART I

Context for the Study

This is a book about the restructuring of American schools, a topic that has received considerable attention from policymakers, school practitioners, and researchers in the last two decades. Although much attention has been directed to this subject, we believe our work adds several new dimensions. Much of the existing writing has focused on the meaning of school restructuring, the reasons American schools have been subject to so much criticism in recent years, and what it is about schools that restructuring is meant to change. Most of this book, however, describes empirical research that investigates the *effects* on students who attend restructured schools, particularly secondary schools. In particular, we explore how membership in schools with particular structures and organizational forms influences how much students learn. In Part I we describe the context in which the empirical work (spelled out in Parts II and III) is embedded. Chapter 1 explains the research background for our empirical work. In Chapter 2 we provide descriptive information about the schools we study and the students who attend them.

CHAPTER 1

Examining School Reform

The beliefs that Americans hold about education are both strong and contradictory. Throughout our history Americans have always had great faith in the power of education as a means to transform society. Americans view education, according to Tyack and Cuban (1995), as "a secular religion." There is a long-standing belief that through the public schools, Americans not only can influence what children (their own and others') learn, but also solve a myriad of social and economic ills. On the one hand, Americans continue to have confidence—even faith—in the power of education to improve society. On the other hand, Americans' support for, and public confidence in, their schools has declined over time. This decline of support has led to increasingly frequent and ever more strident calls to fix the schools, the vehicles to deliver formal education to our citizens.

Calls for school reform are usually issued in response to some problem. For much of our history, a pervasive moral decline has been invoked as a reason that schools should be changed. Although this "problem" has not left the lexicon of public discussions about education, in the last two decades the language surrounding the need for reforming schools has shifted. Currently, the rationale for reform—the problem to be fixed—is defined more often in economic than in moral terms. In what Tyack and Cuban (1995) call "a fire-and-brimstone sermon about education" (p. 1), the federally sponsored report *A Nation at Risk: The Imperative for Educational Reform* mobilized the nation almost two decades ago to fix its schools or suffer dire economic consequences (National Commission on Excellence in Education [NCEE], 1983). Many voices joined a chorus of blame directed at the schools for inadequate preparation of the U.S. work force, the low position American students attain in international achievement comparisons, and the apparent inability of the nation's students to respond to increasing demands for technological expertise. The chorus is still singing the same song, but the number of voices in the chorus is swelling.

Since the *Nation at Risk* report appeared in 1983, demand for reforming U.S. schools has occurred in two "waves" (Elmore & Associates, 1990). In the first reform wave, which still rolls toward our shores, our citizens have been alerted to the sparse academic content of the high school curriculum; a tightening of standards is called for across the educational system. "Second-wave" reforms demand more fundamental changes in our schools than just stronger curricula and higher standards. The restructuring movement is located within this second wave. The societal problems that motivate a need for reform of U.S. schools continue to be couched largely in economic and competitive terms, with occasional references to social inequality and injustice and to the changing demographic composition of U.S. society. Despite a record-breaking period of economic prosperity, more enduring social and economic problems faced by U.S. society are still seen as dire if we hope to attain (or retain) our first-in-the-world position. Therefore, second-wave reform typically demands fundamental restructuring rather than incremental change in American schools.

WHAT IS SCHOOL RESTRUCTURING?

One feature of the call to restructure schools, and an important reason to explain why support for it is so widespread, is the ambiguity of the term (Conley, 1993; Elmore & Associates, 1990; Fennimore, 2000; Murphy & Hallinger, 1993; Newmann, 1993). Such ambiguity allows people to attach their own meaning to the concept. Conley (1993) defines a hierarchy in types of educational change, what he calls "the three Rs": renewal, reform, and restructuring. Renewal activities, although they help existing organizations function more efficiently, do not really change what those organizations actually do. Reform activities reach somewhat deeper, in that they change existing procedures and rules in an organization in order to help it adapt to changing circumstances. Only the third R, restructuring, involves activities that "change fundamental assumptions, practices, and relationships, both within the organization and between the organization and the outside world, in ways that lead to improved and varied outcomes for essentially all students" (pp. 8–9).

What Needs to Be Reformed?

Beyond general agreement about the value of ambiguity in allowing widespread support for this movement, the writers on this topic generally agree that school restructuring aims to improve both the *level* and the *nature* of what students learn in schools. Almost all writers agree that restructuring involves profound rather than incremental changes in schools, and that radical new models of schooling are needed. Similar to the second-wave reforms described by Elmore and his colleagues (1990) are "second-order" reforms described by Cuban (1988) and Fullan (1991). According to Elmore, they "alter the fundamental ways in which organizations are put together, including new goals, structures, and roles" (p. 29).

Beyond the writers' agreement that fundamental change is needed, they also share opinions about what needs to be changed. The conventional wisdom that developed in the 1980s and early 1990s centered on the need for fundamental change along three dimensions that define how schools are organized: (1) how educational organizations are *governed* (including changes in authority stuctures), (2) how students' and teachers' *work is organized*, and (3) the incentive stucture and standards around which student and school *performance* is organized (Elmore & Associates, 1990; Newmann & Associates, 1996).

Providing a Conceptual Framework for Reform

Much of what has been written about school restructuring in the last decade has aimed to provide a theoretical framework for the concept. Conley (1993) compiled what he calls a "roadmap to restructuring." His comprehensive book, aimed at a practitioner audience, attempts to provide both a conceptual history of the movement and an extensive compilation and summary of writings about it. Elmore and his colleagues (1990) provide very useful conceptual models to flesh out the construct. In an edited volume, Hallinan (1995) compiled a group of essays that describe promising practices that fall under the umbrella of school restructuring.

Two books (Elmore, Peterson, & McCarthey, 1996; Murphy & Hallinger, 1993) provide descriptive case studies of several elementary schools that have restructured, one of which focuses on only one dimension: teaching and learning (Elmore & Associates, 1996). In a series of thoughtful books, Theodore Sizer (1984, 1992, 1996) spells out his vision of structural reform in secondary schools (the Coalition of Essential Schools) that is conceptually consistent with other writings about school restructuring. A summary of research about (or consistent with) the Coalition of Essential Schools also draws on several writings about restructuring (MacMullen, 1996). Two influential foundation reports recommend fundamental changes in U.S. middle-grade and secondary schools that are consistent with restructuring (Carnegie Council on Adolescent Development, 1989; National Association of Secondary School Principals [NASSP], 1996). Another book suggests that recent educational reforms are heavily influenced by the involvement of American businesses (Fennimore, 2000). This involvement extends to the language used to talk about reform; the term restructuring came from, and is still quite common in, the business world (Ellis & Fouts, 1994).

Taken as a whole, this body of writing has been extremely useful in clarifying ideas about the meaning and purpose of the school restructuring movement. Attempting to present some first-level empirical data about this topic, some authors have provided useful information about particular sites where restructuring has occurred. However, none of these writings claims to present empirical research that investigates how restructuring affects the school members who experience it (beyond the few case-study descriptions). Useful as these writings are, they provide little information about the effectiveness of restructuring in the settings where it has occurred. In fact, most of these writings describe the difficulty of actually instigating and sustaining fundamental change in schools and explore why such change is so difficult.

GROUNDING FOR OUR STUDY

The empirical research that we present in this book, which focuses on how attending restructured schools influences the students in those schools, was sponsored by the Center on Organization and Restructuring of Schools (CORS). The intellectual underpinnings for this book spring from a very fruitful association with CORS researchers and especially with Fred M. Newmann, who served as the director of this federally funded research center at the University of Wisconsin from 1990 through 1995.

The CORS Research Programs

Newmann and the CORS research team have greatly influenced three major areas of the restructuring movement. First, CORS developed a detailed definition of school restructuring around which the center's work was organized. Second, the center also sponsored a series of empirical studies that investigated the functioning of school restructuring and how it influences students and teachers. Third, CORS disseminated the findings from this research and spelled out the conceptual underpinnings of school restructuring to a broad network of school practitioners, educational researchers, and the interested public.

Two large and complementary programs of research were sponsored by CORS over the center's 5-year life (Newmann & Wehlage, 1995). The major program, the School Restructuring Study (SRS), involved an in-depth study of 24 U.S. public schools (8 elementary, 8 middle, and 8 high schools) that had adopted unconventional organizational features proposed by advocates of restructuring. These included "site-based management, shared decision making, teacher teaming, sustained student advisory groups, coordination of social services, and school choice" (Newmann & Associates, 1996, p. xii). The second major program of research under CORS sponsorship is the set of studies we undertook and report on in this book.

The CORS Concept of Restructuring

Our own conceptualization of restructuring was developed and refined during our 5-year participation in CORS, where we attended monthly meetings where all phases of the full research program were discussed. Recognizing that there is no general agreement about the criteria that define a restructured school, the CORS team started with the fact that a school cannot be classified as either restructured or conventional. Rather, restructuring should be seen as a continuum of *departures from conventional practice*.

Restructuring can occur in many settings. Some schools "restructure themselves" when they engage in major reforms along several structural dimensions. In an attempt to impose some order on the possibilities for restructuring schools, CORS defined four reform dimensions: (1) student experiences; (2) teachers' professional lives; (3) the governance and management of schools; and (4) coordination of community resources around schools (Wisconsin Center for Education Research, 1990).

Although some schools change from existing to new structures, other restructured schools begin anew, organizing themselves in new ways. In fact, a subtantial proportion of the 24 schools in the SRS were of this sort: new or completely reconstituted schools, rather than schools that had moved themselves gradually from one form to another. Although those 24 schools shared no single or common set of structural features, each had implemented a number of changes of six different types. Moreover, the changes schools selected were seldom grouped into only one of these types.

1. Some schools had found ways to personalize students' experiences, to bring school members into more frequent and more sustained contact with one another.
2. Many SRS schools organized their teachers into interdisciplinary or grade-level teams, teachers who often worked collaboratively with a relatively small group of students.
3. Most of the students in SRS schools were instructed in heterogeneously grouped classes; the schools had either eliminated or substantially reduced tracking and ability grouping.
4. Many schools had imposed common standards for student learning, often accompanied by new forms of assessment.

5. Most of the schools in the SRS had obtained some degree of autonomy from their districts or states, with considerable local contol over curriculum, budgets, and staffing.

6. Many SRS schools involved their students in community-based learning (Newmann & Associates, 1996).

As will be apparent in later chapters, where we describe how we captured the concept of measured school restructuring in the several studies in this book, all of these dimensions were considered as criteria for selecting reform practices that we defined as examples of restructuring. Both the SRS and our work were conducted over the 5 years of CORS; the two programs of study advanced simultaneously. Almost every detail of the research studies described in this book was discussed in depth at the monthly meetings of CORS senior research staff. Although all CORS staff struggled with the ambiguity of the restructuring concept in the studies they worked on, the advantage of such a process is that we can report considerable internal consistency among the CORS-sponsored research in how we have defined it.

EMBEDDING RESTRUCTURING IN ORGANIZATIONAL THEORY

Beyond writings about school restructuring and the conceptual work from CORS, we also embed our work in a larger and more theoretical body of research, mostly sociological in nature, that focuses on features of school organization. An organization's structure refers to the relationships between members around its technical core of work (Perrow, 1967; Simon, 1976). The "technical core" refers to the major work accomplished in schools: the organization and implementation of instruction.

A Useful Organizational Contrast

Because the research described in this book links the organizational form of schools to the achievement of their students, we rely on a theory focusing on how the instructional "core technology" of schools is organized: as a bureaucracy or as a community. The grounding for this contrast has been developed by such classical sociologists as Max Weber, Emile Durkheim, Talcott Parsons, Pitirim Sorokin, and Ferdinand Tonnies. The theory in a form that applies to schools was articulated by Bryk and Driscoll (1988).

As the two organizational forms hold different conceptions of the core technology, their assumptions about knowledge, learning, and teaching are quite different. The bureaucratic form assumes a technology that is routine, clear, and stable. The communal form assumes a nonroutine core technology (Burns & Stalker, 1961; Rowan, 1990). These assumptions influence the organizational structure of schools. Although the theory is applicable to schools at all levels, our discussion here focuses on high schools. Our conceptualization of schools as communities, as well as our interests in identifying organizational characteristics that are associated with schools being both effective and equitable, was developed over the course of several years' involvement in research that compares Catholic and public high schools (Bryk, Lee, & Holland, 1993).

BUREAUCRATICALLY ORGANIZED SCHOOLS

Work roles in bureaucratic organizations are typically specialized and differentiated, organized into a top-down hierarchy of decision making, and characterized by formal goals and expectations that are codified through affectively neutral rules and codes of behavior (Bryk & Driscoll, 1988; Newmann & Oliver, 1967; Rowan, 1990). Bureaucratic schools would break down knowledge into a curriculum composed of discrete and fixed subjects. Teaching, the core activity in schools, would aim to impart specialized knowledge, with instruction organized into a standardized and sequenced pattern within subjects. Learning would be assessed by measuring mastery of subject matter.

Learners would be sorted into specialized instructional treatments, aimed to appropriately match subject matter to learners based on ability, interest, and plans for the future. The organization of instruction into ability groups and tracks is consistent with a specialization model. Such first-wave reforms as increasing academic standards, tightening graduation requirements, and teacher-proof curriculum materials fit the bureaucratic model.

COMMUNALLY ORGANIZED SCHOOLS

At the other end of this spectrum is the communal form, where tasks are less certain and conditions more changeable and unpredictable (Brown, 1997; Bryk & Driscoll, 1988; Newmann & Oliver, 1967; Plowman, 1998; Rowan, 1990). Organizations with this form would emphasize shared responsibility for work, shared commitment to a common set of goals, lateral communication and power in decision making, and greater personalization and individual discretion in framing expectations and behavior.

In schools with this form, typical of small high schools in the early 20th century (especially those in rural areas), knowledge would be seen as multidimensional and interdisciplinary. Teaching would respond to students' opinions, talents, and tastes. Learning would be built more around concrete "problems" than abstract "subjects," and assessment would be more flexible and less standardized. The communal school might organize its core technology around independent study, interdisciplinary teaching, flexible scheduling, cooperative learning, and mixed-ability classes.

Dominance of the Bureaucratic Form

Theories that define these alternative forms of how schools are organized, and how teaching and learning might reflect these forms, are not new. Rather, the theories are well established in American education; they have undergirded historical and theoretical debates about the proper direction for school reform for at least a century (Cuban, 1984, 1990; Tyack & Cuban, 1995). Although both forms have always been discussed, one form has dominated the organizational structure of secondary schools for at least a century. "Scientific" management of the progressive era aimed to move schools away from their particularlistic (and probably communal) forms and localized designs in a bureaucratic direction. The "perfect" product of progressive educational reforms and of the bureaucratic organizational form is the American comprehensive high school (Powell, Farrar, & Cohen, 1985).

Although many reforms have aimed to make the traditional system "work better" (what Tyack and Cuban [1995] would call "tinkering"), the bureaucratic structure of the U.S. high school was itself assumed to be solid—until the early 1980s. Despite a history of educational discussions that have drawn on both theories, the bureaucratic form still constitutes the "tradition" against which reforms grouped under the restructuring umbrella are targeted. The two theories of school organization provide a useful lens through which to view the restructuring movement. Calls to restructure schools suggest a fundamental shift away from the bureaucratic and toward the communal organizational model. The modern comprehensive high school is a conservative organization, however, where fundamental change is difficult. Much of the criticism of high schools has targeted their bureaucratic form (e.g., Angus & Mirel, 1999; Boyer, 1983; Goodlad, 1984; NASSP, 1996; NCEE, 1983; Powell et al., 1985; Sizer, 1984). Although reform rhetoric is high-pitched, reforms with a communal form are less common than those not meant to disturb the heart of an essentially bureaucratic organization.

Reforms aimed at nudging the organization from a bureaucratic toward a communal form require real effort to initiate, do not take hold easily, are resisted by many, and are firmly in place in a very few high schools. The definition of school restructuring to which we subscribe—substantial departure from conventional practice—captures this idea. This contention is supported by recent research attempting to measure the extent of fundamental school restructuring. Although schoolwide reform is quite rare (Berends &

King, 1994; Brown, 1993; Fink, 2000; Westheimer, 1998), the implementation of practices reflecting the *spirit* of reform may be more common.

Differing Approaches to Student Learning

A primary goal of all schools is that their students learn. Despite similar goals, schools' organizational forms surely influence how they accomplish this goal. One way of capturing this difference is to examine how schools with the two forms might respond to diversity among students. Under the bureaucratic form, the avowed purpose of matching instruction (and content) to students' ability is to maximize the amount of demonstrable learning for each individual—in essence, to develop as much human capital as possible, based on available "raw material." "Diversity" would be defined mainly in cognitive terms, with instruction specialized to best respond to differences in students' ability.

Communally organized schools also aim to maximize learning, but they are more likely to define and emphasize a common set of academic needs seen as appropriate for all students, regardless of cognitive capacity. The curriculum would not depend on students' abilities, preparation, or plans, although the means for arriving at the goal might be responsive to students' skill levels. For example, the pace of moving through the same material could vary. Students would be expected to experience a set of common academic activities in communally organized schools. These different approaches to maximizing student learning might affect schools' average achievement differently. Just as important, these approaches might also influence the distribution of learning among students, based on their academic and social background characteristics.

THE STRUCTURE OF OUR STUDY

As mentioned, the focus of the research described in this book is on high schools and their students. In addition, our work may be characterized along several distinctive dimensions.

Studying Change Over Time

Most of the research we describe is longitudinal in nature; that is, we investigated how students *changed over time*, and how that change was influenced by the schools they attended. We examined the same students at three important time points in their secondary-school trajectory: just before they began high school (the end of 8th grade), midway through their high-school years (the end of 10th grade), and just before they graduated (the end of 12th grade).

Using Large and Nationally Representative Samples

Our work, although conducted under the sponsorship of CORS, differs from the SRS study of 24 of the most restructured schools in the country in several other ways besides the longitudinal nature of our studies and their focus on high schools. We studied a much larger number of schools than the SRS (close to 800 high schools). These schools were representative of the population of U.S. high schools in the early 1990s. Thus, although the large majority of schools were public high schools, included in our sample of schools was also a representative group of Catholic high schools and non-Catholic elite private (so-called independent) schools. We used quantitative methods, organizing our work around a research tradition that is known as "school effects" research.

A major advantage of our work in comparison with other studies of school restructuring is exactly that we studied a nationally representative sample of U.S. high schools and their students as they developed over time. Of course, this broad focus in some sense also restricts our ability for profound study of school restructuring. The CORS staff engaged in a systematic search for schools that were substantially restructured, but they actually found very few (Berends & King, 1994). Because the schools we studied were representative of the population of U.S. high schools, a very small proportion were substantially restructured in ways that would satisfy the CORS definition. That means that we studied a large number of comprehensive high schools.

Focusing on Learning

The longitudinal nature of the data we used allowed us to focus on how students changed over time in a number of ways. Although we investigated change along several dimensions in which adolescents develop, our primary focus in the research reported in this book is on learning. We say "learning," rather than "achievement," because we investigated how students' performance on standardized tests in several subjects (reading, mathematics, science, and social studies) changed over time. Thus, we define learning by investigating change (or growth) in these areas of the curriculum. Some have argued (e.g., Newmann, Marks, & Gamoran, 1996) that the type of learning that restructured schools attempt to induce through "authentic pedagogy" is more appropriately measured by using alternative forms of assessment, rather than standardized tests. In some sense, it could be the case that we systematically underestimated the effects of restructuring on student learning by using such "inauthentic" assessments as standardized and multiple-choice tests.

Focusing on Effectiveness and Equity

The efficacy of any school reform can be assessed using several criteria. Because we focus on achievement and learning, perhaps the most obvious criterion on which to assess whether restructuring "works" is to ask: Do students who attend restructured schools learn more than those who attend schools that have not been restructured? Answering such a question would imply that we focus on the outcome of average learning. If the answer to such a question were yes, then we might conclude that restructured schools were more effective—that is, that students who attend them learn more than those who do not. Of course, we would also need to take into account whether such schools attracted better students in the first place or were favored in some ways other than their restructuring status. This issue, what researchers usually call "selectivity bias," must be carefully considered in research of this type. We explain how we account for selectivity bias throughout the descriptions of our research.

A second criterion for assessing school efficacy might focus on *who* is learning more or less in a particular school. Using this second criterion—which we call equity—we might ask: Are there systematic differences in how much male and female students learn, between minority and white students, or between affluent and poor students? The desirable response to such questions, if a criterion of equity is used, would be no. In this book, we use the dual criteria of effectiveness and equity to assess the efficacy of school restructuring. An ideal school would be both effective and equitable. That is, students would learn a lot in such a school, and the learning would be equitably distributed by students' social background (i.e., by gender, race/ethnicity, and social class). We make use of the method for studying these two criteria of "good schools," reflecting the ideas we spell out here (and the methods we use), that is detailed by Bryk and Raudenbush (1992). In the analyses described in this book, we focus on the dual criteria of effectiveness and equity in assessing how attending restructured schools influences students' learning.

OVERVIEW OF THIS BOOK

The book is organized into four parts. In Part I, which includes Chapters 1 and 2, we lay out the context for the study. In this chapter we have provided some background about the origins of the movement to restructure high schools and described how our work differs from (and adds to) the existing body of writing and research about school restructuring. In Chapter 2, we describe the samples we used for our studies. Because the samples were representative, Chapter 2 also provides a picture of American students in their 8th-grade, 10th-grade, and 12th-grade years.

Parts II and III of the book present the empirical research about restructuring in chronological order. Part II focuses on research that assesses directly how restructuring schools influence the students who attend them. In Chapters 3 and 4, we devote considerable attention to how we measured the construct of "school restructuring." Beyond our focus on learning, measured as change over time in students' performance on tests of academic achievement, in these chapters we also describe our investigations of restructuring effects on several other outcomes. Chapter 3 focuses on what we call "middle-grade schools," schools that include eighth grade. Here, we investigated achievement, at-risk behaviors, and the degree to which students engage with school. Chapter 4 concentrates on students in the first 2 years of high school, and how their learning and engagement with school are influenced by the types of schools they attend. Here again, "types of schools" is defined by the degree to which they were restructured.

In Part III, we examine the idea of school restructuring through a larger organizational lens. Chapter 5, which also examines students in the first 2 years of high school, focuses on another aspect of restructuring: how teachers' work is organized. In Chapter 6, where we broaden our examination to students over their 4 years of high school, we pose two questions. First, we ask whether the restructuring effects we document in Chapter 4 were sustained in the last 2 years of high school. We also introduce into our analyses more fundamental properties of schools—particularly how they are organized in social and academic terms—to ask whether restructuring per se may actually be capturing more fundamental properties of schools. Chapter 7, which also focuses on students in their 12th-grade year, targets a structural feature of high schools that was part of all our analyses: the number of students they enroll.

In Part IV we spell out several larger lessons that we draw from the results of these studies. Although our work is organized around the concept of restructuring, we believe that the lens we have used to investigate contemporary U.S. high schools teaches quite a lot about the direction that reform should take.

CHAPTER 2

Who Goes Where? Characteristics of Students and Schools

The purpose of this chapter is to describe the students and schools we studied and to explain how we selected these samples. Our descriptions focus on adolescents and their schools at two important points in their educational trajectories: at the end of 8th grade (middle school) and in 10th and 12th grade (high school). Because the samples are representative of students in public and private schools in the United States in the late 1980s and early 1990s, we are describing the U.S. school populations during that period. All students were 8th graders in 1988, and most of them graduated from high school in 1992.

SELECTION OF SAMPLES

For all the research described in this book, we have used data from the National Educational Longitudinal Study of 1988 [NELS:88], a general-purpose study of the educational status and progress of a large and nationally representative sample of 8th-grade students in middle-grade schools sponsored by the National Center for Education Statistics in the U.S. Department of Education (Ingels, Abraham, Spencer, & Frankel, 1989). For the NELS sample, about 25 eighth graders in each of about 1,000 American middle-grade schools were randomly drawn in 1988, for an original student sample of about 25,000 students. We have limited our sample of students to those from the original NELS sample who have information available from the three major data sources for NELS: the student survey, the school survey, and scores on tests administered to all students.

The longitudinal nature of NELS:88 means that the same students were re-surveyed and re-tested in 8th grade, 10th grade, and 12th grade. For various reasons, small numbers of students were lost from the sample along the way. Some dropped out of school, others were left back, and still others changed from one high school to another. Because much of the research described in this book focuses on how *high school* structures influence students' achievement, we restricted our sample to students who stayed in the same high school until they graduated. Thus, although all students in the 12th-grade study (described in Chapters 6 and 7) were also in the 8th-grade study (described in Chapter 3), we did lose some students over the course of our progressive investigations. How, exactly, the makeup of the samples changed over time is discussed below.

The sample for Study 1 (described in Chapter 3) was drawn from the first wave of NELS:88. From these students, we used as our sample all students for whom student, parent, school, and testing data were available (about 12,000 students). In addition to the school survey included in NELS:88, we also used information about the schools from the Hopkins School Enhancement Survey (Epstein, McPartland, & MacIver, 1991). This school survey, not part of the original NELS data-collection effort, was completed in 1990. Moreover, it was not completed by all schools, providing another reason why our student sample is somewhat reduced from the full NELS sample.

Included in the sample for Studies 2 and 3 (described in Chapters 4 and 5) were all 10th graders from the original sample who also had high school data, test scores from 1990, and data from two of their teachers. Between 8th grade and high school, approximately 400 students were lost from the sample, mainly because they were not in high school in 1990, the year of the NELS:88 first follow-up (Ingels, Scott, Lindmark, Frankel, & Meyers, 1992). The studies of 12th graders (described in Chapters 6 and 7) saw the sample reduced again, this time by about 2,200 students (down to a little less than 10,000—Ingels, Dowd, Baldridge, Stripe, Bartot, & Frankel, 1994). Again, the primary cause for losing students from our analytic sample was because these students were not seniors in 1992; some dropped out of school, others were retained in grade. Although it is not the focus of our studies, it is surely of interest to policymakers that about a quarter of a nationally representative sample of 8th graders in 1988 did not finish high school 4 years later.

INFORMATION ABOUT STUDENTS

The students we studied were all in eighth grade in school year 1987–88. Beyond that commonality, several characteristics distinguish their social and academic backgrounds. In this section we describe the student sample in terms of background characteristics, particularly the characteristics that we have used consistently in the research described in the book.

Demographic Characteristics

Whenever researchers study academic performance, they are confronted with the reality that the students being compared are not comparable on many other characteristics related to school performance. Especially important here are students' social backgrounds. Throughout our investigations, we explored differences in student achievement as it relates to a small set of social-background characteristics: gender, racial/ethnic background, and socioeconomic status of parents. Socioeconomic status is a composite variable constructed from several indicators, all of which were drawn from data on the survey of students' parents: family income, parents' highest level of education, parents' occupational status, and the number of educationally related possessions in the home (e.g., 50 or more books, a dictionary, an encyclopedia, a calculator, and a computer).

In Table 2.1 we display these characteristics of our sample of students for the three time points measured in NELS: 8th grade, 10th grade, and 12th

Table 2.1. Gender, Ethnicity, and SES Characteristics Across the Three Study Samples

Variables	8th grade	10th grade	12th grade
Number of Students	12,020	11,692	9,631
Female (%)	50	51	51
Family size	4.65	4.25	4.13
Ethnic Group			
White (%)	67.5	72.2	73.1
African-American (%)	12.8	9.4	9.4
Hispanic (%)	13.4	12.4	11.5
Asian (%)	6.3	6.0	6.0
Socioeconomic Status			
Parent's education[a]	14.3	14.4	14.6
Family income 1988	$44,146	$45,840	$47,958
SES composite[b]	0.00	0.04	0.09

[a] Years of education of the more educated of the two parents, if both parents' education was reported.

[b] This is a standardized composite (M [mean] = 0, SD [standard deviation] = 1) that includes family income, parents' occupational prestige, parents' education, and the number of educational possessions in the home.

grade. Gender and racial/ethnic distribution are shown as percentages within each sample. Socioeconomic status (SES) is displayed in two ways: broken into its component parts and as a composite measure. The composite measure of SES was standardized to a mean of zero and a standard deviation (SD) of one (often called a "z-score"). In a sense, a score of 0 on the composite measure of SES can be thought of as a middle-class family, while 2 SD would reflect upper-class and –2 SD would reflect lower-class status. In general, the sample changed a bit with each round, becoming slightly more selective at each successive time point.

Although the sample at each grade level remained well balanced by gender, the racial/ethnic composition changed; the high school sample contained progressively more White students, with lower proportions of African Americans and Hispanics. The small proportion of Asian students remained stable over the three time points. However, the average SES of the samples rose slightly between 8th and 12th grade. This shift suggests that those students who graduate from high school 4 years after finishing 8th grade are from somewhat more advantaged households, with slightly higher family income and with parents with slightly more education, compared with the group who entered high school (or, technically, at the end of Grade 8).

Academic and Personal Background

In addition to their social backgrounds, students differ in important ways in terms of their academic backgrounds, their attitudes toward school, and their involvement in disruptive or anti-academic behaviors. One aim of the studies described in Chapters 3 to 7 was to determine how students' achievement varied in each school as a function of these different background characteristics.

THE TESTS

In NELS, students' academic achievement was measured at 8th, 10th, and 12th grade through four subject-specific and timed multiple-choice standardized tests. These tests examined students' knowledge and skills in the major content areas of the middle- and high school curriculum: reading comprehension, mathematics, science, and social studies. The number of questions on each test varied: 21 items in reading, 40 items in mathematics, 25 items in science, and 30 items in social studies. Over the three testing periods, although the number of items remained constant, individual test items varied somewhat. More difficult items were included at later years and simpler items were dropped. Although a general interpretation of the scores reported in this and other chapters is that they represent the number of right answers on each test, the actual scores were scaled with Item Response Theory, in order to equate the test score scales over different time points. This scaling was necessary to enable researchers to estimate subject-specific learning gains over the high school years—a major goal of NELS. A thorough discussion of the cognitive tests used in NELS is provided by Rock and Pollack (1995).

ACADEMIC BACKGROUND AND STUDENT SES

In Table 2.2 we show how students' academic characteristics at 8th grade are related to their SES. As our research focused on how students from different social backgrounds perform in school, we broke down these other background measures to better show initial differences between low-, average-, and high-SES students. For purposes of this comparison, we collapsed levels of "agreement" (for engagement) and "frequency" (for misbehavior) to show the percentage in each group who agreed (or agreed strongly) with the statements listed in Table 2.2, or frequently engaged in the behaviors shown.

It is clear that both school performance and frequency of misbehavior in eighth grade were related to SES. Only in the statements of student engagement—looking forward to classes and considering them useful to the future—was social class not important. Achievement scores, self-reports of grades from sixth to eighth grade, and history of retention were each based on different metrics. However, the pattern of differences from low- to high-SES students was the same for each behavior and performance measure. Students with more advantaged parents (i.e., higher SES) also do better in school. Similarly, the percentage of each group who reported engaging in misbehaviors "sometimes" or "often" declined as students' family SES got higher. Considering these two sets of results, it is quite interesting that all these students describe themselves very similarly in their interest in and perceived need for a good education, regardless of SES.

INFORMATION ABOUT SCHOOLS

In this section, we shift our attention from the students to schools, describing the characteristics of the schools that the students attended. We address the differences between middle-grade and high schools by examining the structures, compositional characteristics, and academic organizations of the schools at both middle- and high school levels. Although the majority of the research reported in this book focuses on students during their high school years, the original design of the NELS:88 study targeted a representative group of eighth graders. This sampling allowed us to consider students' social and academic status just before they entered high school and also when they were in high school, which we describe in Chapter 3.

Table 2.2. Achievement Level, Engagement, and Misbehavior in 8th grade, Compared Across Different Levels of SES[a]

Variables	Low SES	Average SES	High SES
Achievement Level[b]			
Math test score	11.5	16.2	23.8
Reading test score	8.4	10.6	13.8
Social studies score	12.5	15.4	19.7
Science test score	7.8	10.0	13.3
GPA, 6th–8th grade (4-pt scale)	2.72	2.89	3.26
Held back at least 1 grade by 1988 (%)	29	16	7
Engagement: Percentage who agreed or strongly agreed with the following:			
Look forward to math class	59	55	53
Math useful in future	86	88	86
Look forward to English class	61	52	54
English useful in future	82	81	85
Look forward to social studies class	57	57	59
Social studies useful in future	59	56	60
Look forward to science class	59	55	62
Science useful in future	66	64	70
Never bored with school	52	53	52
Misbehavior: Percentage who report sometimes or often doing the following:[b]			
Cut or skip classes	6	4	2
Come late to school	16	12	9
Come to class without pencil or paper	37	24	12
Come to class without books	18	12	9
Come to class without homework	32	25	17
Sent to office for misbehaving	37	32	23
Parents warned about attendance	16	10	7
Parents warned about behavior	25	22	17
Got into fight with another student	28	21	17

[a] Students in the low-SES group have an average family income of $18,800, and their parents have 11.9 years of education. Those in the average-SES group have an average family income of $36,800 and parental education of 13.7 years. The high-SES students, on average, have family income of $75,000 and parental education of 16.8 years.

[b] Differences between the three groups were statistically significant at $p \leq .001$.

The Schools Eighth Graders Attended

Not all of the students in our sample attended middle schools (Grades 6–8) or junior high schools (Grades 7–9). Some of our students also came to high school directly from elementary schools (Grades K–8), and a few didn't change schools at all—they attended comprehensive schools (Grades K–12).

Figure 2.1 shows the distribution of the types of middle-grade schools attended by our student sample when they were eighth graders. As the NELS:88 design targeted a nationally representative group of eighth graders, this picture shows the types of schools attended by U.S. eighth-grade students. The pie chart on the left shows how *students* were distributed in schools; the one on the right shows the distribution of the *schools* in our sample.

Slightly over half of the eighth graders in our sample (58%) attended schools that exclusively enroll early adolescents, spanning grades 6–8, 7–8, 8–9 or 7–9. Interestingly, only 41% of the schools in the sample are these types (note in particular that 6% of the schools are junior high schools, but they enroll 17% of the students). The difference in the proportions indicates that the these types of schools are much larger than either elementary or K–12 schools (we discuss issues of size below). That means that almost half of the eighth graders in our sample attended schools with grade combinations other than those that cover just early adolescence. Of particular interest are the 26% of eighth graders who attended some form of elementary school. It could be argued that these students made the most dramatic transition as they moved into high school. They had to make a change from the more intimate and connected (not to mention small) learning communities typically found in elementary schools (Firestone & Herriot, 1982) into more specialized, departmentally structured, more bureaucratic, and almost certainly much larger high schools.

FIGURE 2.1. Types of middle-grade schools attended by 8th graders.

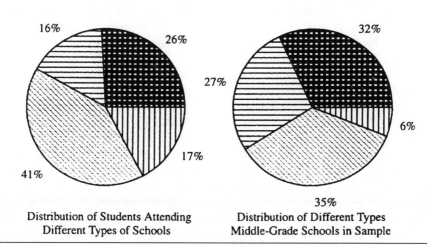

Distribution of Students Attending
Different Types of Schools

Distribution of Different Types
Middle-Grade Schools in Sample

School Structure

The structure of a school refers to basic organizational principles that are constant, regardless of the ebb and flow of people who move through the schools. For example, although there are different students in eighth grade every year, the number of students, the number of teachers, the general configuration of the school year, and the division of the schedule into subject areas all remain roughly constant from year to year. Similarly, although different teachers hold different jobs in the school, the mechanisms for making decisions about curriculum, management, and the other tasks that comprise teaching remain fairly stable. In fact, this second set of characteristics is most commonly targeted in efforts to "restructure" schools (Elmore, 1990). However, over the course of our research on this topic, we have focused on two characteristics about school structure that are typically considered separate from the other domains of school restructuring efforts: (1) the number of students served by the school (size), and (2) the goverance structure of the school (sector).

SIZE

The size of a school is the number of students it enrolls. Figure 2.2 shows how enrollment size is distributed over different types of schools. Most K–12 and elementary schools attended by our sample of students were small (averaging fewer than 600 students), particularly when compared with the size of other grade-level configurations. The schools that exclusively enroll young adolescents typically had between 300 and 900 students, although some of these schools were quite large (two enrolled over 3,000 students!). On the other hand, most high schools enrolled more than than 1,250 students. This size difference is even more striking when we remember that there are only three or four grade cohorts in high school, compared with the usual six to nine grades found in elementary schools.

To get a better sense of what the transition to high school entails, it is useful to compare the *change* in cohort size that students experience. The cohort size represents the number of students in a single grade. Figure 2.3 displays the change in cohort size from 8th to 10th grade experienced by students in each transition type: from a school enrolling young adolescents (7–9, 6–8) into high school; from elementary school into high school; and no change in schools at the beginning of high school (K–12 or 7–12 grade span). Though each type of middle-grade school is represented in this figure, the right-hand group of students made no transition at high school entry—the school they attended in 8th grade was the same one they attended in 12th grade. For this reason, the cohort size stayed essentially the same.

Figure 2.2. Distribution of different grade configurations across enrollment size.

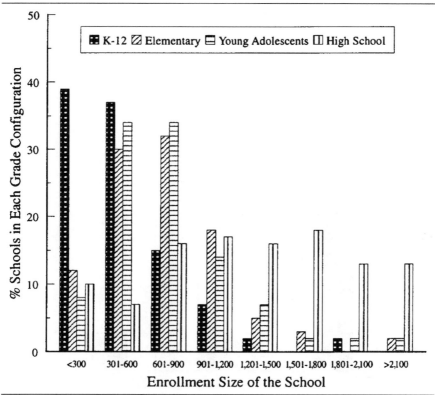

Most notable in this picture is the dramatic difference in eighth-grade cohort size between middle schools/junior high schools (labeled "Young Adolescent") and elementary schools or K–12 schools. When the number of *grades* served by a school decreases, this tends to raise the number of *students* per grade in that school. Imagine the experience differences when a student finds him or herself among 250 other students in the same grade, compared with only 50! A student is much more likely to become "lost in the crowd" when the number of other same-age students is large. On the other hand, activities such as athletic teams, musical groups, debate, or forensics might not be available if there were only a few students in the talent pool. Clearly, there are both advantages and disadvantages for students in the different grade-span approaches.

Another important observation from Figure 2.3 is that students who attended young-adolescent schools also moved into larger high schools (i.e.,

Figure 2.3. Number of students in grade cohort from 8th to 10th grade broken down by type of transition.

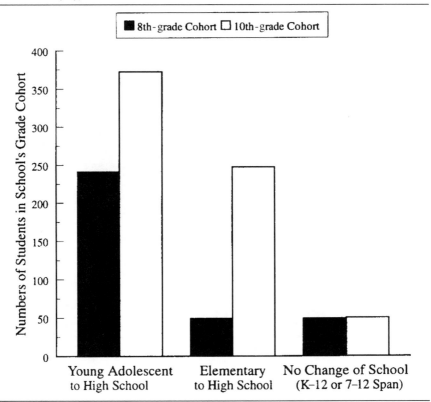

larger grade cohorts) than did students who came to high school from elementary schools. This size difference could come about in different ways. For example, some of these students may have shifted from Catholic elementary schools (typically K–8) to Catholic high schools, which are generally small. In addition, in the case of public schools, the difference could be predicted from the general policy followed when communities grow. When a community population starts to grow, the school district typically looks first for ways to reduce overcrowding in elementary schools, which is where the bulge would first show up. They usually accomplish this goal by moving older students (young adolescents) into separate buildings. Thus, students in this sample who made a transition from public elementary schools to public high schools may also have been residents of smaller communities than those who go from middle schools or junior high schools to high school.

Finally, this figure demonstrates an issue we raised earlier—that the shift into high school generally involves adjusting to a much larger school environment. In particular, students who move directly from elementary schools into high schools are typically confronted with a dramatic increase in the student population. In the average elementary school in this sample, there were probably two classrooms of eighth graders (based on an estimate of 25 students per class). While it might have been feasible in some cases to sort these students into different ability groups for mathematics, English, social studies, or science, it is likely that the differences between the groups are not very large.

In addition, because there were fewer students, a smaller number of teachers would have been needed to teach eighth-grade classes. Fewer teachers makes it much easier on a practical level to coordinate instruction. It is also likely that these teachers know all the students at that grade level better, having seen them in their building for the past 8 years. However, when such students go to high school, the situation is quite different. There are, on average, five times more students in their own age group than they knew a year or two earlier. Instead of knowing one or two teachers with a long history in the school, the student now confronts five or six teachers, each of whom sees that student for less than an hour a day. Even though the high school itself is relatively small, the shift in cohort size suggests a very different culture that the student must manage.

GOVERNANCE STRUCTURE

In addition to the number of students in the school, another characteristic taken into consideration throughout our research was the goverance structure, called the "sector" of the school. In one sense, there are only two types of school governance—public and private. However, the governance of private schools itself differs, based on whether that administration is dictated by the Catholic Church or by the independent groups (which may or may not be religiously affiliated) working to meet parents' needs. Thus, in both our eighth-grade study (Chapter 3) and our investigations into these students' high school experiences (Chapters 4 through 7), we took into account whether the student attended a public, a Catholic, or an elite private school. We decided to focus on only two types of private schools: Catholic and elite private schools. All schools in the latter group, sometimes called "independent" schools, are members of the National Association of Independent Schools (NAIS). Private schools that do not fall into these two categories are typically small, and they represent a very heterogeneous group of schools. Thus, we eliminated the rather small number of such schools from our samples.

Figure 2.4 shows the distribution of these three types of schools attended first by the eighth graders in our study, then again when these same students were in high school. The major finding here concerns the substantial decline in the proportions of students in Catholic and elite private schools between middle-grade and high schools. The shift in distribution in part shows differences in types of schools in the different sectors chosen by students at these two grade levels. In general, we considered explicitly and systematically the role played by sector in our studies, although it was never a major focus of our subsequent analyses.

Student Body Composition

In addition to the schools' structural differences, we also considered the student body composition of the school as part of the background to our studies. In particular, for most comparisons between schools, we examined the possible influence of minority student concentration, the average SES of students attending the school, and the average ability of students. Table 2.3 compares these student-body-composition characteristics among K–12 schools, elementary schools, schools educating only young adolescents, and high schools.

Figure 2.4. Proportion of students in public, Catholic, and elite private schools at 8th and 10th grades.

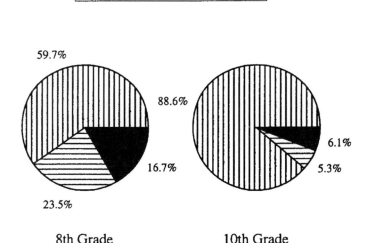

□ Public ⊟ Catholic ■ Elite Private

8th Grade   10th Grade

Table 2.3. Student Body Composition for Different Types of Schools

Variables	K–12 Schools	Elementary Schools	Middle and Junior High Schools	High Schools
Minority concentration				
White (%)	86.3	78.7	69.0	70.6
African American (%)	6.9	10.4	16.4	13.5
Hispanic (%)	2.6	8.2	10.6	10.8
Other (Asian, Native American) (%)	4.2	2.6	4.0	5.1
Socioeconomic Status				
Free lunch (%)	14.9	17.9	26.6	21.5
Average SES	0.13	0.04	-0.14	-0.22
Student ability				
GPA, 6th–8th grade	2.99	3.12	2.11	2.97
Average achievement, 8th grade[a]	52.9	54.1	49.9	51.3
Academic heterogeneity[b]	8.03	7.45	9.88	8.65

[a] Average of the reading and mathematics test scores.
[b] School SD in student test scores.

It is clear that K–12 and elementary schools have a rather different student body composition from the other two types. They are more White, enrolling fewer African-American and Hispanic students than either of the other two school types. In addition, their socioeconomic status is higher—seen both from the rather blunt measure of the percentage of students on free lunch and the more specific aggregate of student SES. Students' average test scores and average grades are also slightly higher in such schools, and the scores are somewhat more homogeneous than in the other two school types. K–12 and elementary schools enroll more similar and more advantaged students than do the other two types of schools. This may be because these schools are more likely to be private than are the other groups. In general, these comparisons demonstrate systematic links between the type of school and the characteristics of students attending those schools, links that are important to keep in mind for later analyses.

Academic Organization

We also took the academic organization of the school into account in the studies detailed in Chapters 3 through 7. "Academic organization" describes how schools deliver instruction to their students: the type of grouping or tracking used, the departmentalization of the school, the number of academic courses available, and the variation in students' courses of study in the same school. As middle-grade schools and high schools usually deliver instruction in very different ways, we have elected in this section to examine each separately rather than try to make comparisons between middle-grade and high schools. In addition, we build on the differences according to social class discussed earlier in this chapter. Instead of considering individual differences in student status, as we did in Table 2.2, here we consider school aggregates as characteristics of schools. We consider school average SES as a proxy measure for the resources available to the school. Thus, whereas before we were comparing affluent, average, and poor *students*, here we contrast students attending advantaged, average, and poor *schools*.

MIDDLE-GRADE SCHOOLS

Three measures typify the academic organization of most middle-grade schools: the degree of departmentalization, the use of ability grouping in classes, and the use of team-teaching or block scheduling, which typically combines different teachers in one subject area. This set of comparisons is found in Table 2.4.

Every middle-grade school in our sample used a departmental structure in eighth grade. However, some schools were departmentalized only for certain subjects. A "departmentalized" school had separate departments for each

Table 2.4. Middle-grade Academic Organization Measures Broken Down by School Socioeconomic Status

Variables	Low SES Schools	Average SES Schools	High SES Schools
Number of schools	188	624	126
Departmentalization			
Fully departmentalized (%)	79	69	61
Semi-departmentalized (%)	21	31	39
Ability Grouping			
Using no ability grouping (%)	14	19	39
Using ability grouping only in math and reading (%)	32	40	53
Using ability grouping for most or all subjects (%)	54	41	8
Shared Instruction			
Using team-teaching and/or block scheduling (%)	36	52	63
Using 1 teacher/subject (%)	64	48	37

subject. A school that is "semi-departmentalized" combined departments for math and science, another for English and social studies, and then had one or two departments covering all other subjects (for example, home economics, shop, music, foreign languages, and art). Shifts toward combining teachers into broader departmental divisions were clearly linked to the average SES of students attending the school, which in turn may be linked to both size and sector. Those schools where the average SES was low were also more likely to be fully departmentalized, with the structure shifting more toward semi-departmentalization for higher SES schools.

Similarly, lower-SES schools were most likely to use ability grouping in some or all subjects. As the SES level of the school increased, there was less grouping, with almost 40% of the high-SES schools using no ability grouping for any subject and another 53% using it only in reading and mathematics. The use of shared teaching was also related to the average SES of the students. Team-teaching and block scheduling were used in schools of all SES levels, but these techniques were more common in higher- than lower-SES schools.

In general, academic organization in middle-grade schools is somewhat related to the SES level of students. In those schools more commonly attended by less-affluent students, the academic structure was also more differentiated, with teachers divided by departments, students divided by ability, and instruction isolated by subject matter (i.e., one teacher per topic). Schools attended by more-advantaged students were also places where teachers were more connected with one another (via reduced departmentalization and more shared instruction) and where there was more interaction among students of differing skill levels (via reduced or no ability divisions). These features characterizing differences between middle-grade schools' academic organization will be revisited in Chapter 3.

HIGH SCHOOLS

When compared with middle-grade schools, high schools appear very similar in their academic organizations. All the high schools in our sample were fully departmentalized, with almost no shared instruction across subject areas. The major differences in academic organization at the high school level instead occurred across curricular programs or "tracks." Therefore, we explored the academic organization of high schools through the proportion of students taking courses in different tracks, the average number of mathematics and science courses taken by students, and the variation in the number of these courses taken by students in the same school. We used mathematics and science courses to reflect average course taking because these courses were clearly identified in students' transcripts as either academic or nonacademic. English and social studies courses, on the other hand, are more difficult to identify as academic or nonacademic. To verify our assumption that mathematics and science courses reflect an academic orientation, we ran random checks at both extremes of this measure. In each case, the number of mathematics and science courses was highly correlated with the number of college-prep or academic courses taken by that student.

Figure 2.5 shows the proportion of students in different curricular programs in schools with different SES compositions. In schools attended by low-SES students, only a small portion of students were enrolled in college-preparatory or "academic" programs (12%). This portion increased as the SES level of students attending the school increased. In average-SES schools, 25% of the students were in the academic track. In high-SES schools, roughly half of the students followed an academic program. Similarly, the portion of students in the vocational track shrank as the SES level of students in the school increased.

Figure 2.6 uses three lines to display both the average number of mathematics and science courses students take and the variation in that number for students in low-, medium-, and high-SES schools. The middle line represents the average number for students in schools of each SES level, whereas the upper

FIGURE 2.5. Distribution of curricular programs for students enrolled in low-, average-, and high-SES high schools.

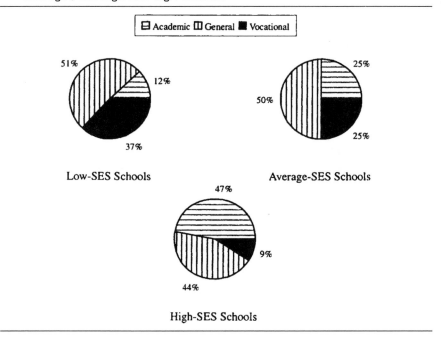

Figure 2.6. Distribution of mathematics and science courses taken by students in low-, average-, and high-SES high schools.

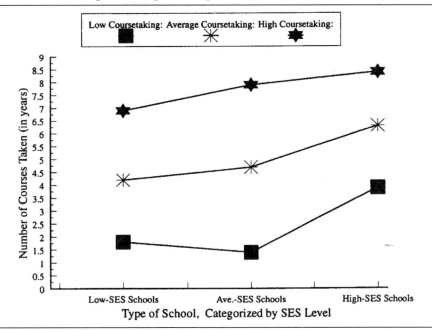

and lower lines represent course taking that is one standard deviation above and below that average for students in the three types of schools. The end point at the right of the top line shows the number of mathematics and science courses typically taken by students in high-SES schools, while the end point of the lower line represents the lowest level of courses in high-SES schools. The average number of mathematics and science courses students took in a school was related to the average SES of the school (i.e., all three lines have positive slopes), with more affluent schools showing a higher average. In fact, the average number of courses taken was strongly correlated with the average school SES (r = .59). Interestingly, the variability in students' course taking was more constrained both at the high and the low ends of the SES spectrum, with the widest variation found average SES schools.

SUMMARY OF SAMPLE CHARACTERISTICS

In this chapter, we have provided descriptive background about the students and schools that comprise the samples we used in the major analyses in this book. We also used the comparisons in this chapter to provide readers with a general picture of the academic and social characteristics of U.S. students and schools between 8th and 12th grade. In each section, we have drawn out the comparisons in social and academic background that we thought should be taken into account as we examined the types of school structures that worked best for students. As we move into the first exploration of school restructuring in middle-grade schools (Chapter 3), the student and school characteristics discussed here provide a framework for assessing critical comparisons.

PART II

A Focus on School Restructuring

The major aim of Part II of this book is to examine how students who attend schools that have been restructured are affected by that experience. Within this aim, there are two fundamental questions we hope to answer in the chapters in Part II. First, precisely what *is* school restructuring? These chapters spell out our definition of this construct, which we have developed to be consistent with, and grounded in, contemporary writings about school reform. Beyond defining the restructuring construct, we also describe how we have operationalized it using data from nationally representative samples of schools. Second, how does restructuring influence students? We present our empirical research in which we examine how attending schools whose organizational practices are consistent with this definition of restructuring influences students. In Chapter 3, which focuses on eighth-grade students in middle-grade schools, we examine how *restructuring practices* influence student development, broadly defined as achievement, engagement with school, and behaviors that put students at risk of school failure. In Chapter 4 we take a similar approach, except that here we examine the same students 2 years later, when they are 10th graders in high school. Thus, the focus here is on *high-school restructuring*. We continue to focus on how students who attend both restructured and traditional secondary schools—both compared with schools that have implemented moderate reforms—are influenced in terms of their development.

CHAPTER 3

Restructuring in the Middle Grades

Just as we begin our investigation with students in eighth grade, we also focus our inital attention on schools that serve middle-grade students. There are two major types of school organizations, namely "elementary school" and "high school." Elementary schools typically are small, teach basic skills in different subjects in one classroom (often with a single teacher), and tend to be characterized by an intimate social environment. By comparison, high schools are typically large, teach specialized skills in different subjects in different settings, and operate on a more bureaucratic and impersonal social level (Firestone & Herriot, 1982). Between these two types of school organizations, there is a transitional stage that we refer to in this book as "middle-grade schooling." The use of this phrase should be taken to identify any schools that contain Grades 7 and 8, possibly also Grade 6 and Grade 9. Such schools are variously indentified as "junior high schools," "middle schools," "elementary schools," or "comprehensive schools," depending on the grade span. The phrase "middle-grade schooling" is meant to include all of these structural forms.

The major function of middle-grade schooling is to provide learning experiences for young adolescents that will help them make a successful transition into high school and, more generally, into adolescent and adult roles. The aim is to provide relevant learning experiences for young adolescents, encouraging both improved achievement and greater engagement in school. For most of this century, the common approach to improving middle-grade schooling has been to change *who attends* the school rather than to change the *way education is structured* in such schools.

A common method to accomplish the change-who-attends goal is to change the grade span of the school (cf., Ames & Miller, 1994; Ayres, 1909; Blyth & Karnes, 1981; Briggs, 1927; Conant, 1960; Oakes, 1993). In fact, much of the research on middle-grade schooling focuses on the ideal combination of grade levels that might produce optimal outcomes for students (Anderman & Midgley, 1997; Blyth, Hill, & Smyth, 1981; Eccles, Lord, & Midgley, 1991; Epstein, 1990). Currently in the United States, there are about 30 different grade spans in schools that enroll seventh graders (Epstein, 1990). Based on evidence about middle-grade schools gathered in a large survey by the Center for Research on Elementary and Middle Schools at Johns Hopkins University, Epstein (1990) argues that although schooling practice is somewhat related to grade span, the critical change needed to generate effective middle-grade schooling is to alter what happens to students in school, rather than altering to whom it happens.

UNDERSTANDING RESTRUCTURED PRACTICES

Current efforts to restructure practices in middle-grade schools typically flow in a particular direction: They emphasize smaller learning communities that feature a core academic program followed by all students. In part, these efforts also address the empowerment of teachers and administrators to first become trained, and then empowered, to make good choices to address the needs of young adolescents (Carnegie Council on Adolescent Development, 1989). Our approach is to target the technical core of schooling, that is, how teaching and learning occur. The elements of restructured practice we consider can be organized into two larger areas, each with its own body of research: (1) changing how *instruction is organized* (who is taught what) and (2) changing how *teachers are organized* to deliver instruction (who does what teaching) (see also Lee & Smith, 1993).

The Organization of Instruction

At the heart of the goal to provide every student with a common academic program rests a dilemma: Not all students perform with the same level of competence on the same activities. The most common response to this difficulty— grouping students by ability for instruction—seems to be a logical and efficient response to this dilemma. However, it is also wrought with problems. A persistent finding in recent research is that tracking is one of the most powerful predictors of academic performance in high school (Braddock, 1990; Gamoran, 1987; Lee & Bryk, 1988; Lucas, 1999; Oakes, 1985; Oakes, Wells, Jones, & Datnow, 1997). In particular, this practice usually intensifies negative consequences for less-able students while providing little or no benefit for more-able students (Anderson & Barr, 1990; Braddock, 1990; Guiton, 1995; Hoffer, 1991). In addition, tracking magnifies social differentiation in achievement over time, such that early differences related to parental background or race/ethnicity become quite large by the end of high school (Braddock, 1990; Eccles, 1997; Ferguson, 1998; Hanson, 1990; Lee & Bryk, 1988; Lucas, 1999; Oakes, 1985). Consequently, the Carnegie Council on Adolescent Development (1989) vilified this practice, describing tracking as one of "the most divisive and damaging school practices in existence" (p. 49).

Our study of restructured practice in middle-grade schools thus included a focus on those characteristics of schools' academic organization that emphasize shared learning between diverse sets of students around core academic programs. Among the practices we investigated are:

- Exploratory classes in academic specialties
- Special projects developing depth of knowledge for all students as part of the regular curriculum
- Heterogeneous grouping for all academic subjects (mathematics, English, social studies, and science)
- High levels of student participation in ungrouped academic instruction
- Cooperative learning techniques used in classrooms
- Shared instruction among teachers across grade levels
- Shared instruction among teachers across subject matter (i.e., interdisciplinary teams that share the same students)
- Policies discouraging punitive eighth-grade retention

In addition, the focus on shared (or integrated) instruction for all students carries with it a concern for increased social connections between students and among students and teachers. To accomplish this purpose, middle-grade schools have considered organizational changes that keep students and teachers together for longer periods of time, while at the same time reducing the numbers of students with whom a teacher or a student interacts. These restrucutured practices include:

- Keeping the same classmates for all classes
- Placing students in smaller schools within the school
- Giving students the same homeroom teacher or advisor for all middle-school years

Considered alongside, but separate from, these practices is the size of the grade cohort, that is, how many students there are in a school's eighth grade. Although school or cohort size is not typically addressed as a restructuring *practice*, we argue that the impact of this structural characteristic—the number of students—is important to consider. Although we discuss school size throughout this book, we consider it in more detail in Chapter 7.

The Organization of Teachers' Work

The "work" done by teachers in middle-grade schools is also structured by how schools operate. Teachers' work is typically isolated (in classrooms). Teachers have little opportunity to share information, either among themselves or across departments or specialties. Bidwell (1965) describes the typical teacher's work as quite formal and bureaucratic. In fact, many schools and districts are trying to make teaching more standardized, more systemized, and (as much as possible) a uniform effort. Although there may be some benefit to centralizing and routinizing work in factories, most educators agree that teaching children is, for the most part, not an easily standardizable activity. It requires much personal flexibility, professional decision making, and constant on-the-spot judgments over the course of a single day (Korda-lewski, 2000; Westheimer, 1998). Consequently, research exploring how to restructure middle-grade teachers' work quite consistently favors increased collegiality, more shared decision making, and increased emphasis on staff-development activities geared toward the special needs of young adolescents. One goal of such practices is to establish professional communities, where work that is shared among teachers is directed toward the best professional understanding of teaching and learning. Among the practices focusing on restructuring middle-grade teachers' work, we investigated:

- Common planning time for department members
- Flexible time scheduling of classes
- Reducing departmental divisions between teachers
- Staff-development activity directed toward issues concerning the op-timal development of young adolescents
- Team-teaching, either within or across departments

The Extent of Restructuring Implementation

Thus far in our discussion, we have mentioned 16 restructured practices fa-vored by much recent research that has explored the educational needs of young adolescents. In Figure 3.1 we show how these restructured practices are distributed in the nationally representative sample of middle-grade schools we are studying. These distributions are drawn from simple yes/no responses by the school administrator of each school in our sample about whether his or her school had implemented each practice.[1] We considered many ways to combine these practices. Though at first it seemed reasonable to explore logi-cal combinations of these practices from a theoretical standpoint (i.e., group-ing practices that may go together conceptually or statistically), we found that schools' implementation of these restructured practices followed a less logical structure. For example, although about 40% of the schools reported using interdisciplinary team-teaching and about 50% of the schools reported students sharing instruction across different subjects, only 24% of the schools engage in both practices. In general, an exploratory analysis of the incidence of all these practices reveals three general areas around which the practices

FIGURE 3.1. Distribution of individual restructured practices across schools.

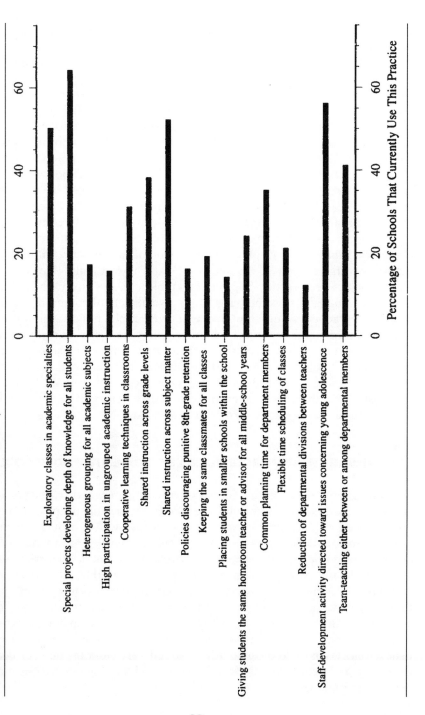

can be clearly associated: reduced departmentalization, team-teaching, and heterogeneous grouping for instruction.

Schools' *implementation* of these practices, however, did not seem to occur in these groupings. That is, the practicalities of putting restructured practices in place in schools typically do not follow a program organized around only one of these groupings. Although we originally had planned to combine schools' restructuring around these groupings, we found that this was not a reasonable course to follow. Instead, our major approach was to consider the degree to which a school had engaged in these practices in toto.

We constructed the "Restructuring Index" to measure schools' implementation of the restructured practices, where we simply summed the number of practices the school reported using (out of a total of 16). The index provides information about the middle-grade school's overall involvement with the reforms recommended by the Carnegie Council on Adolescent Development (1989). In Table 3.1 we display the proportion of each practice implemented in schools with very few (1–3), some (4–6), and a great many (7 or more) of the 16 restructured practices in place. This table indicates how each practice is distributed, along with some sense of the overall school commitment to restructured practices in different arenas. For example, policies discouraging retention in the eighth grade and schools-within-schools are quite uncommon across all schools, whereas shared instruction and special projects are quite common in schools with many of these practices in place. Staff development focused on young adolescents is relatively common in all schools. (Details of the construction of our restructuring measures, as well as all variables used in the analyses in this book, are provided in Appendix A.)

EXAMINING THE CHARACTERISTICS OF STUDENTS AND SCHOOLS

Our intent in the eighth-grade study was to investigate whether students who attend middle-grade schools that have incorporated some or most of the 16 restructured practices actually benefit, either academically, through improved attitudes toward schooling (we call this "engagement"[2]), or in reduced levels of disruptive behavior in school (we call these "at-risk behaviors"[3]). Some technical details about the construction of these variables are provided in Appendix A. Although we narrow our focus toward a primary concentration on achievement in subsequent chapters, in this chapter the set of outcomes we examine is broad, including achievement, engagement, and at-risk behaviors. Our reason for using a broader set of outcomes here is that we believe that young adolescents' attitudes and behaviors in the year before they enter high school are likely to be associated with their subsequent academic performance.

Table 3.1. Frequency of Each Restructuring Practice in Schools with Different
Overall Levels of Restructuring

| | *Levels of Restructuring Practice* | | |
Individual Restructured Practice	Schools with Few	Schools with Some	Schools with Many
Exploratory classes in academic specialties	.28	.53	.69
Special projects developing depth of knowledge of all students	.44	.71	.82
Heterogeneous grouping for all academic subjects	.34	.57	.73
High students participation in nongrouped academic instruction	.11	.33	.64
Cooperative learning used	.18	.35	.42
Shared instruction across grade levels	.28	.27	.50
Shared instruction across subject matter	.18	.55	.86
Policies discouraging 8th-grade retention	.05	.13	.21
Keeping same classmates for all classes	.06	.19	.37
Schools within the school	.06	.12	.23
Students have same homeroom teacher/advisor for all middle-school years	.12	.25	.38
Common planning time for teachers	.16	.36	.59
Flexible time scheduling of classes	.05	.19	.46
Reduction of departmental divisions	.08	.24	.57
Staff development on issues concerning young adolescence	.49	.62	.61
Team-teaching either between or among departmental members	.10	.39	.72

Our investigations are structured around a basic model that examines
the characteristics of students and their schools that are likely to contribute
to student development, captured by their academic achievement, engagement, and at-risk behavior. With this model, we estimated these contributions above and beyond the degree of restructuring in the school. To conduct these analyses, as well as most of the analyses in this book, we have
used an analytic technique called "hierarchical linear modeling" (HLM).
School effects research questions such as those we explore in this book, where
we investigate how characteristics of *schools* influence the development of
their *students*, are by their nature multilevel; that is, students are "nested"
in schools. Such HLM analyses typically are conducted at two levels: within
schools (Level 1) and between schools (Level 2). Readers who are unfamil-
iar with this technique but who are interested in a bit of detail about how

HLM works are referred to Appendix B, where we spell out some typical HLM models. Those who wish more detail are referred to Bryk and Raudenbush's (1992) book on HLM or to an article that spells out the application of HLM to a substantive educational question (Lee & Bryk, 1989).

The Relationship Between Student Characteristics and Development

Table 3.2 shows the results of the first step of our analyses. We focused on how student characteristics are associated with the outcomes we use to measure student development: academic achievement, engagement, and at-risk behaviors. In more technical terms, Table 3.2 displays three separate within-school (Level 1) HLM models for these outcomes. The coefficients indicating the relationship between background characteristics and each outcome vary in magnitude, direction, and statistical significance. A positive coefficient indicates that the particular background characteristic is associated with a higher score on the outcome, whereas a negative coefficient indicates association with a lower score. Both the magnitude of and the asterisks attached to each coefficient indicate the strength of association. Coefficients with at least one asterisk are significantly associated with the outcome; more asterisks indicate stronger associations. Coefficients at or near zero indicate little or no association between the background characteristic and the outcome.

To varying degrees (and in different directions), students' gender, ethnicity, academic background, and social class are associated with their development,

Table 3.2. Within-school Model of Student Characteristics and 8th-grade Outcomes—Achievement, Engagement, and At-risk Behaviors

	Outcomes		
	Achievement	Engagement	At-risk behaviors
School Average	-.08	-.16	.16
SES slope	.18***	.06***	-.09***
Female differential[a]	.01	.19***	-.37***
Minority differential[a]	-.36***	-.06	.18***
Academic background[a]	.34***	.15***	-.22***
Between-school variance of school average	.22***	.10***	.05***
Between-school variance of SES slope	.02***	.00	.02***

[a] The assocation of these variables with the outcome has been constrained from varying randomly between schools. Thus, they represent pooled within-school effects.
*** $p \leq .001$

measured in terms of achievement, engagement, and at-risk behaviors. Students from higher-socioeconomic-status (SES) families have higher achievement, are more engaged in school, and engage in fewer at-risk behaviors. Whereas female students are significantly more engaged and have fewer at-risk behaviors, minority students have lower achievement and more at-risk behaviors. Students with more favorable academic backgrounds (we use this as a proxy for students' ability) demonstrate higher achievement, are more engaged, and have fewer at-risk behaviors.

The relationship between SES and achievement (what we call "the SES/ achievement slope") is an important idea that we pursue consistently throughout this book. We use this as a measure of social equity in school outcomes. This relationship is perhaps most easily understood graphically. In Figure 3.2 we display the relationship between students' SES and their achievement at the end of 8th grade. This is a "net" relationship, in that we have also taken into account students' academic background, their gender, and their race/

FIGURE 3.2. Distribution of student achievement across social class divisions.

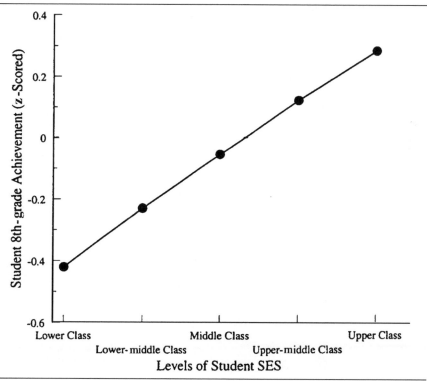

ethnicity. As is clear in this graph, the slope of the line that captures the relationship between SES and achievement is positive—students with higher SES levels also have higher achievement. This relationship is an example of what we described in Chapter 1 as "the social distribution of achievement." Throughout the book, including in this chapter, we examine this measure of social equity in schools as a function of school restructuring.

The Relationship Between School Characteristics and Restructuring

As our discussion in Chapter 2 implies, we need to isolate the impact of restructured practice on students in a school. This means that we must take into account other characteristics of schools that may be related to their willingness or ability to implement these practices. To estimate the effects of middle-grade school restructuring, we also take into account several demographic and structural characteristics of schools: average SES, minority concentration, the number of students in the eighth-grade cohort, sector, and the academic heterogeneity of the student body. The latter characteristic is measured by the standard deviation of achievement in each school—that is, a higher number means that the levels of academic achievement of students varies widely. Table 3.3, shows the distribution of these school characteristics in four groups: the three groups of schools shown in Table 3.1, as well as schools in the sample that had implemented none of the restructuring practices.

In Table 3.3, the first column of figures lists the characteristics of schools that in 1988 had implemented none of the restructured practices. Column 2 displays the characteristics of schools with very few restructuring practices;

Table 3.3. Characteristics of Schools with Different Levels of Restructuring

| | Levels of Restructuring Practice | | | |
	Schools with No	Schools with Few	Schools with Some	Schools with Many
Average School SES[a,b]	.08	-.12	-.05	-.03
Percent Minority[a]	12	24	23	25
8th-grade size[a,b]	180	238	197	163
Sector[a,b]				
Public (%)	73	90	78	68
Catholic (%)	11	5	7	15
Elite private (%)	16	5	14	17
SD, Achievement	9.08	8.58	8.51	8.23

[a] Differences between NO restructured practices and other groups significant at p≤.01.
[b] Differences between FEW, SOME, and MANY restructured practice schools significant at p≤.01.

Column 3 displays the characteristics of schools that had implemented some practices; and Column 4 displays the characteristics of schools that had many restructuring practices in place. We tested two contrasts for statistical significance. Contrast a indicates whether characteristics of schools with no restructuring practices in place were different from the other schools, whereas contrast b tests whether there were differences in the characteristics of schools with few, some, and many restructuring practices in place.

Those schools that have implemented very few practices (1–3) serve slightly more disadvantaged students. They have larger eighth-grade cohorts, and they are mostly composed of public schools (although a few Catholic and other private schools are in this group). At the other end of the spectrum, schools that have implemented many restructuring practices (7 or more) serve more advantaged students (although their average SES is lower than those with no practices in place). This group also has smaller eighth-grade cohorts than any other category, and, although the majority is composed of public schools, contains a higher proportion of Catholic and elite private schools. As the number of restructuring practices goes up, so also does the academic homogeneity of the school's student body. It is clear that several demographic and structural characteristics of schools are related to their willingness to implement (or interest in implementing) restructuring practices of the sort we investigate. Therefore, in subsequent analyses, where we investigate the net effect of restructuring practices on students' achievement, engagement, and at-risk behaviors, we have to take these school characteristics into account.

WHAT DID THE EIGHTH-GRADE STUDY REVEAL?

The purpose of this section is to describe how the degree to which middle-grade schools had implemented the restructuring practices described earlier in this chapter influenced student development, defined in terms of achievement, engagement, and at-risk behaviors. Because both student background and school characteristics were shown to be associated with the degree to which U.S. middle-grade schools implemented restructuring practices, our multilevel analyses incorporated both student and school characteristics.

Overview of Model Structure

HYPOTHESES OF THE EFFECTS OF RESTRUCTURING

In at least three respects, the final analyses in this investigation are complex. First, we evaluated the relationship of restructuring to two types of outcomes: (1) the school average of each outcome (achievement, engagement, and at-risk behaviors) and (2) the social distribution of these outcomes by student SES. This results in six different outcomes. We pose several hypotheses about these results. We expect that more restructuring practices in a school simultaneously demonstrate two sets of relationships: (1) a positive relationship with achievement and academic engagement and a negative relationship with at-risk behaviors, and (2) a negative relationship with the social distribution of achievement and engagement by SES and a positive relationship to the social distribution of at-risk behaviors. In the first set, more practices should raise average achievement and engagement; in the second set more practices should demonstrate a more equitable distribution of achievement, engagement, and at-risk behaviors by student SES.

DIFFERENT APPROACHES TO MEASURING RESTRUCTURING

The second type of complexity in these analyses involves dividing the restructuring practices into the logical groupings we described earlier. Our first set of HLM analyses evaluated the relationship of the Restructuring Index on each of our six outcomes, looking for the patterns we hypothesized. We also considered restructuring as three separate submeasures: reduced departmentalization, heterogeneous grouping, and team-teaching. Our logic is as follows: Although individual practices are related to one another, they could also influence the outcomes differently. For that reason, we conducted each analysis four different times, first with the Restructuring Index, and once with each of the three subgroups of restructuring practices.

TAKING CHARACTERISTICS OF STUDENTS AND SCHOOLS INTO ACCOUNT

There is a third level of complexity to our analyses. As the results in Tables 3.2 and 3.3 show, several characteristics of students and schools must be taken into account in each analysis. Therefore, estimating the effects of restructured practices on the outcomes, whichever way we conceptualized the construct of restructuring, must also take account of the student and school characteristics shown in those tables. The number and complexity of the submodels led us to simplify the presentation of our results as much as possible. Results of the analyses on achievement and the social distribution of achievement by student SES are presented in Table 3.4, engagement and its social distribution in Table 3.5, and at-risk behaviors and their social distribution in Table 3.6. Although all analyses are two-level HLMs that include adjustment for the characteristics of students and schools, we have streamlined our presentation by omitting the effects of these factors in these tables. Interested readers are referred to Lee and Smith (1993) for the full HLM model results.

Table 3.4. Final HLM Models of the Influence of Restructuring on Student Achievement

Parameters	Gamma Coefficient
A. Influence of Composite Restructuring Measure	
Average achievement	.10
Restructuring index	.01
SES/achievement slope	.18***
Restructuring index	.09
B. Influence of Reduced Departmentalization	
Average achievement	.08
Reduced departmentalization	.08**
SES/achievement slope	.19***
Reduced departmentalization	-.07**
C. Influence of Heterogeneous Grouping	
Average achievement	.09
Heterogeneous grouping	.02
SES/achievement slope	.19***
Heterogeneous grouping	-.04**
D. Influence of Team-teaching	
Average achievement	.09
Team-teaching	.06**
SES/achievement slope	.18***
Team-teaching	-.01

**p≤.01; ***p≤.001

Restructuring and Achievement

The effects of restructured practice (measured in the four ways indicated above) on student achievement are shown in Table 3.4. The social distribution of achievement by SES is positive (.18, $p \le .001$—exactly the same as shown in Table 3.2). That is, students of higher SES achieve at higher levels than their lower-SES colleagues. The Restructuring Index (Table 3.4, Panel A) is unrelated to either average achievement or the SES slope. However, when we "unpacked" the composite, we found that reduced departmentalization (Table 3.4, Panel B) shows the desired pattern. That is, students in middle-grade schools with less rigid departmental structures achieve at higher levels (.08, $p \le .01$) and the social distribution of achievement by SES is also more equitable (–.07, $p \le .01$).

This combined effect of reduced departmentalization is perhaps easier to understand in a graph (see Figure 3.3). The largest achievement advantage from being in schools with reduced departmentalization accrues to low-SES students. As individual student SES increases, the advantage of being in a school with low departmentalization is reduced. For students from the highest SES families, departmentalization may actually be an advantage. In general, reducing departmentalization in middle-grade schools increases student achievement and also increases social equity. That is, reduced departmentalization advantages most students, in terms of achievement, but it is most advantageous for the most economically disadvantaged students.

The pattern of effects for heterogeneous grouping is somewhat different (Table 3.4, Panel C). Although heterogeneous grouping is unrelated to school average achievement, it influences the social distribution of achievement. In

FIGURE 3.3. Distribution of student achievement across social class levels in schools with rigid compared with flexible department structures.

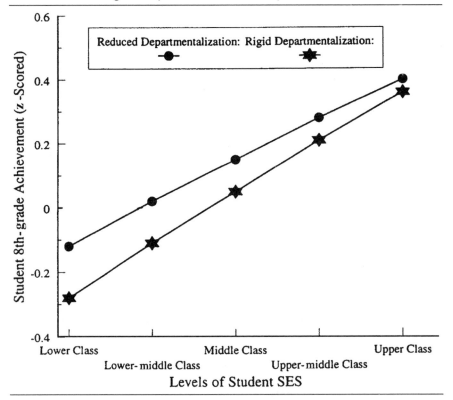

schools where students are grouped heterogeneously for instruction, achievement is more equitable for students from different SES levels ($-.04$, $p \le .01$). In schools that practice team-teaching (Table 3.4, Panel D), on the other hand, students have higher achievement ($.06$, $p \le .01$). However, team-teaching is unrelated to the equitable distribution of achievement within schools.

Restructuring and Academic Engagement

Using the same four-part presentation as in Table 3.4, the effects of school restructuring on student engagement are shown in Table 3.5. As we saw for achievement, students from higher-SES familes are more engaged with school than their less-advantaged counterparts ($.08$, $p \le .001$). In comparison with academic achievement, we see that restructuring (whatever its form) is only

Table 3.5. Final HLM Models of the Influence of Restructuring on Student Engagement

Parameters	Gamma Coefficient
A. *Influence of Composite Restructuring Measure*	
Average engagement	-.18
Restructuring index	.04**
SES/engagement slope	.08***
Restructuring index	-.01
B. *Influence of Reduced Departmentalization*	
Average engagement	-.17
Reduced departmentalization	-.04
SES/engagement slope	.06*
Reduced departmentalization	.03
C. *Influence of Heterogeneous Grouping*	
Average engagement	-.17
Heterogeneous grouping	.04
SES/engagement slope	.09***
Heterogeneous grouping	-.02
D. *Influence of Team-teaching*	
Average engagement	-.17
Team-teaching	.06~
SES/engagement slope	.06*
Team-teaching	-.06*

~$p \le .10$; *$p \le .05$; **$p \le .01$; ***$p \le .001$

modestly related to engagement and its social distribution. However, all statistically significant relationships follow the hypothesized patterns. Students were more engaged in schools with more restructured practices (Table 3.5, Panel A; .04, $p \le .01$).[4] However, none of the specific restructuring groupings is associated with school average engagement. Notably, although the Restructuring Index is not related to the social distribution of engagement (nor is hetergeneous grouping or reduced departmentalization), in schools with team-teaching engagement is more equitably distributed by student SES (Table 3.5, Panel D; –.06, $p \le .05$). Moreover, in schools with team-teaching, students are marginally more engaged (.06, $p \le .10$).

Restructuring and At-risk Behaviors

Our investigation of restructuring practice on students' at-risk behaviors, the results of which are shown in Table 3.6, demonstrates that these practices are only modestly related to this aspect of student behavior. Although achievement and engagement were positively related to student SES, at-risk behaviors decline as student SES goes up (–.07, $p \le .001$). Moreover, the few effects of restructuring practices were not in the hypothesized direction. In schools with less departmentalization (Table 3.6, Panel B) and with more team-teaching (Panel D), students were *more likely* to engage in at-risk behaviors (effects of .11 [$p \le .001$] and .10 [$p \le .01$] respectively). In addition, schools that practice team-teaching (Table 3.6, Panel D) evidence a more socially inequitable distribution of these behaviors. The relationship evidenced for schools with and without team-teaching in place is shown graphically in Figure 3.4. Schools with team-teaching are quite inequitable, especially for low-SES students. We are at a loss to explain these relationships. On the one hand, it may be that the reporting of at-risk behaviors is more stringent when there are more adults responsible for students in a given classroom. Conversely, these classrooms may have looser standards for student conduct. More finely tuned research, perhaps through frequent and extended classroom observations in schools with and without team-teaching, might untangle this vexing finding.

Effects of Grade Size

We also examined how eighth-grade cohort size influences our outcomes. Based on our own and others' research on school size, we hypothesize that achievement and engagement are higher, and at-risk behaviors lower, in schools with smaller eighth grades. Moreover, we hypothesize that these outcomes are more equitably distributed in middle-grade schools with fewer eighth graders. From the full analyses, portions of which are presented in Tables 3.4–3.6, we concentrated on Panel A, where results for the Restructur-

Table 3.6. Final HLM Models of the Influence of Restructuring on Student
At-risk Behaviors

Parameters	Gamma Coefficient
A. Influence of Composite Restructuring Measure	.
Average at-risk behaviors	.15
Restructuring index	.01
SES/at-risk behaviors slope	-.07***
Restructuring index	.01
B. Influence of Reduced Departmentalization	
Average at-risk behaviors	.12
Reduced departmentalization	.11***
SES/at-risk behaviors slope	-.08***
Reduced departmentalization	.00
C. Influence of Heterogeneous Grouping	
Average at-risk behaviors	.16
Heterogeneous grouping	.06~
SES/at-risk behaviors slope	-.07***
Heterogeneous grouping	.01
D. Influence of Team-teaching	
Average at-risk behaviors	.12
Team-teaching	.10**
SES/at-risk behaviors slope	-.05**
Team-teaching	-.08*

~$p \leq .10$; *$p \leq .05$; **$p \leq .01$; ***$p \leq .001$

ing Index are displayed. In HLM analyses reported in this chapter, we included a statistical control for the size of the eighth-grade cohort. Here we
single out the influence of this structural characteristic of schools, which we
consider worthy of highlighting. We present an overview of these effects in
Table 3.7. Similar to presentations in Tables 3.4–3.6, our results here take into
account the full set of student and school characteristics described earlier, as
well as the effects of the Restructuring Index (Tables 3.4–3.6, Panel A).

Grade size is marginally but positively associated with achievement (.04,
$p \leq .10$), a finding that does not support our hypothesis. This indicates that
students in schools with larger eighth grades have slightly higher achievement. However, grade size is negatively related to engagement ($-.06$, $p \leq .01$),
suggesting that in schools with larger eighth grades students are less engaged
in school (here, our hypothesis is confirmed). However, our hypothesis about

Figure 3.4. Distribution of students' at risk behavior across social class levels in schools with and without team-teaching in place.

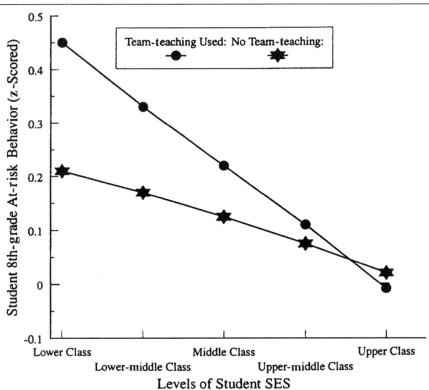

grade size, social equity, and achievement is confirmed. In schools with large eighth grades, achievement is less equitably distributed (.05, $p \leq .01$). In other words, in schools with large eighth grades, a student's SES is more strongly associated with his or her achievement. Grade size is not associated with at-risk behaviors.

Eighth-grade size may serve as a proxy for either grade-grouping or school size. We interpret our results as suggesting (albeit indirectly) that schools that serve *only* early adolescents (middle schools or junior high schools) influence their students in an opposite direction to what we hypothesized as optimal for restructuring practices. Isolating young adolescents in this manner clearly increases the size of the grade cohort, a practice that may result in negative effects on student development over the long run. We explore the issue of how size influences achievement and its social distribution in more depth in Chapter 7 (concentrating, at that point, on the size of *high schools*).

Table 3.7. Final HLM Models of the Influence of 8th-grade Size on All Outcomes

Parameters	Gamma Coefficient
A. Influence of 8th-grade Size on Achievement	
Average achievement	.10
8th-grade size	.04~
SES/achievement slope	.18***
8th-grade size	.05**
B. Influence of 8th-grade Size on Engagement	
Average engagement	-.18
8th-grade size	-.06**
SES/engagement slope	.08***
8th-grade size	-.01
C. Influence of 8th-grade Size on At-risk Behaviors	
Average at-risk behaviors	.15
8th-grade size	.00
SES/at-risk behaviors slope	-.07***
8th-grade size	.00

~$p \leq .10$; **$p \leq .01$; ***$p \leq .001$

Summary

The pattern of associations for restructuring practice shown in this chapter offers general support for our hypotheses concerning middle-grade restructuring and achievement. Although the magnitude of relationships is generally modest, restructured practice (in one or another of the forms we investigated) is associated with higher achievement and with a more equitable distribution of achievement. Students in middle-grade schools where team-teaching is practiced evidence higher achievement. Important findings also concern how middle-grade schools match students to coursework. Schools that practice less grouping by ability and less departmentalization appear to promote social equity in achievement among their students, although such organizational structures are generally unrelated to higher average achievement.

The association between school restructuring and student commitment to school, characterized by either engagement or at-risk behaviors, is less straightforward. Students who attend schools with more restructuring practices in place (from the index) are more engaged in academic work, but also engage in more at-risk behaviors. The Restructuring Index is unrelated to social differentiation in engagement, though socially advantaged students are more engaged. Students who attend less departmentalized schools and schools with team-teaching seem to engage in more at-risk behaviors. Neither semi-departmentalization nor heterogeneous grouping is associated with engagement or its social distribution. Thus, although attending restructured schools may positively influence student engagement, this increased positive attitude toward school may coexist with higher levels of at-risk behaviors.

IMPLICATIONS FOR MIDDLE-GRADE SCHOOLING

In light of the findings from our eighth-grade study, what can we recommend to educators and policymakers about the restructuring of middle-grade schools? Before offering some recommendations, we note a few caveats to our study that stem from using survey data, like the National Educational Longitudinal Study of 1988 (NELS:88), that were not designed specifically to study school restructuring.

A full evaluation of the effects on students of attending schools that structure their instructional activities in ways that vary from the organizational norm would certainly benefit from information not available to us from this general-purpose national survey. For example, we are not sure whether the samples of students in schools where administrators report that they engage in practices like heterogeneous grouping or team-teaching actually encounter instruction of this type. Nor do we know the level of implementation of these practices. Nor can we tell whether teachers who work in teams use other than traditional didactic methods. Moreover, it is unclear whether less departmentalization is associated with other aspects of instruction. In general, a more intense investigation of a smaller number of schools and classes, particularly focusing on schools that identify themselves as highly restructured, would add considerably to our knowledge of the effects of restructuring.

Which Elements of Restructuring Should Middle-grade Schools Consider?

In general, the Restructuring Index shows fewer significant associations with the outcomes we considered than the measures with a more focused conceptual rationale. This finding suggests that simply adopting more elements of restructuring, without linking them to an overall vision of how to improve school functioning, may not be a productive way for schools to approach the task of improvement. Rather, *which* experiences of students are restructured and *how profoundly* these experiences are restructured is more important than *how many* experiences are restructured. Therefore, we qualify our conclusions about the submeasures somewhat. Despite variation in the relationship patterns for the submeasures, their sizable intercorrelations limit our ability to make strong claims for the independent effectiveness of one form of restructuring over another. As defined at the outset, our conceptualization of restructuring for middle-grade schools is in a particular direction, which we mean to be consistent with policy recommendations about the reform of schools serving young adolescents. Given that vision, it is not surprising that we find interrelationships among measures.

Moreover, our restructuring measures are imprecise in some cases. These limitations, together with the caveats spelled out earlier, would combine to underestimate the relationships between school restructuring and student outcomes that we investigated here. Thus, we suggest that the results documented here should be seen as lower bounds for actual relationships between restructured schooling and student outcomes for the middle grades. Although the size of relationships is generally modest, their pattern is rather consistent.

Restructuring Toward What End?

The movement to restructure American middle-grade schools is not advocating change for the sake of change. Restructuring students' experiences is meant to move toward infusing the learning process with more meaning for the learner, to create less differentiated learning experiences (especially corresponding with social background), to emphasize the quality rather than the quantity of products, to integrate learning across disciplines, and to loosen the hierarchical barriers between adult and student members of school communities.

In sum, our results lend empirical support to the movement to restructure middle-grade schools. Changes that make schools that serve young adolescents less like comprehensive high schools and more like "small societies" are in order. Students who attend schools that are less bureaucratically structured achieve somewhat higher and engage more, and the distribution of these outcomes is somewhat more equitable in such schools. We suggest that the results of these analyses of restructuring in middle-grade schools represent only one piece in a larger puzzle.

CHAPTER 4

Restructuring in the Early Years of High School

The theoretical base for school restructuring is thin. As we explained in Chapter 1, rather than forging a coherent theoretical argument from the disparate sources from which this idea has been drawn, we locate our work on high school restructuring within a related theory: the contrast between bureaucratic and communal organizational forms of schooling. Beyond a weak conceptual grounding, evaluation of the effects of high school restructuring on students is complicated by at least three other factors. First, there is little agreement on what educational practitioners, policymakers, and researchers mean by school restructuring. Second, there are currently very few secondary schools that could be defined as "fully restructured" or even as actively "restructuring," regardless of the definition. Efforts to evaluate the degree of implementation of the restructuring reform have concluded that the fundamentally restructured school (especially a high school) is very rare. Third, for the more numerous schools that have only recently implemented reforms in the spirit of restructuring, it may be premature to evaluate effects of these organizational changes.

Given these difficulties, in this chapter we continue the somewhat eclectic approach to evaluating the effects of school restructuring introduced in Chapter 3. That is, we investigate how school organizational forms that are consistent with the *intent* of the restructuring movement influence their students, although these forms are not necessarily newly implemented (i.e., the schools are not always restructured from a different form). Thus, rather than evaluating the restructuring reform per se, we examine how practices consistent with the movement affect high school students' development, in particular their learning and development (see also Lee & Smith, 1995). Although we focus here on the same students that were part of the 8th-grade study described in Chapter 3, now they are 10th graders and almost all of them are in different schools.

56

REFORMING THE AMERICAN HIGH SCHOOL

The organization of secondary education has been subjected to reform almost from its inception. As Tyack (1974) points out, the separation of secondary schooling from the traditional village school into a more formal and systematized, and ultimately bureaucratic, organization was itself a significant educational reform in the late 19th and early 20th centuries. Over the last two decades, important social critics (e.g., Boyer 1983; Fullan, 1991; Goodlad, 1984; National Commission on Excellence in Education (NCEE), 1983; Sizer, 1984, 1992) have described the secondary school as so fundamentally linked to the success of our economic and political future that its failure jeopardizes the future of the nation itself. Its multiple ailments have prompted constant and strident calls for reform, revision, and restructuring. Almost no one argues that U.S. high schools are "working." Over the last few decades, their basic foundations have been questioned.

Beyond claims about weak academic programs, the American high school increasingly is being criticized for offering inappropriate responses to the human concerns of its members (e.g., Newmann & Oliver 1967; Oliver 1976; Phelan, Davidson, & Yu, 1998; Tyack 1974). Another complaint focuses on the large size of most U.S. high schools. Big schools may not be better, in terms of either economic efficiency (Clinchy, 2000; Fox, 1981; Guthrie, 1979) or academic development (Ayers, Klonsky, & Lyon, 2000; Gooding & Wagner, 1985; Haller, Monk, Spotted Bear, Griffith, & Moss, 1990; Monk, 1987). Moreover, a standard of equity in the distribution of school outcomes has joined the classic standard of excellence in assessing the effectiveness of schools (Coleman et al., 1966; Edmonds, 1984; Purkey & Smith, 1983).

INTRODUCING THE 10TH-GRADE STUDY

The way we define school restructuring in this chapter focuses on the structural practices that govern high schools. Our focus is on practices that differentiate the academic and social organization of schools between traditional or bureaucratic organizations, on the one hand, and communal organizations on the other. We consider practices that move the organization of schools toward more communal structures to be consistent with our definition of restructuring. Four ideas guided our work:

• *Idea 1 focuses on the prevalence of organizational practices aimed at changing the structure of high schools.* Here we suggest that the probability that an average high school adopts fundamental reforms aimed at moving schools toward the communal form is lower than the probability of adopting reforms aimed at change within the bureaucratic form.

• *Idea 2 centers on organizational practices with a communal form.* We suggest that students who attend schools with educational practices of the communal form are affected favorably, compared with those who attend schools with reform practices that aim to move student experiences in more traditional or bureaucratic ways. We expect positive effects in both the cognitive and noncognitive domains: on learning in several subject areas and on engagement with academic life. We also expect positive effects on the social distribution of these outcomes, in the direction of more social equity.

• *Idea 3 focuses on organizational practices with a bureaucratic form.* We expect that students in schools with structural practices consistent with the bureaucratic form are favored, compared with those in schools engaging in none of the practices identified as structural reforms. Effects are suggested on the same outcomes described above.

• *Idea 4 centers on school size.* We suggest that students who attend smaller high schools are advantaged by that experience, above and beyond other reform practices in which the school engages. We expect that attending small schools has positive effects on cognitive and noncognitive outcomes, as well as a more equitable distribution of these outcomes.

We begin to examine these ideas in this section, after briefly describing the sample we have used for the 10th-grade study. First, we present our definition of high school restructuring, which is based on the types of reform practices schools have in place. Second, we evaluate how the reform practices consistent with this definition have taken hold in the nation's high schools. Third, we examine the characteristics of students and schools in the 10th-grade study and how these characteristics are distributed across schools with different types and levels of restructuring.

The sample for the analyses in this chapter was drawn from the base year and first follow-up of the National Educational Longitudinal Study of 1988 (NELS:88). Beyond the general sample information in Chapters 2 and 3, it is important to know that the sample of NELS:88 10th graders used here has passed through four data filters: (1) students had cognitive test scores from both the base year and first follow-up; (2) data from their high schools and teachers were available; (3) students were enrolled in public, Catholic, or elite private secondary schools; and (4) they attended high schools with at least five NELS-sampled students. As many of these filters also applied to the sample in Chapter 3, when students were 8th graders, we are essentially studying the same *students* 2 years later. However, almost all are in different *schools*. Our sample includes 11,794 sophomores in 820 high schools. Most schools (717) are public, with fewer Catholic (54) and independent (49) schools.

Restructuring Practices

The logic underlying the construction of our measures of school restructuring rests on two criteria: (1) the distinction between bureaucratic and communal school organization from the literature, and (2) specific definitions of restructuring developed by the Center on the Organization and Restructuring of Schools (CORS) (Newmann, 1993). We drew up a list of 30 organizational practices included in the 1990 NELS data that describe school structure and that capture important elements of American secondary school reform. Although our work in this chapter describes high school restructuring, it is consistent with the definition of restructuring for middle-grade schools we spelled out in Chapter 3. Principals who completed the questionnaires indicated whether each practice was currently in place in their high schools.

We grouped the practices according to their adherence to (or departure from) a bureaucratic structural form. Practices reinforcing a top-down power flow (from administrators to teachers and students) include strong departmentalization, emphasis on teacher expertise and specialization, emphasis on rigid instructional requirements for students (i.e., tracking), and recognition programs for teachers that operate within the worker-reward paradigm. A natural extension of this structure to the external community would view parents as recipients of information provided by teachers and administrators.

We grouped practices that shift schools from the bureaucratic toward a communal form into three domains: (1) those aimed at *reorganizing instruction* (mixed-ability classes, cooperative learning focus, independent study in different curriculum areas, flexible time for classes); (2) those meant to *alter authority and expertise* in the school (interdisciplinary teaching teams, students evaluating teachers, staff solving school problems); and (3) those aimed at *personalizing relationships* within the school (using parent volunteers, students' keeping the same homeroom for several years, common planning time for teachers, schools-within-schools). We hoped that sorting these practices into these groups would provide some conceptual clarity. Together they represent movement toward a communal school organization in the areas of instruction, authority, and human relations. Details of the construction of our restructuring measures, as well as other variables used in these analyses, are found in Appendix A.

Prevalence of Reform Practices

If the comprehensive high school model were dominant in American education, communal reform practices would be less common than reforms within the traditional bureaucatic model. To test this hypothesis—within the first idea we spelled out above—we examined the prevalence of each practice in the high schools in our sample as a probability (i.e., the proportion of average NELS high schools reporting the practice). Probabilities for individual practices range from .09 to .85. The average school has 12 of the 30 reform practices in place. Individual structural practices, ordered by the frequency with which they occur in U.S. high schools, are listed in Table 4.1.[1]

Table 4.1. Prevalence of Structural Practices in "Average" U.S. High Schools (n = 820 schools)

Structural Practice	Probability
Traditional Practices	
Departmentalization with chairs	.85
Common classes for same curricular track	.76
Staff development focusing on adolescents	.66
PTA or PTO	.64
Parent-teacher conferences each semester	.64
Focus on critical thinking in curriculum	.64
Common classes for different curricular tracks	.62
Increased graduation requirements	.62
Recognition program for good teaching	.56
Parents sent information on how to help students study	.56
Moderate Practices	
Parent workshops on adolescent problems	.46
Student satisfaction with courses important	.42
Strong emphasis on parental involvement	.38
Strong emphasis on increasing academic requirements	.35
Student evaluation of course content important	.35
Outstanding teachers are recognized	.34
Emphasis on staff stability	.34
Emphasis on staff-development activities	.32
Restructured Practices	
Students keep same homeroom over high school	.30
Emphasis on staff solving school problems	.29
Parents volunteer in the school	.28
Interdisciplinary teaching teams	.24
Independent study, English/social studies	.23
Mixed-ability classes in math/science	.21
Cooperative learning focus	.21
Student evaluation of teachers important	.20
Independent study in math/science	.18
School-within-a-school	.15
Teacher teams have common planning time	.11
Flexible time for classes	.09

The probabilities in Table 4.1 show a pattern: Practices that fit our definition of restructuring are the least common reforms in U.S. secondary schools. That is, communal reforms are considerably less common than bureaucratic reforms. We grouped together the structural practices that represent communal reforms (the third group in Table 4.1) and labeled them "restructured practices." These practices represent substantial departure from conventional practice (in terms of their low frequencies). Practices that adhere to the bureaucratic form were grouped under the "traditional" or "moderate" labels. We divided traditional and moderate practices probabilistically rather than conceptually. Neither of these reform categories represents a shift away from traditional forms of instruction, authority, or human relations. Moreover, such practices are not unusual in high schools.

CLASSIFYING SCHOOLS BASED ON PRACTICES

Although Table 4.1 describes reform *practices*, we wanted to categorize *schools* in terms of their current practices. Though our aim in this chapter is to evaluate the effectiveness of the restructuring reform movement, this is difficult because only a tiny fraction of U.S. high schools could actually be called "restructured." Thus, we shifted our attention to evaluating the effects on students of attending schools implementing reforms consistent with our definition of restructuring.

Unfortunately, schools are not consistent in the types (or numbers) of reforms they implement. Exploratory analyses of schools focusing on the reform practices listed in Table 4.1 revealed that schools typically adopt several of these practices simultaneously, rather than one at a time. We found, for example, that besides the relatively low probability of schools' engaging in any single restructuring practice, those that do are also likely (1) to adopt more than one restructuring practice, and (2) to adopt several traditional or moderate practices. On the other hand, we were suprised that more than a trivial number of schools report having in place *none* of the 30 practices listed in Table 4.1. Based on exploratory analyses, we classified the schools in our sample into three categories:

• Unrestructured schools. Twelve percent (97) of the 820 sample schools did not report that they engaged in any of the 30 practices listed in Table 4.1.
  • Schools with traditional practices. These schools (346, or 42%) reported engaging in one or several moderate or traditional practices, but did not report engaging in a meaningful number of practices we classified as consistent with restructuring (see below).

• Schools with restructuring practices. Schools in this category (377, or 46%) reported at least three of the restructuring practices in place, as well as several practices we listed as traditional or moderate.

Although any group that includes almost half of the sample can hardly be called unusual, grouping schools in this way held together conceptually and statistically. Focusing on the practices listed in Table 4.1 that are consistent with restructuring, we investigated the proportions of schools engaging in several practices simultaneously. As the number of practices increased, the proportions dropped steeply. This suggests that sustaining many restructuring reforms is difficult.[2] Readers may wonder, "Why three reforms?" We provided more detail on the logic for our deciding on this cut-point in Lee and Smith (1995). We have used these categories of schools-by-practices both to organize descriptions of students and schools and for the contrasts we used to evaluate the effects of school restructuring. We used two school-level contrasts in our analyses: (1) no reforms compared with traditional reforms and (2) restructuring also compared with traditional reforms.

CONSIDERING SCHOOL SIZE

A movement away from large comprehensive high schools is consistent with efforts to restructure schools along other dimensions. Thus, in addition to the restructuring contrasts we also investigated the effects of high school size.[3] We considered small school size a facilitating factor for school restructuring. The communal organizational form is more common, and probably easier to implement, in smaller schools (Bryk et al., 1993; Lee, Bryk, & Smith, 1993).

Students, Schools, and School Restructuring

The major aim of this chapter is to examine the effects of attending schools that are either unrestructured or restructured in the direction of a communal organizational form (both compared with schools with traditional reforms) on students' academic and social development. However, before investigating such effects, we examined the characteristics of students and schools that were associated with these three types of schools.

What kinds of students attend schools without reform practices, with traditional reform practices, and with restructured practices? Are other school characteristics associated with schools grouped by the reform practices they have implemented? These were substantially fewer students (11%) in schools without reform practices, and the proportion of schools of this type was smaller (12%) than the other two school groups. Schools with traditional practices represented slightly less than half the schools (42%) and students

(45%). Almost half the schools (46%) and students (44%) were in our target group—schools with restructured practices.

ANALYSIS STRATEGY AND PRESENTATION

Consistent with other multivariate analyses in this book, in our analyses in this chapter we use hierarchical linear modeling (HLM). In Appendix B, we present a brief description of this methodology, organized around the research questions in this chapter. We present results to test Ideas 2–4 that examine these effects in both numerical and graphic form. Although we are anxious to tell the complete story revealed by our analyses, we have also attempted to keep the presentation of numerical results as straightforward as possible. We refer readers interested in a more extended discussion of the numerical results to Lee and Smith (1995).

In most analyses in this chapter, we have taken into account important characteristics of students and schools. For students, we controlled for socioeconomic status (SES), minority status, gender, and academic status (ability and engagement) at the beginning of high school. Our models also included a common set of controls for demographic and structural characteristics of schools: average school SES, school minority concentration, Catholic and independent sector (compared with public schools), and two controls that described the academic character of high schools.[4] School size, which we view as a restructuring rather than a control variable, was also included.

STUDENTS IN THE THREE GROUPS OF SCHOOLS

We investigated restructuring effects on five dependent variables, all of which measure change between 8th and 10th grades. Four were achievement tests (in mathematics, reading, history, and science); the fifth measured students' engagement with school. Beginning in this chapter, we consider achievement in particular subjects, rather than composite achievement, as we considered in Chapter 3. We computed achievement gains as differences between students' scores on the same tests in each subject at 8th and 10th grades. Our engagement measure was composed of eight variables that: (1) measured students' behaviors and attitudes about their current high school classes, (2) reflected the frequency of these attitudes and behaviors, (3) were associated with the same subjects measured by the NELS tests, and (4) assessed whether students worked hard and felt challenged.[5]

Panel I of Table 4.2 describes the average characteristics of students in the three types of schools. For the outcomes (Panel I-A), the general pattern in the mean differences among students shows that students attending schools without reform practices were consistently less advantaged and less engaged

Table 4.2. Characteristics of Students and Schools Associated with Various Levels of Practices Associated with Restructuring

	Level and Type of School Restructuring		
	Schools without Reform Practices	Schools with Traditional Practices	Schools with Restructured Practices
Student Sample	$n = 1,280$	$n = 5,353$	$n = 5,161$
School Sample	$n = 97$	$n = 346$	$n = 377$
I. Variables Describing Students			
A. Outcomes			
Math gain	4.74	5.28	5.49
Reading gain	2.18	2.53	2.39
History gain	1.92	2.21	2.33
Science gain	2.11	2.26	2.57
Engagement	.055	-.051	-.003
B. Student Controls			
Engagement, 8th grade	-.07	-.11	.24
Social class[a]	-.232	-.101	.049
Minority status (%)	34.9	15.9	20.8
Female (%)	52.5	50.6	50.2
Ability controls, 8th grade:[a]			
Test composite	-.20	-.05	.14
Reading control	-.21	-.04	.14
Math control	-.21	-.04	.12
History control	-.20	-.05	.13
Science control	-.21	-.05	.14
II. Variables Describing Schools			
School Controls			
Average SES[a]	-.41	-.18	.30
Minority (%)	33.5	12.9	16.4
Average Achievement, 8th grade	-.48	-.15	.27
Math/science courses[b]	2.37	2.48	2.69
Variability in course taking[c]	1.46	1.32	1.16
School size	1,095	633	764
School sector:			
Public (%)	98.7	95.5	82.6
Catholic (%)	0.8	4.1	10.4
NAIS (%)	0.5	0.5	7.0

[a] Variables are z-scored, M = 0, SD = 1.
[b] Mathematics and science courses taken by students were summed and averaged.
[c] The standard deviation (SD) of math/science course taking.

than those in traditional practice or restructuring schools. Moreover, students in schools with restructured practices typically gained more in terms of achievement than their counterparts in schools with traditional practices or without reforms. Achievement gains were slightly larger in restructuring than in traditional practice schools, although engagement varied little between the groups. Although most differences were statistically significant, they were also quite small—usually no larger than .15 SD.

Students' demographic and academic characteristics (Panel I-B of Table 4.2) followed a similar pattern: Those in schools without reform practices were of lower SES, were more likely to be members of minority groups, and came to high school less engaged and with lower ability in eighth grade than their peers in traditional practice or restructuring schools. In general, students in schools without reform practices ranked below, and those in restructuring practice schools ranked above, those attending schools with traditional reforms. Group differences in the control variables, although not large, were typically larger than group differences in the outcomes (.2-.3 SD).

SCHOOL CHARACTERISTICS OF THE THREE GROUPS

Reflecting the student characteristics, schools without reform practices were significantly disadvantaged compared with traditional practice and restructured schools in terms of SES and minority enrollment (Panel II of Table 4.2). The proportions of schools from the three sectors in these groups may explain some of the social background differences. Although 14% of the schools were private, very low proportions of Catholic and elite private schools were in the group without reform practices. However, a relatively high proportion of restructuring practice schools were private. In fact, over half (52%) of the Catholic schools and three-quarters (74%) of the independent schools were in this group. The overwhelming majority of all groups (over 80%), however, were public schools.[6]

The academic character of the schools, defined by students' average coursework in mathematics and science, was also related to restructuring. Schools without reform practices were typified by less, and restructuring practices schools by more, academic course taking. Moreover, the amount of variation among students in their course-taking behaviors was also important. Course taking in schools without reform practices was more variable than in traditional schools, and in restructuring schools course taking was more homogeneous. School size followed a different pattern. Traditional practice schools were smaller than either restructuring or no-reform schools.

The numbers in Table 4.2 show that the characteristics of students and schools were considerably different among schools without reform practicies, with traditional practices, and with restructuring practices—in terms of demographic factors, sector, cognitive and noncognitive status as students enter high school, and differences in schools' academic emphases. In fact, mean differences among the three groups of schools in students' cognitive gains in Table 4.2 were less than might be expected, considering the group mean differences in the student and school characteristics. Such differences among the groups in student and school characteristics suggest the importance of taking these factors into account in analyses that aim to evaluate the effects of school restructuring.

THE EFFECTS OF SCHOOL RESTRUCTURING ON STUDENT DEVELOPMENT

In the last section, we described how we measured school restructuring. We also described how students and schools differ, based on whether the schools had no reform practices, had implemented only traditional reforms, or were restructured according to our definition. In this section, we explore how attending restructured schools and no-reform schools (each compared with traditionally reformed schools) influenced students' development in terms of gains in achievement and engagement between 8th and 10th grade. We evaluated these effects with multilevel methods. How we present our results in this section reflects the three-step multilevel model approach we used. First, we describe the partitioning of variance in the outcomes into within- and between-school components. Second, we explore how students' outcomes were influenced by their demographic characteristics. In the third section, we describe the effects of school restructuring on student outcomes after controlling for both student and school characteristics. Only when differences between students and schools are taken into account can restructuring effects be accurately evaluated.

Variance in the Outcomes Between Schools

We performed most HLM analyses in this book in three steps. In the first step, we partitioned the variance in the five outcomes into two parts—the proportion that was between students in the same schools and the proportion that was systematically between schools (called the "intraclass correlation" within HLM). It is only the between-school component of the variance in the outcomes that may be influenced by restructuring (or any other school factor). Our outcome set included achievement gains in mathematics, reading, history, and science over the first 2 years of high school. The between-school proportion of variance in these outcomes was modest—15% for reading, 16% for mathematics and history, and 20% for science. The between-school proportion of variance in engagement was even less (13%). Although low, these proportions were adequate to proceed. However, such low proportions also suggest that school factors (such as restructuring) are able to influence student development only modestly.

Taking Students' Demographic and Social Characteristics into Account

In the second step of our HLM analyses, we estimated a set of within-school HLM models. Here we introduced controls for the variables describing students' social and academic background discussed earlier and listed in Panel I-B of Table 4.2. Results of this within-school HLM model, displayed in Table 4.3, show that most of these demographic and academic background factors were significantly related to gains in engagement and achievement. Once ability status was taken into account on the gain-score outcomes,[7] gender was unrelated to learning except in science; females learned significantly less in this subject. Engagement prior to high school was positively related to all five outcomes. The fact that ability was positively related to engagement and science gain suggests that more able students were more engaged and learned more in science. However, ability was only modestly related to learning in mathematics, reading, and history.

In the HLM analyses, we paid special attention to the relationship between student SES and these outcomes, as we did in Chapter 3. SES was significantly and positively associated with engagement and gains in the four subjects. We interpret this finding as indicating that learning and engagement are inequitably distributed in U.S. high schools; more advantaged stu-

Table 4.3. Within-school Model for the Effects of School Restructuring on Gains in Engagement and Achievement, 8th–10th grades

Independent Variables	Dependent Variables				
	Academic Engagement	Gain in Mathematics	Gain in Reading	Gain in History	Gain in Science
Intercept (School average)	.00	3.22^{***}	2.22^{***}	1.76^{***}	2.86^{***}
Engagement, 8th grade	1.16^{***}	$.16^{***}$	$.08^{*}$	$.05^{*}$	$.07^{*}$
8th-grade ability	$.48^{***}$	$-.04^{*}$	$.07^{\sim}$	$-.07^{**}$	$.21^{***}$
Social class	$.77^{***}$	$.14^{**}$	$.04^{\sim}$	$.11^{\sim}$	$.12^{**}$
Minority status	$.82^{***}$	$-.04$	$-.23^{*}$	$-.12^{\sim}$	$-.68^{***}$
Gender (female)	1.22^{***}	$-.10$	$-.04$	$-.07$	$-.37^{***}$

$^{\sim}p \leq .10$; $^{*}p \leq .05$; $^{**}p \leq .01$; $^{***}p \leq .001$

dents learn more and are more engaged in the first 2 years of high school. We hypothesized that school restructuring also influences the social distribution of these outcomes; we expect that restructuring practices consistent with a communal organization are associated with a more equitable distribution of these outcomes. That would mean that the relationship between SES and, say, gains in mathematics achievement would be lower in schools with more restructured practices.[8]

Taking Schools' Compositions and Structures into Account

The results of our between-school HLM analyses on the five outcomes are presented in Tables 4.4 and 4.5. In Table 4.4, we present the effects of school restructuring (and school controls) on average gains in engagement and achievement. In Table 4.5, we present the same set of effects on the relationship between SES and the five outcomes. The results in Table 4.4 focus on *effectiveness* (i.e., school average learning in the four core subjects and in engagement), whereas the results in Table 4.5 focus on *equity* (how the outcomes are distributed among students of different SES levels in each school). Although the results for each outcome in Tables 4.4 and 4.5 were estimated

Table 4.4. Between-school Model for the Effects of School Restructuring on Gains in Engagement and Achievement, 8th–10th grades

	Dependent Variables				
	Academic Engagement	Gain in Mathematics	Gain in Reading	Gain in History	Gain in Science
Effects on Mean Between-school Outcome					
Average Intercept	-.89***	2.92***	1.94***	1.71***	2.95***
A. School-level Controls					
School SES	-.08	-.02	.08	.10	.27***
Minority concentration	.03~	.00	.10	.03	-.23~
Catholic high school	-.07	.49*	.32~	-.01	.33
NAIS high school	1.23***	.18	.44~	.03	.45~
Academic emphasis	.26***	.21**	.18*	.13*	.56***
Course variability	-.17*	-.07	-.06	-.09~	.26**
B. Effects of School Restructuring					
School size	-.19*	-.39***	-.32***	-.36***	-.37***
Schools without reform practices	-.14*	-.21~	-.20~	-.15*	-.10
Restructuring practice schools	.37**	.49***	.37***	.35***	.59***

~$p \leq .10$; *$p \leq .05$; **$p \leq .01$; ***$p \leq .001$

Table 4.5. Between-school Model for the Effects of School Restructuring on Equity in Gains in Engagement and Achievement, 8th–10th grade

	Dependent Variables				
	Engagement/ SES Slope	Gain in Mathematics/ SES Slope	Gain in Reading/ SES Slope	Gain in History/ SES Slope	Gain in Science/ SES Slope
Effects on SES-Differentiation					
Average SES Slope	1.59^{***}	$.43^{***}$	$.51^{*}$	$.36^{*}$	$.61^{***}$
A. School-level controls					
School SES	$.63^{**}$	$.39^{\sim}$	.19	.20	.06
Minority concentration	.25	.26	.44	-.27	-.05
Catholic high school	-.82	-.26	$-.68^{*}$	-.70	-.06
NAIS high school	.03	.75	.25	-.28	-.70
Academic emphasis	$-.94^{**}$	$-.27^{*}$	$-.34^{*}$	-.13	$-.46^{*}$
Course variability	$.34^{\sim}$	.02	.09	.20	.12
B. Effects of school restructuring					
School size	.10	$.03^{*}$	$.34^{**}$	$.22^{*}$	$.25^{*}$
Schools without reform practices	.16	$.18^{*}$	$.54^{*}$	$.33^{*}$	$.47^{\sim}$
Restructuring practice schools	$-.54^{***}$	$-.33^{**}$	$-.38^{*}$	$-.32^{*}$	$-.30^{**}$

$^{\sim}p \leq .10$; $^{*}p \leq .05$; $^{**}p \leq .01$; $^{***}p \leq .001$

together, we separate them here to simplify the discussion. In all analyses, we have also taken into account all the student characteristics shown in Table 4.3, although we have not displayed those here.

SCHOOL RESTRUCTURING, LEARNING, AND ENGAGEMENT

We focus on three measures of school restructuring, two of which are contrasts (the third is school size). One measure contrasts schools with no reform practices with schools with traditional reforms. The second contrast (and the one of most interest here) is between restructured schools and traditional practice schools. The effects of restructuring on learning and engagement we called "effectiveness" earlier.

The pattern of results in Table 4.4 is quite consistent. Over their first 2 years of high school, students learned more, and were significantly more engaged, in restructured than in traditional schools. On the other hand, students in schools without reform practices learned significantly less than their counterparts in traditional schools. The magnitude of effects for the restructuring/ traditional contrast was considerably larger than the no reform/traditional contrast, although both contrasts were statistically significant on all outcomes.

RESTRUCTURING AND THE EQUITABLE DISTRIBUTION
OF LEARNING AND ENGAGEMENT

Our exploration of social equity is structured similarly to that in Chapter 3, in that we investigate the relationship between students' SES and the outcomes. A variable that is negatively associated with the SES/outcome slopes would indicate more social equity, in that it lessens that relationship. The results in Table 4.5 again show a consistent pattern. Compared with traditional high schools, restructured high schools induced a more socially equitable distribution of learning in mathematics, reading, history, and science, as well as in engagement. Correspondingly, schools without reform practices were more socially inequitable in terms of these distributions (i.e., the effects were positive).

SCHOOL SIZE, LEARNING, ENGAGEMENT, AND SOCIAL EQUITY

Other consistent patterns concern the effects of school size. Results in Table 4.4 indicate that in all four subjects, students learned less in larger than in smaller schools. Students were also less engaged in larger than in smaller schools. From Table 4.5, we see that larger schools were also more inequitable in terms of the distribution of engagement and learning by student SES. These size effects on equity are larger for learning in reading, history, and science than in mathematics. Students who attended smaller high schools were favored in terms of both effectiveness and equity. That is, students who attended small schools learned more, and their learning was less differentiated by social class. Because these analyses also took into account school sector, the fact that private schools are typically smaller does not explain this finding. Because of the way we explored school size in these analyses, we were unable to translate our results directly into actual school enrollments. We explore these findings about school size in more detail in Chapter 7, where we discuss actual school sizes.

The hypotheses we posed early in this chapter about communal and bureaucratic organizational structure, and about school size, are supported by these results. The consistent pattern of the effects shown in Tables 4.4 and 4.5 suggests that restructuring can have important consequences for student learning and engagement. High schools that implement practices consistent with the restructuring reform movement fit the set of double qualifications for "good schools" we spelled out earlier—schools like this are simultaneously more effective and more equitable in terms of their students' engagement and learning. This is also true for smaller high schools.

Revisiting the Effects of School Restructuring

The substantive meaning of these results may be clearer when displayed graphically. Figures 4.1 through 4.4 depict achievement gains in the four subjects for students from lower-SES, middle-class, and upper-SES families in three types of schools: those without reform practices, those with traditional practices, and those with practices in place that are consistent with restructuring.[9] In these graphs, "lower-SES students" are those whose SES is 1 SD below the mean; "middle-class students" are those whose SES value is the mean (0); and "upper-SES students" are those whose SES is 1 standard deviation (SD) above the mean. Achievement gains are the averages for students of various SES levels who attend schools of the three types. The three lines shown on each graph, one for

FIGURE 4.1. Mathematics learing in the first two years of high school for students of different SES in no-reform, traditional, and restructured schools.

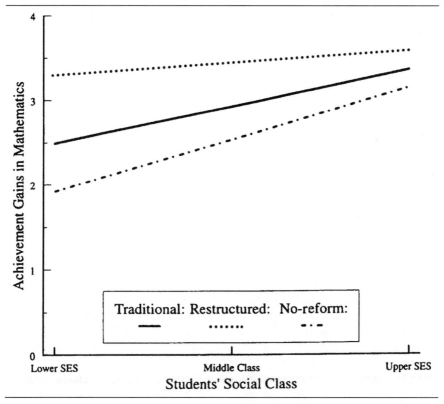

FIGURE 4.2. Reading learning in the first two years of high school for students of different SES in no-reform, traditional, and restructured schools.

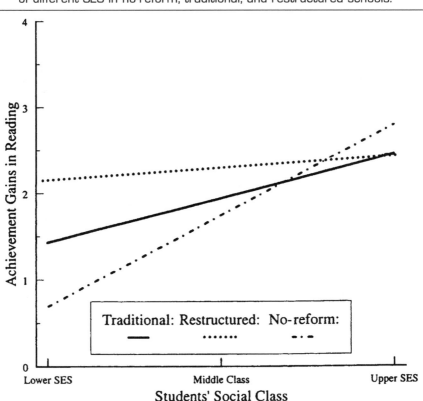

each type of school, are a visual respresentation of the numerical results presented in Tables 4.4 and 4.5.[10]

Three important trends are evident from these graphs. First, the relationship between SES and achievement gain was positive in all types of schools and all subjects. Second, in all four subjects, almost all students learned the most in restructured schools and the least in schools without reform practices. Third, the advantage of attending a restructured school was most striking for lower-SES students. The fact that the slopes of the lines, in all four subjects, were flatter in restructuring schools suggests that student learning is less influenced by students' SES in such schools. That is, students who attended restructuring schools, compared with their counterparts in traditional schools (and especially in schools without reform practices) were advantaged in two ways: Not only did all students learn more, but learning

Figure 4.3. History learning in the first two years of high school for students of different SES in no-reform, traditional, and restructured schools.

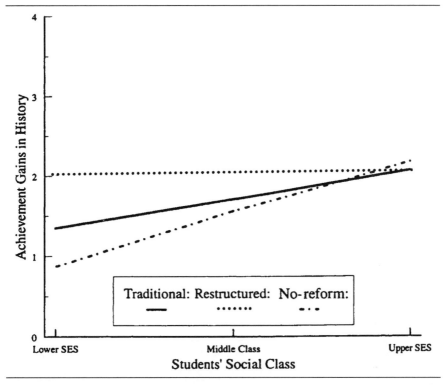

was more equitably distributed. These results led us to conclude that restructured schools are both more effective and more equitable.

Summary of the Findings

Under the theoretical contrast of bureaucratic and communal organization, we used two dimensions to evaluate high school restructuring. One focused on structural practices, which we categorized by their form (communal or bureaucratic), and included the idea of "substantial departure from conventional practice" (i.e., unusualness). We grouped high schools, by the number and type of reform practices, into three categories: restructuring practice schools, traditional practice schools, and schools without reform practices. The second dimension focused on the size of high schools. Here we considered smaller size as a feature of school structure that facilitates a more communal organization.

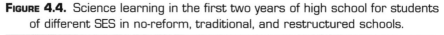

FIGURE 4.4. Science learning in the first two years of high school for students of different SES in no-reform, traditional, and restructured schools.

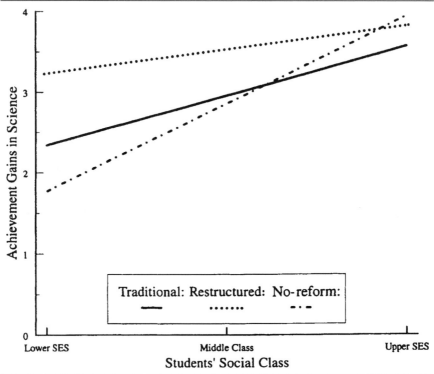

Effects on cognitive learning early in high school followed a clear and consistent pattern. Students who attended schools with several restructuring practices learned more in mathematics, reading, history, and science, whereas students attending schools without reform practices learned less. We found similar advantages for students in smaller schools (above and beyond whether they are restructured). We also considered how attending certain types of schools affected the *distribution* of learning among students from different social backgrounds. Effects here were also consistent. Learning in the four subjects was more equitably distributed in smaller schools. Schools with restructuring practices were more equalizing environments in terms of the social distribution of cognitive gains, and schools without any of these reforms were more stratifying environments. Our results regarding students' engagement with academic learning early in high school were similar to those for cognitive development. Students in small schools were more engaged in their studies, and engagement was higher and more equitably distributed in schools where restructuring practices were common.

IMPLICATIONS FOR HIGH SCHOOL RESTRUCTURING

Based on the strength and consistency of the findings of the 10th-grade study, we draw some general conclusions about the organizational structure of high schools: Students learn more, and are more engaged, in smaller schools and in schools with several practices that are consistent with restructuring. Schools organized in this way are also more equitable environments.

How Many Reforms?

We are concerned that our results here might lead school practitioners to jump to a conclusion that we do not think is justified: "Pick any three reforms from this list, and a high school will be both more effective and more equitable." We conducted a series of sensitivity analyses to explore the implications of such a decision. The results of our sensitivity analysis demonstrated clearly that the simultaneous implementation of many restructuring reforms (more than three on most outcomes) did not increase either effectiveness or equity. However, our sensitivity results also showed that implementing only one or two was not as advantageous as implementing three or four. The results of these sensitivity analyses justify our construction of the restructuring contrasts, as well as having practical implications for the implementation of reforms in high schools.

Two studies of school restructuring in local contexts support these findings. A study in Kentucky (Kyle, 1993) reported that schools in the early stages of reform (elementary, middle, and high schools), particularly those that had dabbled in a wide range of reforms, had less advantageous outcomes than schools with sustained commitment to fewer reforms. A study of the emerging effects of reform in Chicago's elementary (K–8) schools labeled some "Christmas trees. . . . 'showcase' schools with many new programs, multiple 'add-ons' with little coordination, and little attention to strengthening the organizational core" (Bryk, Easton, Kerbow, Rollow, & Sebring [1993], p. 15). Such schools were compared with those with a shared and unified school vision. These authors found that outcomes in the latter types of schools were more favorable.

We suggest that the lessons to be drawn from our analyses and other studies are that school practitioners should think about the *direction* and *consistency* of the reform orientation in which they want to take their schools, and we suggest that the direction should be consistent with moving schools toward a more communal organization. Moreover, we suggest the importance of a consistent vision of reform, one that schools stick with over time and that they work hard to make successful. This means that jumping on a lot of reform "bandwagons" simultaneously is not a good idea.

Is Reducing School Size Really the Issue?

Although the restructuring practices we investigated here have implications for the conceptual direction of school reform, we suggest that it does not make sense to consider our findings about school size in a similar "reform light." Would reducing the size of high schools really "cause" students to learn more? The structure of our analyses, where we estimate the *direct* effect of school size on the outcomes, would suggest that this would be so. However, we urge readers not to draw this simple conclusion from our results. In fact, we suspect that none of these schools had recently reduced their size as a reform strategy. Rather, we interpret the findings about size as indicating that enrollment size acts as a facilitating or debilitating factor for other desirable practices. For example, we know that collegiality among teachers, personalized relationships, and less differentiation of instruction by ability (to name a few restructuring practices) are more common and easier to implement in small schools. Reducing school size, while a potential structural reform in its own right, is unlikely to increase student learning per se. We take up this topic in more depth in Chapter 7.

What Should We Conclude?

We think that it is more appropriate to draw broad, rather than narrow and prescriptive, recommendations from our results. We feel confident in concluding that something important is happening inside the schools with multiple restructuring practices that encourage their students to demonstrate more learning, which is also more equitably distributed. The results here are stronger, and more consistent, than the results in Chapter 3, where we explored similar reform effects in middle-grade schools. However, results from both studies point in a consistent direction—in favor of moving toward communal school organization. For us, the results provide empirical support for moving schools in that direction and away from the bureaucratic form that has characterized the U.S. comprehensive high school for a century. The results also suggest that schools should target their reform efforts around a modest number of single practices of this type, practices that should probably be adopted neither singly and serially, nor in large numbers to "showcase" a school's superficial commitment to reform. Our results also provide support for smaller learning environments.

We admit to some frustration about our lack of empirical success in grouping restructuring reform practices into those targeted on instruction, autonomy, and community. Thus, we caution readers against trying to extract specific recommendations from our results about *which* of these reforms, considered individually, are better than others, or even about *how many* reforms are optimal. In the next section of this book, we focus on trying to understand more about the internal workings and organizational forms of those schools we classified as "restructuring practice schools."

PART III

School Social Organization and Restructuring

The three chapters in Part III of this book expand our work beyond the focus of Part II (Chapters 3 and 4), where we have examined how attending schools whose practices were consistent with the school restructuring movement influenced students' engagement and achievement. Although we continue to explore how characteristics of schools influence the students who attend them, in Part III (Chapters 5, 6, and 7) we broaden our definition of "school characteristics." Here we give closer attention to other aspects of school organization beyond demographic composition and restructuring (at least as we defined it in Part II). Chapter 5 centers on the *social organization of schools*, in particular on how the organization of teachers' professional lives influences their students. Chapter 6 returns to the theme of school restructuring, as we defined it in Chapter 4, but here we locate our notion of school restructuring within a *more broadly defined concept of school organization*. We also focus (in Chapters 6 and 7) on the same group of students, now in their last year of high school. In Chapter 7 we provide a closer look at a particular aspect of school structure that has been part of all our analyses, *school size*, again investigating how it influences students' learning over the 4 high school years. Our purpose in Part III is to embed our exploration of school restructuring within more enduring, and perhaps more fundamental, aspects of U.S. secondary schools: how they are organized academically, socially, and structurally.

CHAPTER 5

The Organization of Teachers' Work Lives

It is axiomatic that the main work of schools—teaching and learning—revolves around teachers. Although most of our discussion about reforming high schools through restructuring has thus far focused on features of school organization and structure, many restructuring conversations also include suggestions that focus on changing procedures, principles, rules, roles, and relationships within schools. These types of conversations often target teachers and teaching. Calls for reforms involving teachers and instruction have been issued by such prestigious groups as the Carnegie Task Force on Teaching as a Profession (1986) and the National Commission on Excellence in Education ([NCEE], 1983), and several aspects of instruction have been embedded in our measures of restructuring used in Chapters 3 and 4. One of the four dimensions of reform spelled out by the Center on the Organization and Restructuring of Schools (CORS) involved changing the professional lives of teachers. This chapter focuses on that dimension of restructuring.

Whether the locale is inside or outside the classroom, whether the focus is on the academic or social dimensions of schooling, the work done by teachers is pivotal in the education of students. Moreover, teachers transmit much more than mere factual information to their students. The work teachers do—instruction—is influenced by the conditions within which they perform their tasks. The focus of most studies of teachers' work is on how changes in the structure of their lives influence their own behaviors and attitudes about their work. However, a common assumption among reform proposals that address the work of teachers is that, either implicitly or explicitly, such reforms aim to improve learning for all students. Consistent with that assumption, and with the focus of this book (on student achievement), in this chapter we explore how characteristics of teachers' work lives influence how much their students learn. We capture the notion of teachers' professional lives in several ways: how they define their work; how they interact with their students, their colleagues, and their superiors; and the degree to which they feel control over their work.

STUDYING TEACHERS' WORK LIVES

Before discussing our empirical examination of the link between teachers' professional community and student learning, we briefly review the relevant research about three concepts that characterize teachers' work environments: cooperation among teachers, how much of their work lives teachers control, and their attitudes about their students.

Division and Sharing of Work

Instruction in high schools is typically specialized by subject matter and departments, with teachers cast in the role of knowledge experts. The typical public high school has a bureaucratic structure, a mechanistic task structure, and a base of shared authority resting on specialized knowledge and expertise (Rowan, 1990). Teachers' work lives in such organizations are complex. Although a professional authority structure would imply autonomous and self-monitored work, the isolation and vulnerability built into the structure of teaching may inhibit or limit professional development. The solitary nature of teaching can be ameliorated through face-to-face relationships with colleagues and by leaders who support the important work of the school (Herriot & Firestone, 1984; Lortie, 1975; Westheimer, 1998). Developing a professional community in a school requires both deprivatizing practice and increasing collaboration among teachers across disciplines—in essence, dissolving the specialized task structures that typify most secondary schools. These types of cooperation mutually reinforce instructional goals and activities. Rather than imposed by controls or sanctions, these goals are professionally supported through observation and affiliation (Little, 1990; Louis, Marks, & Kruse, 1996; Westheimer, 1998).

Besides the obvious personal benefits that accrue to teachers through social contact with their peers, cooperative professional relationships are also important in developing an effective school culture (Barry, 1995; Leonard & Leonard, 1999; Lieberman, 1995; Little, 1982). These affective ties among individuals become linked to the structure of work, creating a network of associations that may enhance teachers' academic efforts. Collegial and supportive interactions foster the sharing of information and advice about teaching (Lee, Bryk, & Smith, 1993; Roth, Masciotra, & Boyd, 1999; Rowan, 1990).

The evidence that positive consequences accrue to students who are enrolled in schools characterized by collaborative and supportive structures rests mainly on observations in schools undergoing specific reforms directed to these ends (Kruse & Louis, 1993; Lieberman, 1990, 1995; Shedd & Bacharach, 1991; Westheimer, 1998). A link between professional cooperation and student learning rests on the assumption that such interactions either improve instruction or reduce teacher stress and burnout caused by professional isolation. Both improved instruction and reduced stress are assumed to increase student learning. The cross-sectional nature of most of this research makes it impossible to determine whether actual changes in teaching result from inducing increased cooperation. However, investigating how student learning differs among secondary schools with different collaborative structures would lend support to the argument.

Control, Decision Making, and Empowerment

The bureaucratic structure of most high schools places decisions about resources with administrators, whereas power over technical skill and curriculum knowledge mostly rests with teachers and/or departments (Mintzberg, 1983). Improving conditions in schools involves both resource allocation and classroom practice. Thus, a division between administrators' authority exercised over resources and teachers' authority over practice may lead to conflict. Many reforms that focus on teachers and their work emphasize shifting basic decisions about resource allocation and other school policies from the central office to building-level administrators, and even to teachers. Often referred to as "empowerment," "shared decision making," or "site-based management," this reform strategy argues for making teachers more active decision makers. It rests on the idea that increased participation will raise teachers' investment in the "business" of schooling (Johnson & Pajares, 1996; Shedd & Bacharach, 1991). Teachers' control of their classrooms rests, ultimately, on cooperating with their students (Metz, 1993). A downward shift of power would redefine the formal positions of both teachers and administrators by altering functional control over important organizational domains: resources and management (French & Raven, 1968; Mintzberg, 1983). We borrow McNeil's (1988) terminology— "control"—and expand the notion beyond management decisions to include teachers' influence on a wide range of school issues (including how instruction is organized).

Although researchers have suggested that teacher control is associated with student outcomes (Ashton & Webb, 1986; Rosenholtz, 1989), this link has not been demonstrated directly. Rather, teachers' control or influence over their work has been shown to influence their *perceptions* of their own effectiveness in teaching (Conway, 1984; Imber & Duke 1985; Imber & Neidt, 1990; Lee, Dedrick, & Smith, 1991; Newmann, Rutter, & Smith, 1989; Shedd & Bacharach, 1991). Teachers *feel* more effective when they control curriculum, teaching methods, and the classroom environment (Kelchtermans & Strittmatter, 1999; McNeil, 1988; Miller, 1999; Mohrman,

Cooke, & Mohrman, 1978). However, the link to student outcomes may be indirect, through teachers' becoming more committed to their work. Thus, empowering teachers could induce commitment, and commitment would in turn influence student learning.

Norms, Goals, and Attitudes

In any organization (not just schools), individual commitment to organizational goals develops in response to uses of power, commonly exercised through decision-making strategies, sanctions, and norms (Etzioni, 1975; Schwartz, 1999; Yukl, 1981). Although commitment increases when individuals are empowered, in high schools this is countered by a hierarchical institutional structure and normative emphasis on expert authority (Greene & Podsakoff, 1981). If many teachers are committed to the goals and values of their schools, commitment becomes a normative feature of the school's culture (Terry, Hogg, & Duck, 1999; Wyner, 1991). In professional communities, there is an emphasis on both the *content* and the *sharing* of norms. A positive school professional community requires commitment to certain values. Norms must include an institutional focus on learning, one that emphasizes growth, development, and engagement in academic pursuits for all students (Louis, Marks, & Kruse, 1996). Beyond providing information to be digested and procedures to be mastered, teachers in professional communities also communicate their own attitudes toward particular students and toward the learning process. These attitudes represent an important dimension of classroom and school culture. They are instrumental in how students construct knowledge and learn (Brophy, 1986).

EFFECTS OF TEACHERS' ATTITUDES ON STUDENTS

Rosenthal and Jacobsen's (1968) seminal study of the self-fulfilling prophecy of expectations showed that experimental manipulation of teachers' beliefs about the abilities of their students substantially influenced actual learning. Despite the controversy and research that study sparked among psychologists about the effects of teacher expectations on student outcomes, its conclusions have been confirmed (see, for example, Brophy, 1983; Cooper, Findley, & Good, 1982; Cooper & Tom, 1984; Raudenbush, 1984). Teachers' beliefs about students' ability to learn influence achievement. This result suggests that teachers' expectations about their students, as well as their willingness to assume personal responsibility for the results of their teaching, have important consequences for learners. Students not only become more engaged in school under those circumstances (Firestone &

Rosenblum, 1988; Gill & Reynolds, 1999); they also learn more (Cooper & Tom, 1984; Rogers, 1998).

Studies of teaching in schools where tracking and ability grouping are common have concluded that teachers' negative attitudes and expectations about their students' ability to learn potentially distance all but the most able students from high-level learning (Ennis, 1994; Oakes, 1985). Teachers' negative projections can also alienate students, which negatively influences their learning (Firestone & Rosenblum, 1988; Newmann, 1981). In short, evidence supporting the impact of teacher expectations on student learning is compelling. Students fulfill their teachers' prophecies, performing up to, or down to, the projections and standards held for them.

ATTITUDE AS AN ORGANIZATIONAL PROPERTY OF SCHOOLS

Whereas much of the research reviewed above has been conducted by psychologists, we locate the research described in this chapter (and the rest of the book) within a sociological framework. We expand the notion of teachers' expectations for students to a larger context: school culture centered around expectations. We also shift our focus from teachers' "expectations for learning" to their "responsibility for learning." The top of this spectrum would include teachers who take personal responsibility for the success or failure of their own instruction. Such teachers would view teaching and learning as an interactive process, rather than a one-way flow of information, with students cast as active participants (Brattesani, Weinstein, & Marshall, 1984). Assuming more responsibility for learning also implies that such teachers have greater confidence in their own ability to affect outcomes of the instructional process (i.e., learning) for *all* students, not just the most able or motivated. When teachers are responsible for learning, their expectations about their students' ability to learn might be linked to their own sense of efficacy in teaching: a personal attitude that teaching is worth the effort. The message of expectancy might be embedded in a teacher's self-efficacy to generate an attitude of organizational commitment or responsibility (Maehr & Braskamp, 1986).

Within this framework, we consider teachers' attitudes in the aggregate, as a feature of the social organization of the school. We argue that students and teachers alike are influenced in their personal commitment to education by the extent to which the faculty in their school feels that teaching is worth the effort. This collective attitude is part of a larger community dynamic that invests the technical core of schooling with value and worth (Bryk & Driscoll, 1988). Considered in this way, teachers' willingness to take responsibility for their students' learning indicates a collective commitment to all students' school success.

EXAMINING COLLECTIVE RESPONSIBILITY FOR LEARNING

As noted earlier, in this chapter we investigate the link between high school students' learning during their first 2 years of high school and the social organization of their schools, defined by teachers' work. We used teachers' reports of their beliefs about students, the collaborative nature of staff relationships, and the degree to which teachers see themselves as in control or empowered in their classrooms and in their schools to define these elements of school social organization. Although we investigated these three elements of teachers' work lives, our major focus was on school norms that reflect teachers' attitudes about students—what we call "collective responsibility." This dimension of teachers' work lives might influence students in two ways. Most obviously, when a school's teachers as a group believe that their own efforts are crucial in the learning process, student learning could increase as a result. Moreover, when responsiblility is assumed for all students, regardless of their academic qualifications or social characteristics, learning might be more equitably distributed across the school's student body. In such schools, students' social background would be only weakly related to their learning. Three ideas have guided our analyses:

• *Idea 1 focuses on responsibility and student background.* Here we examine teachers' attributions of responsibility for the success or failure of their teaching. We ask whether teachers consider this responsibility to lie with the students or within themselves. We suspect that schools where teachers assume responsiblity for learning enroll students who typically do better in school. This would suggest that these are schools with more advantaged students, in terms of race, social class, or ability. It seems reasonable to assume that teachers would be more willing to assume personal responsibility (or take credit) for learning for students who are, in fact, learning well, but would ascribe to children and families that responsibilty (or guilt) if learning does not occur.

• *Idea 2 relates teachers' work life and student learning.* Here we ask whether the organizational features of schools defined by teachers' work lives actually influence student learning. We suggest that in schools where teachers take more responsibility for the results of their teaching, students learn more. Similarly, we suggest that in schools with high levels of collaboration among staff, or where teachers believe they have more control, students learn more.

• *Idea 3 explores how teachers' work lives influence the equitable distribution of learning.* Although the second idea focuses on the *level* of student learning in a school, here we consider the *distribution* of learning. The social organization of schools may either facilitate or debilitate the learning of disadvantaged students. We suggest that high levels of responsibility for learning are associated with student learning that is equitably distributed within the school according to students' background. Staff collaboration and control may also be associated with a more equitable social distribution of learning.

The school and student samples used for the analyses in this chapter are identical to those described in Chapter 4, where we also examined achievement growth during the first 2 years of high school. We studied 11,692 10th-grade students in 820 schools drawn from the first two waves of NELS:88. Information on teachers' work lives was drawn from teachers' reports. The NELS:90 sampling design called for collecting data from two of each student's teachers at each wave, in either English or social studies or in either mathematics or science. Of this sample of 9,904 teachers linked to our student and school samples, 32% taught English, 31% taught mathematics, 15% taught social studies (mostly history), and 22% taught science. We investigated whether our sample comprised a representative sample of teachers of these core subjects and concluded that it did.[1]

Measures of Teachers' Professional Community

We captured features of teachers' professional community with four composite measures drawn from teachers' reports. We followed a three-step process to create the measures: (1) We selected items that seemed to tap the ideas we wished to capture from the teacher questionnaire data; (2) we constructed psychometrically and distributionally appropriate composite measures using factor analysis; and (3) we aggregated these measures to the school level.[2]

One measure, *collective responsibility for learning*, included several related ideas: teachers' internalizing responsibility for the learning of their students, rather than attributing learning difficulties to weak students or deficient home conditions; a belief that teachers can teach all students; a willingness to alter teaching methods in response to students' difficulties and successes; and feelings of efficacy in teaching.[3] Besides how schools differ on levels of collective responsibility, we were also interested in whether this attitude was consistent among teachers in the same school. Thus, in addition to an aggregate that captures the mean level of collective responsibility in a school, we also included a second measure of this construct: its within-school standard deviation. This second measure captured the *degree to which teachers in the same school shared these attitudes*. It is also possible that this measure could capture differences in attitudes among teachers in different departments.

A third measure, *cooperation*, captured teachers' views about supportiveness of the principal; cooperation among teachers, administrators, and unions;

common knowledge about and support for innovation and experimentation. A fourth composite, *teacher control*, included items querying teachers' perceptions of their degrees of influence and control in the school in two areas: over conditions in their classrooms (teaching, content, materials, homework policy, and discipline) and over policies affecting the school (discipline policy, student assignment to ability groups, and curriculum policy). Details of the construction of all measures used in these analyses are provided in Appendix A.

Measures of Student Outcomes

Similar to the analyses in Chapter 4, we investigated the effects of school social organization on student learning in four subject areas: mathematics, reading, history, and science. Again, we measured learning with a simple gain score between students' tests in each subject between 8th and 10th grades.

Analysis Strategy and Presentation

As mentioned, our major focus is on collective responsibility for learning. To examine whether school demographic and academic characteristics were associated with this measure of teacher professional community (Idea 1), we present descriptive information about students and schools separately for three groups of schools: those that have high levels of collective responsibility for learning (one or more standard deviations [SD] above the mean on that variable), schools with medium levels of collective responsibility (within one SD above and below the mean), and schools with low collective responsibility (more than one SD below the mean).

As before, we used hierarchical linear modeling (HLM) to evaluate the effects of school professional community on student learning. More details on the statistical and analytic properties of this methodology, focused around a model that reflects the research questions in the book, are provided in Appendix B. Not only were we interested in whether these features of teachers' professional communities were associated with average student learning in the four core subjects (Idea 2), but we were also interested in whether professional community was associated with a socially equitable distribution of learning in these subjects (Idea 3).

Most analyses in this chapter took into account other characteristics of students and schools, as we know that student learning is influenced by many factors other than characteristics of teacher professional communities. Student characteristics included demographics (gender, socioeconomic status [SES], and minority status), as well as several measures of students' academic status at the beginning of high school: ability,[4] engagement in school in the eighth grade, and high school track placement. We also included a set of statistical controls for the characteristics of schools: school composition (average school SES, minority concentration), school ability level (average eighth-grade achievement), academic emphasis (proportion of students in the academic track), school sector (Catholic and independent schools compared with public schools), and school size. We have attempted to keep the numerical information from these complex analyses to a minimum, but augment those results with graphic interpretations from the full-model HLM analyses. Readers interested in a more thorough discussion of the numerical results are referred to Lee and Smith (1996).

Characteristics of Students and Schools

What kinds of students attend schools where collective responsibility for learning is quite common, compared with schools where these attitudes are average or unusual? Are other characteristics of schools associated with schools differentiated by levels of collective responsibility? Information describing the students and schools we studied, in three groups of schools characterized by low, medium, and high levels of collective responsibility, is presented in Table 5.1. The method we used to create these categories resulted in about two-thirds of the schools (and three-fourths of the students) in the middle category.

Students attending schools with high levels of collective responsibility were, in general, quite advantaged both socially and academically, compared with students in schools with the lowest levels of collective responsibility (see panel I of Table 5.1). This pattern was reflected in achievement gains for all subjects. Demographically, schools with high levels of collective responsibility enrolled students from families of higher SES. In terms of their academic status as they entered high school, students attending schools typified by high levels of collective responsibility were more able (in all subjects), were more engaged in school, and were more likely to be in the academic than the vocational track. Schools in the three categories, however, were well balanced by gender and by general-track enrollment. Schools of medium collective responsibility enrolled slightly more minority students than the schools at either extreme.

Unsurprisingly, the pattern of differences among students was generally reflected in the characteristics of schools, except that group differences were typically even larger (Panel II of Table 5.1). For the four measures of teacher professional community we have investigated in this study (Panel II-A), schools with high levels of collective responsibility were also characterized by more cooperation and higher levels of teacher control. This pattern suggests that these measures of teacher professional community were related to one another. The high variability among teachers in their willingness to take responsibility

Table 5.1. Characteristics of Students and Schools for Three Levels of Collective Responsibility for Learning

	Level of Collective Responsibility for Learning		
	High	Medium	Low[a]
Student sample	$n = 1,226$	$n = 8,801$	$n = 1,665$
School sample	$n = 134$	$n = 548$	$n = 138$
I. Variables Describing Students			
A. *Outcomes*			
Math gain	6.57	5.39	4.95
Reading gain	3.70	2.51	1.61
History gain	2.95	1.51	1.26
Science gain	3.43	1.54	1.33
B. *Student Controls*			
Engagement, 8th grade[b]	0.24	-0.01	-0.12
Social class[b]	0.46	-0.03	-0.21
Minority status	0.16	0.20	0.18
Female	0.50	0.51	0.51
Ability Controls, 8th grade[b]			
Math control	0.45	0.0	-0.10
Reading control	0.50	0.06	-0.11
History control	0.50	0.07	-0.11
Science control	0.51	0.06	-0.11
Curriculum Track, 10th grade			
Academic track	0.42	0.38	0.34
General track	0.49	0.50	0.51
Vocational track	0.09	0.12	0.15
II. Variables Describing Schools			
A. *Characteristics of Professional Community*			
Average collective responsibilty[b]	0.87	0.02	-0.49
Variability in collective responsibility	0.47	0.48	0.61
Cooperation[b]	0.66	-0.05	-0.66
Control[b]	0.80	-0.04	-0.48
B. *School Controls*			
Average SES[b]	0.77	-.083	-0.37
Minority (%)	21.54	24.28	23.98
Academic track (%)	70.46	48.26	33.15
Average achievement, 8th grade	55.22	50.98	49.83
School size	844	1,280	1,077
School Sector			
Public (%)	44.05	91.90	98.86
Catholic (%)	21.43	4.54	0.00
Elite private (%)	34.52	3.57	1.14

[a] School categories created as follows: Low = < 1 SD below sample mean on collective responsibility; Medium = between -1 SD and +1 SD from the mean; High = > 1 SD above the sample mean.
[b] Variables are z-scored, M = 0, SD = 1.

for learning in schools with lower levels of collective responsibility means that teachers were less likely to *share* these attitudes in low-responsibility schools.

Particularly striking were group differences in average SES. In high-responsibility schools, average SES differed from that in their low-responsibilty counterparts by over one SD, a large difference. Such schools also enrolled students with higher average ability. Compared with the medium- and low-responsibility schools, there was a high proportion of private schools (both Catholic and elite private schools) in the group of high-responsibility schools. School size, however, was associated with collective responsibility in a slightly different pattern: The largest schools were in the medium category; schools with high levels of collective responsibility were the smallest.

Differences among students and schools displayed in Table 5.1 provide evidence to support Idea 1. High schools with high levels of collective responsibility enrolled more socially and academically advantaged students. Collective responsibility was also associated with school sector, with private schools considerably more likely to have been characterized by collective responsibility at a high level. These social and academic characteristics of students, and compositional and structural characteristics of schools, must be taken into account in analyses that attempt to isolate the effect of teacher professional community on student learning.

THE EFFECTS OF PROFESSIONAL COMMUNITY
ON STUDENT LEARNING

This section presents results of our analyses that test Ideas 2 and 3. That is, we investigate whether the social organization of schools, defined by their professional communities, influences how much students learn in the first 2 years of high school and how equitably that learning is distributed. Our analyses followed the same multilevel strategy spelled out in Chapters 3 and 4. As described earlier, HLM analyses are typically performed in three steps. In the first step, variance in the outcome measures is partitioned into its within- and between-school components. Because our sample and outcome measures in the chapter were almost identical to those presented in Chapter 4, the results of step one of the HLMs were also similar.

Taking Students' Demographic and Social
Characteristics into Account

The second step in these HLM analyses involved estimating within-school HLM models, where we introduced the controls for student social and academic background described earlier. Our within-school models closely resembled those described in Chapter 4, with one exception: Here we included an additional statistical control for students' track placement. Virtually every demographic and academic background characteristic was related strongly to achevement gains in the four subjects (mostly below the .001 probability level). For all subjects, academic (compared with general) track placement was strongly and positively associated with achievement gains, whereas vocational (compared with general) track placement was negatively associated with achievement gains. Because the results were very similar to those presented in Table 4.3, we have not presented numerical results of the within-school models here.

We gave special focus in our within-school HLM models to the relationship between SES and achievement gains, as we did in Chapters 3 and 4. For all four subjects, SES was significantly and positively related to gains, meaning that in U.S. secondary schools students from families of higher social class learned more than their less-advantaged classmates in mathematics, reading, history, and science in the first 2 years of high school.[5] The ideas around which these analyses were organized focus on the effects of teachers' professional community on both learning and on its equitable distribution. Therefore, we also investigated the relationship between SES and achievement gains as outcomes.

Taking School Composition and Structure into Account

The results of the between-school HLM analyses are presented in Tables 5.2 and 5.3. Table 5.2 displays the results of school professional community (and school-level controls) on average gains in achievement. Table 5.3 displays the effects of the same independent variables on the relationship between SES and achievement gains, which measured educational equity. We have separated the results into two tables mainly to simplify our discussion of the results. In each analysis, the full set of controls for students' academic and social background was also included (although we did not include these results in our tables).

PROFESSIONAL COMMUNITY AND STUDENT LEARNING

Among the four measures of school professional community, the results in Table 5.2 indicate that only responsibility for learning was consistently, positively, and significantly related to achievement gains in all four subjects. Moreover, variability within schools on this measure was negatively associated with achievement gains in mathematics and reading. This finding suggests that when teachers do not share common attitudes about responsibility for students' learning, students learn less. Taken together, our findings indicate

Table 5.2. Between-school Model for the Effects of Teachers' Professional Community on Gains in Achievement

	Math	Reading	History	Science
		Dependent Variables		
		Gains in		
EFFECTS ON MEAN BETWEEN-SCHOOL GAIN				
Average Intercept	2.97***	2.70***	2.02***	3.41***
School-level Controls				
School SES	.03	.49**	.16	.38**
Minority concentration	.08	.13	.03	-.06
Average achievement	-.21	-.24~	-.06	.01
Academic track (%)	.03	.05	.01	.01
Catholic high school	.13	-.45	.47~	.37
Elite private high school	-2.42**	.38	-.21	-.35
School size	-.47*	-.20*	-.15*	-.15**
Effects of School Professional Community				
Responsibility for learning	.33***	.27***	.18*	.16**
Variability in responsibility				
for learning	-.24*	-.17*	-.07	-.08
Cooperation	.15	.18~	.12~	.13~
Teacher control	-.09	-.09	.01	.08

~$p \leq .10$; *$p \leq .05$; **$p \leq .01$; ***$p \leq .001$

that students learn more in schools where more teachers (and where teachers more consistently) report a willingness to assume responsibility for their students' learning. Other measures of teacher professional community had few effects, once collective responsibility was taken into account. For example, more cooperation among teachers was only modestly related to learning. Teachers' control over school matters was unrelated to learning.

Among the school-level controls, the associations between student learning and school composition and structure were inconsistent. For example, school average SES was strongly related to learning in reading and science, but unrelated to mathematics and history learning. When individual students' ability was taken into account, school average achievement generally was unrelated to learning. However, consistent with results in Chapters 3 and 4, school size showed a consistent, negative, and significant relationship to learning. Students in larger schools learned less in all subjects.

Table 5.3. Between-school Model for the Effects of Teachers' Professional
Community on Equity in Achievement Gains

	Dependent Variables			
	Gains in			
	Math/ SES slope	Reading/ SES slope	History/ SES slope	Science/ SES slope
EFFECTS ON SES DIFFERENTIATION				
Average SES Slope	.18**	.18*	.09*	.23***
School-level Controls				
School SES	.05	.03	.08	.38*
Minority concentration	-.13	.13	-.25	-.10
Average achievement	-.39~	-.13	.05	-.21
Academic track (%)	-.18	-.21	-.23	.05
Catholic high school	-.42	-.03	-.38	-.24
Elite private high school	.63	-.02	.20	-.45
School size	.22~	.16	.25~	.31*
Effects of School Professional Community				
Responsibility for learning	-.30*	-.30*	-.33*	-.38*
Variability in responsibility for learning	.19	.16	.08	.14
Cooperation	-.22	-.10	-.35*	-.21
Teacher control	.03	.08	.05	.14

~$p \le .10$; *$p \le .05$; **$p \le .01$; ***$p \le .001$

PROFESSIONAL COMMUNITY AND THE EQUITABLE
DISTRIBUTION OF LEARNING

Again similar to our approach in Chapters 3 and 4, we also explored the
relationship between SES and learning in each school. The results shown in
Table 5.3 indicate that only one school characteristic, collective responsibility for learning, was consistently, negatively, and significantly related to the
social distribution of learning in all subjects.

The results in Tables 5.2 and 5.3, taken together, tell a consistent story:
In schools where collective responsibility is high, students learned more and
learning was less related to students' social background. Effects of our other
measures of school professional community on learning and its distribution
were either small, inconsistent, or statistically nonsignificant. These findings
should *not* be intepreted as indicating that these features of teacher professional community are unimportant. Rather, the various measures of this
construct are strongly correlated with one another, which the descriptive

results in Table 5.1 suggest. Another finding was consistent: Students learned more in smaller schools.

Revisiting Collective Responsibility for Learning

These relationships may be displayed graphically. Figures 5.1 through 5.4 depict achievement gains in mathematics, reading, history, and science for low-SES students, students from middle-class families, and high-SES students in schools whose levels of collective responsibility were low, medium, and high. In these graphs, low-SES students were one SD below the mean; middle-

FIGURE 5.1. Achievement gains in mathematics for students of varying levels of SES in schools with different levels of collective responsibility.

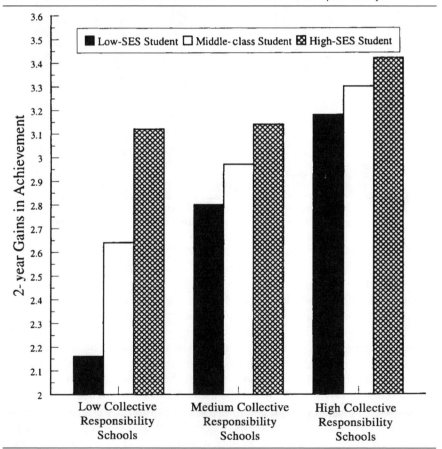

FIGURE 5.2. Achievement gains in reading for students of varying levels of SES in schools with different levels of collective responsibility.

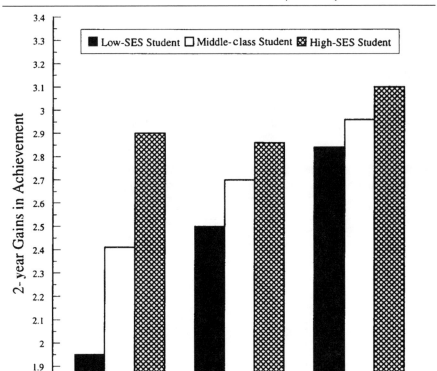

class students were those whose SES value was the mean SES for the entire sample; and high-SES students were those whose SES was one SD above the mean. Achievement gains for these three types of students were based on both their SES and on the level of collective responsibility in the schools they attended. These levels were constructed in the same way: Low collective responsibility schools were one SD below the mean on this variable; medium collective responsibility schools were at the mean; and high collective responsibility schools were one SD above the mean. The heights of the bars in these graphs were computed from the numerical results in Tables 5.2 and 5.3.[6]

Figure 5.1 focuses on students' achievement gains in mathematics between 8th and 10th grade. Two main trends are observable: (1) students with

FIGURE 5.3. Achievement gains in history for students of varying levels of SES in schools with different levels of collective responsibility.

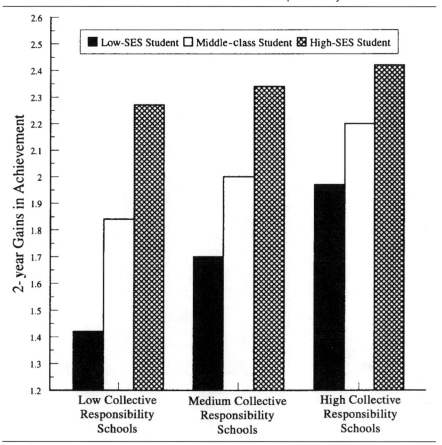

higher SES learned more mathematics than their lower-SES peers; and (2) students in schools with high levels of collective responsibility learned more than their counterparts in low collective responsibility schools. However, there is another observable trend: There were larger differences in achievement gains between low-, middle-, and high-SES students in low collective responsiblity schools than in schools where the level of collective responsibility was high. That is, SES made less difference in determining how much mathematics students learned in schools where teachers took more responsibility for their students' learning. High-SES students learned more in all types of schools. But students' mathematics learning, especially low-SES students, was quite strongly influenced by the type of school they attended. When

Figure 5.4. Achievement gains in science for students of varying levels of SES in schools with different levels of collective responsibility.

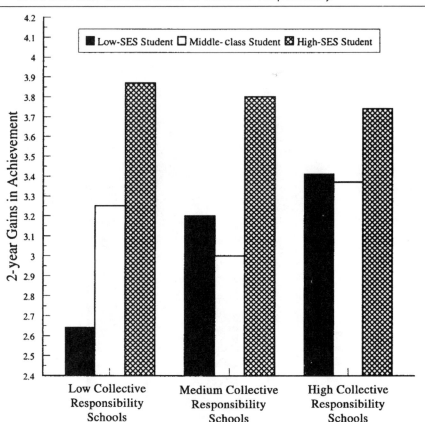

low-SES students attended schools with high levels of collective responsibility, they actually learned as much, in the early years of high school, as high-SES students in schools characterized by lower collective responsibility.

The patterns for learning in reading (Figure 5.2) and history (Figure 5.3) were quite similar to the pattern in mathematics, although the actual size of achievement gains was different. Variation in magnitude of the gains across the four subjects depended, in part, on the number of items on the tests in each subject: Students could gain more if the tests had more questions. The pattern was slightly different in science. From Table 5.2, we see that the magnitude of the effect of collective responsibility on average science learning (.16) was about half the size of the same effect on average learning in mathematics (.33). However, the relationship of SES to learning (the average SES slope in Table 5.3) was larger in science (.23) than in mathematics (.18). Moreover, the social equity effects on the distribution of science learning by student SES (also in Table 5.3) indicate that the effect of collective responsibility on the SES/science slope was also larger (–.38) than it was for mathematics (–.30). This different pattern of results is reflected in Figure 5.4. Here we see that although high-SES students may have learned slightly less in high collective responsibility schools, their low-SES and middle-class classmates learned somewhat more than their counterparts with similar SES in schools with less collective responsibility for learning.

CHANGING THE SOCIAL ORGANIZATION OF SCHOOLS

We are somewhat troubled by the strength and consistency of the findings reported in this chapter—that the degree to which the teachers in a school were willing to take responsibility for learning actually drove student learning. Why does this trouble us? A major reason is our finding that high schools varied markedly on collective responsibility. That is, in many U.S. high schools (particularly those enrolling academically and socially disadvantaged students), teachers' beliefs about the limitations of their students' ability to learn (and of teachers' ability to teach them effectively) were quite prevalent. We believe that high school teachers *should* assume responsibility for their students' academic progress, along with the students themselves. The fact that there was so much variation in this measure among the nation's high schools, and that schools where teachers were less willing to assume such responsibility were those that enrolled large proportions of disadvantaged students, is troubling.

How Do We Change Teachers' Attitudes About Their Students?

Of the four elements of teachers' work lives we considered in this chapter, collective responsibility for learning overwhelmed cooperation and empowerment in multivariate analyses. Although recent calls for school reform have suggested specific strategies to increase cooperation among school staff and to increase teachers' influence over school conditions that affect their work, we know of few articulated reform strategies that aim to fundamentally change teachers' beliefs about their students' capacities to learn and about their own ability to affect the learning of all students. An intervention program described in a study of one inner-city high school (Weinstein, Madison, & Kuklinski, 1995) is an exception, but the authors also commented on how difficult it was to actually change these attitudes. In a related discussion, Fennimore (2000) argued for changing how school professionals, policymakers, and researchers usually describe poor children in educational settings (what she called "deficit language"). However, the author did not mention reforms aimed at changing teachers' attitudes in this regard. Although many reforms stress how important it is that school staff members support the notion that "all children can learn," few suggestions are made about how to actually induce teachers to really believe this and to act on their beliefs. Our results demonstrate the importance of teachers' attitudes for students' learning, but how to change these attitudes is less obvious.

The findings in this chapter are consistent with research that demonstrates that cooperative, collegial, and communal school environments have strong effects on student engagement and teacher commitment (Bryk & Driscoll, 1988; Bryk et al., 1993). Our findings about the organizational effects of teachers' work lives on student learning extend this line of inquiry. Although it seems reasonable that the effects of teachers' attitudes on their students' learning would be linked primarily through the instructional process (which we were unable to explore),[7] our results suggest that they also influence students as features of the social organization of schools.

What About Causal Order?

How we structured our analyses implies a clear causal direction: Teachers' attitudes influence student learning (and not the reverse). The structure of the NELS:88 data, where students are followed longitudinally over time, allows us to study cognitive change in students. However, to study how teachers' attitudes develop and change, we would have to follow the same *teachers* over time, not students. Thus, it is possible that teachers' attitudes would change in response to their students' actually making progress. The evidence that collective responsibility for learning is higher in schools with more able students (Table 5.1) suggests the possibility of a reversed causal order.

Despite the possibility of an alternative causal direction, there are three reasons why we nevertheless feel comfortable about the order we have imposed on this study. First, we conceptualized collective responsibility for learning as an organizational property of schools rather than a psychological attribute of individuals. Second, our multivariate analyses took into account not only students' ability but the average achievement level of the school. A third reason why our interpretation seems reasonable is temporal. In high schools, students pass in and out of classes and through the influence of many teachers. Thus, teachers may actually interact with a particular student for only a year (or even a semester). Students' experience with the teachers in the entire school is more enduring (2 years in this study). In a high school, teachers know students for only a short time, and a single teacher may have only limited effects on his or her students, but the teaching staff in the aggre-gate is enduring.

The Importance of Professional Community

The Center on Organization and Restructuring of Schools advocated devel-opment of a professional teaching community (Louis et al., 1996; Newmann & Associates, 1996). Several elements of professional community, as those authors have defined it, were captured here: Louis and her colleagues (1996) listed "collective focus on student learning" and "collaboration" as two of five critical elements defining a professional community. Among several struc-tural elements necessary for this type of community to develop and grow within schools, they listed "teacher empowerment and school autonomy." Our findings offer some empirical support for restructuring the work lives of teachers in secondary schools in the direction laid out by these authors. Schools whose teachers interact as a community benefit their students, in terms of both higher learning and more social equity. It is clear to us that how schools are organized socially influences both *how much* students learn and *which* students learn what.

CHAPTER 6

Cumulative Effects of Restructuring

When considered together, the studies described so far in this book—which have focused on the same students in middle-grade schools and during the first 2 years of high school—have yielded three major findings. First, both 8th graders in middle-grade schools and 10th graders in high school who attended restructured schools benefited in terms of learning and engagement. Second, our analyses in Chapter 5 suggested that at least one feature of high schools' social organization—the degree to which teachers take responsibility for their students' learning—also increased students' learning. Third, our several studies have shown that both school restructuring and collective responsibility foster a more equitable distribution of learning as well as increasing learning.

Thus, we have some hints that school restructuring, as we have defined it, is related to some broader organizational features of schools. Our purpose in this chapter is to probe the association between school organization and restructuring, and their separate influences on students, in more depth. We want to understand the deeper meaning of the findings from Chapters 4 and 5. Throughout our investigations in this book, we have seen that other organizational features also characterize the high schools we define as "restructured." We located our work on school restructuring within a theoretical framework that contrasts two organizational frameworks that define schools: bureaucracies and communities.

This chapter both expands and narrows our study of the effects of school restructuring. First, although we continue to examine the school progress of the same students and schools that we have focused on throughout this book, here we look at these students 2 years later than our investigations in Chapters 4 and 5; now these same students have reached their last year of high school. Second, although we continue our examination of the effects of school restructuring that we explored in Chapters 3 and 4, here we investigate whether the restructuring effects we isolated earlier are, in fact, related to other organizational features of those high schools. Third, we limit still further the outcomes we consider. We confine these to achievement (as we did in Chapter 5), but narrow our outcomes set still further to achievement in mathematics and science. Fourth, our study is also narrowed in terms of the sample; here we focus only on students who have remained in high school until graduation (and in the same high school for the last 2 years); those who dropped out after 10th grade are removed.

Despite the strength and consistency of the findings from Chapter 4, we were plagued by lingering doubts about how to interpret them. Are there other things about these high schools, beyond their adopting several reform practices of a particular type, that might account for their effectiveness? We were surprised that our results did not produce evidence showing that schools actually adopted either restructuring or traditional practices along a single philosophical or pedagogical dimension. Indeed, all the high schools that reported three or more restructuring practices also reported a large number of traditional pratices in place. Our interpretation, echoed by others who commented on that study (Bryk, 1994; McLaughlin, 1994), was that the practices we examined reflect some fundamental differences in how high schools are organized.

REVIEWING SCHOOL ORGANIZATION

The suggestion of a link between school restructuring and other properties of schools led us to adopt a more focused organizational lens in reframing our examination of the link between structural practices and student learning (see also Lee, Smith, & Croninger, 1997). This reframing suggested another body of literature and a broader analytic structure. Before we describe our analyses, we briefly review research along three important dimensions of school organization: social relations, the curriculum, and instruction.

School Social Organization

The bureaucratic structure of most high schools relies on affectively neutral social relationships to facilitate the administration of standardized rules and procedures. Strong personal ties among adults, or between adults and students, make it more difficult for staff to comply with standard practices and procedures. Yet, as we mentioned in Chapter 5 and as Waller (1932) noted long ago, emotional bonds between teachers and students are crucial in engaging and motivating students to learn. The quality of affective ties among staff also influences teacher commitment and indirectly affects student achievement (Barry, 1995; Bryk et al., 1993; Kordalewski, 2000; Lee & Smith, 1999; Rosenholtz, 1987, 1989). The alienating and disengaging qualities of the typical high school are well documented (e.g., Firestone & Rosenblum, 1988; LeCompte & Dworkin, 1991). Many reform proposals have encouraged downsizing schools, mainly to create stronger bonds and more trusting relationships between students and adults, and to facilitate collaboration and cooperation between teachers (e.g., Carnegie Council on Adolesent Development, 1989; Clinchy, 2000; NASSP, 1996; Sizer, 1984, 1996; Westheimer, 1998).

Rather than formal and affectively neutral relationships, members of communally organized schools share a common mission. Staff and students interact outside the classroom; adults see themselves as responsible for students' total development, not just for the transmission of lessons. Teachers share responsibility for students' academic success, often exchanging information with colleagues and coordinating efforts between classrooms and across grades. Outcomes are more positive in such schools for both teachers (e.g. satisfaction, morale, absenteeism) and students (e.g., less class-cutting, less absenteeism, lower dropout rates). Attending more positive and caring schools is especially beneficial for disadvantaged students (Battistich, Solomon, Kim, Watson, & Schaps, 1995; Battistich, Solomon, Watson, & Schaps, 1997; Bryk & Driscoll 1988; Bryk et al., 1993; Esposito, 1999).

Organization of the Curriculum

Students' academic experiences are compartmentalized, differentiated, and socially stratified in most high schools. The curriculum is divided into discrete subjects typically organized by departments. Departments organize their subjects into course sequences (i.e., tracks), with access typically determined by ability, performance, prior coursework, and/or aspirations. Such high schools offer students a broad range of courses within each department. Although this type of curriculum provides opportunities to explore numerous interests, the courses vary considerably in their academic content and expectations (Johnson, 1990; Powell, Farrar, & Cohen, 1985; Raudenbush, Rowan, & Cheong, 1993; Siskin, 1997). Expansion of the curriculum both horizontally (in terms of tracks) and vertically (multiple offerings within tracks or even multiple versions of the *same* course with different expectations) creates substantial differences in what students study and learn within the same school (Lee et al., 1993).

Disadvantaged students are especially harmed by a highly differentiated curriculum. More of their courses are low-track offerings that require less academic effort, have lower expectations for achievement, and have less high-level content (Cooper, 1999; Gamoran, 1987, 1989; Lucas, 1999; Oakes, 1985; Oakes et al., 1997; Sedlak, Wheeler, Pullin, & Cusick 1986). There is now considerable consensus among researchers that low-income and minority students are especially advantaged in schools with a narrow curriculum and a strong academic focus. As the courses are more similar in academic content and expectations, students in different classrooms have similar academic experiences. Although this form of academic organization has been associated with Catholic schools, Bryk et al. (1993) suggest that public schools with similar curriculum structures also have high and more socially equitable achievement. Unfortunately, however, not many public schools look like this.

Organization of Instruction

A bureaucratic conception of how knowledge is acquired emphasizes standardizing teaching practices and learning tasks. Evidence is accumulating that such standardization fails to provide opportunities for students to develop more advanced thinking skills, higher levels of proficiency in academic subjects, and a sense of themselves as active learners (Ivie, 1998; McCaslin & Good, 1992; Newmann & Associates, 1996). Another approach to instruction (sometimes called "authentic") requires that students be involved in constructing (rather than reproducing) knowledge through disciplined and sustained involvement in tasks that resemble real-life problems.

Although all students benefit from authentic instruction, there is evidence that such practices may be particularly beneficial for socially disadvantaged students. Such students, however, are especially unlikely to experience authentic instruction (Cole & Griffin, 1987; MacIver & Epstein, 1990; Quality Education for Minorities Project, 1990; Shouse & Mussoline, 1999). Disadvantaged students, often also low-achieving, are typically in classrooms that emphasize lower-order skills, basic knowledge, drill and practice, recitation, and desk work (Knapp & Shields, 1990; Levine, 1988). However, there is evidence that low-achieving students can master more complex and demanding tasks. Moreover, these richer learning environments can lead to dramatic gains in achievement (American Association for the Advancement of Science [AAAS], 1984; Battistich et al., 1997; Gamoran, 1997; Knapp & Shields, 1990; Kozma & Croninger, 1992; Levine, 1988).

INVESTIGATING THE RELATIONSHIP BETWEEN SCHOOL ORGANIZATION AND STUDENT LEARNING

As noted earlier, in this chapter we target the social and academic organization of high schools, which builds on our analyses from Chapter 4. Our interest here is in how organizational elements of high schools, above and beyond the restructuring practices they have adopted, affect student learning and its distribution. We are interested in determining whether the educational advantages of organizational features touched on in our previous empirical work described in this book might explain the educationl advantages we found for students attending schools with many restructuring practices in place. We organize our analyses around three ideas and related questions:

- *Idea 1 focuses on organization and restructuring.* We ask: What are the differences in the social and academic organization of high schools that report different types of structural practices?
- *Idea 2 examines the sustained effects of restructuring.* We ask: Do the benefits for students early in high school of attending high schools that reported several of the practices we classified as "restructuring" persist to the end of high school?
- *Idea 3 relates organizational practices and student learning.* Assuming a positive answer the question posed under Idea 2, we ask: Do the effects of school restructuring on student learning persist once we take into account other elements of the social and academic organization of the schools (particularly those associated with restructuring practices?

If the schools that report many restructuring practices are different from traditional or nonrestructuring schools in terms of their social and academic organization (Question 1), and if these organizational forms explain away or substantially reduce the effects of these practices (Question 3), then we would have evidence that broader differences in school organization—specifically those that center on social relations, curriculum, and instruction—promote desirable outcomes (specifically learning and its equitable distribution).

The student and school samples described in Chapters 4 and 5 are the same as those used in this chapter, with a few additional data filters applied. First, the students we study here are those who remained in high school until graduation. Thus, the student sample from Chapter 4 (11,794) has been reduced by 18%, to 9,631.[1] Our sample of schools has also been reduced slightly, in that we retained only schools for which we were able to catalog their organizational dimensions as well as their structural practices (a 4% reduction, from 820 to 789 schools). However, virtually all students and schools that comprise the analytic sample for this chapter were included in the analyses in Chapters 4, and 5.

Measures and Outcomes

Three reasons underlay our decision to restrict our outcome set to achievement growth in mathematics and science. First, we restricted the number of outcomes simply to limit the complexity of results. Second, we selected math and science because data on classroom instruction at 12th grade that were collected by the National Educational Longitudinal Study of 1988 (NELS:88) were limited to these subjects. Third, available information about students' course taking in these subjects was much more precise than in history and English, both from self-reports and from transcripts.

LEARNING MEASURED AS CHANGE OVER TIME

Consistent with our methodological approach throughout the book, the multivariate analyses here were conducted with hierarchical linear modeling (HLM). However, in this chapter we make use of a three-level HLM model of change over time, described by Bryk and Raudenbush (1992) in Chapter 6 of their book. The technique here is applied somewhat restrictively, given that we have available only three time points in our model (achievement at 8th, 10th, and 12th grades). Each NELS:88 test score positions a student on an absolute scale of performance. We framed differences in scores between time points as "growth," with the difference in scores on the same test between two time points measuring the student's "gain" in performance (or learning). We explored two growth parameters: (1) 8th to 10th grade (early) and (2) 10th to 12th grade (late). Of course, the parameters are not independent, nor is either independent of initial status (achievement measured at the end of 8th grade).

Actually, we investigated four outcomes for these two subjects: early and late achievement gain (Outcomes 1 and 2) and the social distribution of these early and late gains according to students' socioeconomic status (SES) (Outcomes 3 and 4). These outcomes are displayed in Figures 6.1 and 6.2. Figure 6.1 displays Outcomes 1 and 2: early (8th–10th) and late (10th–12th) achievement growth in math and science. Results are reported in standard deviation (SD) units to facilitate comparison across tests with different numbers of items. Figure 6.2 represents Outcomes 3 and 4, which represent the social distribution of achievement gain in mathematics (A) and science (B) within each school.

Three trends are evident in Figure 6.1. First, students learned more earlier than later in high school in both subjects (i.e., the slopes are steeper for Outcome 1 than for 2). Second, students didn't learn very much over either period (i.e., the learning slopes are not very steep). Third, the learning rates were not constant across subjects: Students learned more mathematics than science, particularly in the early high school years. Using ideas we have employed throughout this book, we consider Outcomes 1 and 2 as *effectiveness parameters.*

Figure 6.2 displays the achievement gains for low- and high-SES students in mathematics (Panel A) and science (Panel B) over these two periods, which

FIGURE 6.1. Gains in mathematics and science for grades 8–12.

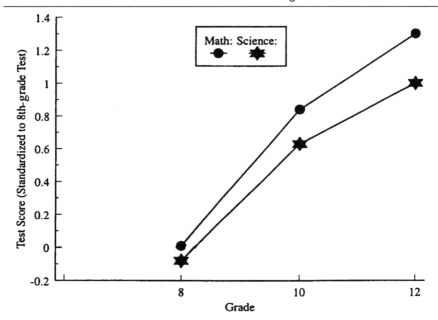

Note: The numbers in this figure are estimated after social class, gender, ethnicity, individual course taking, and 8th-grade ability are taken into account. These scores are then converted to a standard metric based on the 8th-grade test, showing how much students gain in the 10th and 12th grades relative to their initial performance in the 8th grade.

we consider to be *equity parameters*. Outcome 3 represents the SES slope on math and science learning early in high school (the left-hand portion of Panels A and B of Figure 6.2), whereas Outcome 4 is the SES slope on learning in the last 2 years (the right-hand portion of Panels A and B). The results shown in Figure 6.2 suggest that the slope between SES and achievement gain in both subjects varied over time and over SES level. Although it decreased over time, the slope was steeper for higher-SES students than for their low-SES counterparts. The left-hand portions of Figures 6.1 and 6.2 (i.e., the gains between 8th and 10th grades) represent a subset of the outcomes we explored in Chapter 4. That is, in Chapter 4 we explored achievement gains in four subjects, whereas we focus on only two subjects in this chapter.[2]

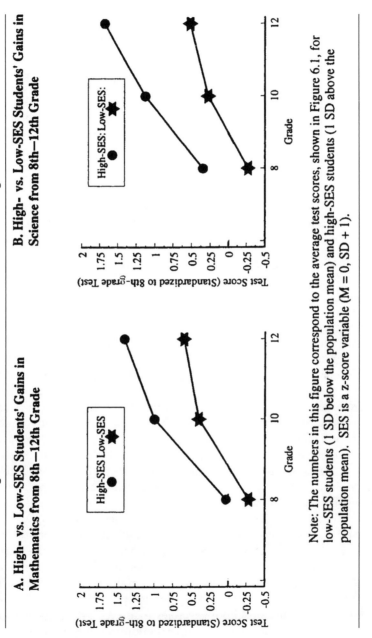

A. High- vs. Low-SES Students' Gains in Mathematics from 8th–12th Grade

B. High- vs. Low-SES Students' Gains in Science from 8th–12th Grade

Note: The numbers in this figure correspond to the average test scores, shown in Figure 6.1, for low-SES students (1 SD below the population mean) and high-SES students (1 SD above the population mean). SES is a z-score variable (M = 0, SD + 1).

VARIABLES DESCRIBING STUDENTS

Controls measured on students were of three types: demographic character-istics, academic status at high school entry, and course taking. Details on the construction of all variables are provided in Appendix A. Demographic controls included SES, student minority status (Hispanic or Black), and gen-der. We use two controls for cognitive status at the beginning of high school: achievement (in either math or science, depending on the outcome) and en-gagement with academic activities. We also included controls for students' course-taking patterns in mathematics (self-reports of courses taken in the first 2 years of high school) for Outcome 1, as well as a measure of all high school courses taken in mathematics and science (from students' transcripts for modeling Outcome 2). Except for course taking, these were the same controls on students that we used in Chapter 4.

VARIABLES DESCRIBING SCHOOLS

The school measures captured ideas that are important in this chapter. We investigate five categories of school variables. The first category, *restructur-ing status*, captured school structure in the same three groups of schools used in Chapter 4. The restructuring contrasts represent a construct of substan-tive interest in this chapter. The second category, *composition and structure*, included school average SES, minority concentration, school sector (two dummy variables for Catholic and elite private schools, each compared with public schools), and school size. As we have done in other chapters, here we included these variables primarily for the purpose of statistical control.

Three sets of variables captured school organization. The third category, *school social organization*, was captured by the same measure of collective responsibility for learning that we used Chapter 5. This variable tapped teach-ers' attitudes about their personal willingness and ability to alter teaching methods to respond to the learning difficulties of their students. School mea-sures in the fourth category tapped the construct of *school academic organi-zation*. One variable in this category measured the school average of students' course taking in academic mathematics and science courses. We also used the standard deviation of course taking to indicate variability (or homoge-neity) in students' intellectual experiences. These two variables, as a pair, represented a proxy measure of the common curriculum. Our measure of school academic press was constructed from principals' reports about the importance their schools places on academic pursuits.

A fifth cateogory of school variables focused on the organization of *in-struction*. One measure, authentic instruction in science and mathematics, included four school-level aggregates of students' and teachers' reports of the frequency of various instructional activities in those two subjects.[3] We considered this composite as an indicator of instructionally rich classrooms that made use of multiple practices associated with constructivist teaching or active learning—what Newmann called "authentic pedagogy" (Newmann, 1993; Newmann, Marks, & Gamoran, 1996). Another variable tapped the variability (or lack of homogeneity) in authentic instruction among teachers in the same school.

School Organization and the Restructuring Categories

To gauge the relationship between school organization and restructuring (Idea 1), we investigated how the several categories of school characteristics described above were related to school groupings by restructuring practices. Specifically, Table 6.1, which displays descriptive information about the 789 schools in the sample, displays information for three groups of schools: schools without reform practices (column 1), schools with traditional practices (column 2), and schools with restructuring practices (column 3). We tested the same contrasts used in Chapter 4: (1) no-reform compared with traditional schools and (2) restructuring practice schools compared with traditional schools. As we saw earlier, almost half (46%) were restructuring practice schools, 43% were traditional practice schools, and 11% were schools without reform practices. The schools' organizational characteristics were distinctive in several ways.

COMPOSITION AND STRUCTURE

Schools without reform practices were quite disadvantaged compared with traditional practice schools on several social demographic factors (more minority students and students of lower ability). More striking, however, was the advantage of restructuring schools compared with the traditional group in terms of average SES and average eighth-grade achievement. Distribution by sector may explain some of the social background differences. Private schools represented 14% of the school sample, the majority of which were restructuring practice schools. Nevertheless, public schools comprised the overwhelming majority of all groups. Traditional schools were smaller than either restructuring or no-reform schools.

SCHOOL ORGANIZATION

School *social organization* focuses on how much responsibility teachers take for their students' learning. The pattern of group differences that favored restructured schools suggests that social organization may be intertwined with

Table 6.1. Organizational Characteristics of High Schools in Three
Restructuring Categories

	No Reform Practices	Schools with Traditional Practices	Restructuring Practices
School Sample Size	$n = 88$	$n = 338$	$n = 363$
A. *Compositional and Structural Organization*			
Average SES[a,b]	-.43~	-.19	.33***
Minority enrollment (%)	34.14***	10.73	13.78
Public (%)	98.80	96.01	83.02***
Catholic (%)	0.85~	3.50	9.73***
Elite private (%)	0.35	0.48	7.25***
Average achievement, 8th grade[b]	-.52*	-.16	.30***
School size	1,091***	632	769**
B. *School Social Organization*			
Collective responsibility for learning[b]	-.74***	-.14	.31***
C. *School Academic Organization*			
Average number of math and science courses, 9th–12th grade	4.52	4.73	5.14***
Variability in math, science course taking[c]	2.05	2.00	1.83***
Academic press[b]	-.25	-.21	.31***
D. *Organization of Instruction*			
Authentic instructional practices, science and math	-1.63***	-.58	1.04***
Variability in authentic instructional practices[c]	.56**	.13	-.26***

[a] Group mean differences were tested with one-way ANOVA and contrasts. Both "No Reform Practices" and "Restructuring Practices" schools were contrasted (separately) with "Traditional Practice" schools. Indications of statistical significance of group means refer to these contrasts.
[b] Variables are z-scores (M = 0, SD = 1).
[c] Variables are standard deviations.
~$p \leq .10$; *$p \leq .05$; **$p \leq .01$; ***$p \leq .001$

school restructuring, although the causal direction of relationships is unclear. A similar pattern was evident among measures of *academic organization*. Restructuring practice schools were significantly advantaged on all these measures: Students took more mathematics and science courses, and there was less variability in course taking. Regarding *the organization of instruction*, teaching was more authentic and authentic instruction was more homogeneous across classes in restructuring practice schools, and these schools also evidenced higher levels of academic press. Although again the causal direction is unclear, the pattern is clear: Restructuring schools have stronger academic organizations.

Several patterns were evident from the descriptive information in Table 6.1. Restructured schools were advantaged in the types of students they enrolled, possibly explained by the the larger proportion of private schools in their ranks. These differences suggest the importance of taking into account the demographic and structural organization of schools in multivariate analyses that compare *schools*, above and beyond controlling for the types of *students* who attend them. As restructuring practice schools were also advantaged in terms of their organizational characteristics, these factors are also important in understanding the mechanism through which school restructuring actually "translates" into student learning.

Organizational Effects on Early and Late Achievement Gains

REVIEWING THE FOUR OUTCOMES

Achievement in NELS was measured for the same students at three important time points: near the end of 8th grade (entry into high school); in 10th grade (midway through high school); and at the end of 12th grade (just before graduation). Recall from our earlier discussion of the results in Figures 6.1 and 6.2 that we investigated four outcomes. Early gains in achievement in mathematics and science we called "Outcome 1" (from 8th to 10th grade); late gains in mathematics and science achievement we called "Outcome 2" (between 10th and 12th grade). Outcomes 3 (early) and 4 (late) focus on the relationship between SES and those gains.

According to the information presented in Figure 6.1, students learned little science over the course of high school, at least as measured by NELS test items; they learned somewhat more in mathematics.[4] Variation of scores between students on early and late science gains were similar (and large), but in mathematics the late gain was less variable than the early gain. All four gains were quite reliable (.85–.95), despite modest between-school variances. However, because the variability between schools in these outcomes was modest, identifying school effects would be difficult. This very difficulty suggests that the school effects we did identify would therefore be quite important.

WITHIN-SCHOOL (LEVEL 2) MODELS

Table 6.2 displays the Level-2 (within-school) HLM models for the four learning outcomes (early and late gains in science and math). Similar to the procedures we followed in previous chapters, we present effects of student characteristics on Outcomes 1 and 2, estimated simultaneously but separately

Table 6.2. Within-school Model for Early and Late Achievement Gains in Science and Math

	Dependent Variables			
	Outcome 1 Early Gain, 8th–10th grade		Outcome 2 Late Gain, 10th–12th grade	
	Science	Math	Science	Math
Fixed Effect[a]				
Intercept (Base)	4.00***	8.90***	1.98***	4.82***
Independent Variables				
Engagement, 8th grade	-.14	-.35*	.06	-.10
Achievement, 8th grade[b]	2.40***	2.33***	-.20	.94**
Academic courses taken in math and science, 8th–10th grade	.08	.51**		
HS academic courses taken in math and science, 10th–12th grade			.30	.17
Social class (SES)	.61***	.75	.74***	1.21***
Minority status	-1.31*	-.56	.63	1.59**
Gender (female)	-1.38***	-.19	-1.41*	-.80*

[a] All effects are presented in a standardized effect-size metric, computed by dividing the HLM gamma coefficient for each outcome by the adjusted HLM school-level standard deviation (SD) of that outcome.
[b] The ability control is constructed as a composite of 8th-grade test scores in the three curricular areas *not* measured by each gain score.
~$p \le .10$; *$p \le .05$; **$p \le .01$; ***$p \le .001$

for each subject, in effect-size (ES) units. We remind readers that these growth models include statistical controls for early gain on late gain, as well as controls for general achievement at eighth grade.

Several patterns are evident. Although engagement had no significant effect on learning, prior achievement (measured at eighth grade in each subject) had a substantial effect. In both subjects, effects of achievement at the beginning of high school were very large on early gains (effects over 2 SD, $p \le .001$). Other student characteristics exerted quite different effects for the two subjects. For example, eighth-grade achievement had no effect on late gains in science, but it had a strong effect on late gains in math (.9 SD, $p \le .01$). Surprisingly, the number of academic courses taken in math and science early in high school had no effect on early science gain. However, course taking was an important predictor of early math learning (.5 SD, $p \le .01$). Courses taken in these subjects in the last half of high school exerted no residual effect on late gains, once other variables were controlled.

Demographic effects differed by subject. The effects of social class were particularly important. We see in Table 6.2 that SES was more strongly associated with late than early gains in both subjects, but especially mathematics. The relationship between SES and early and late gains in mathematics and science represent Outcome 3 and 4. Compared to gains in mathematics, science gain was more similar for the two time periods. Gender differences favoring males were large, especially in science (i.e., males learned more in these subjects over the course of high school). Although gender differences also favored males in math, they were larger for late than early gain. Minority-status differences were unusual. For early gains in both math and science, minority students gained less than their nonminority counterparts, although differences were much larger on early science than math gain. Minority effects on late gains were positive, however. Although these demographic effects were important and interesting, we refrain from discussing them further. Except for SES, demographics are not among our research questions. Nevertheless, the magnitudes of minority- and gender-group differences suggest the importance of statistically adjusting for students' race/ethnicity and gender. We remind readers that the SES effects displayed in Table 6.2 represent Outcomes 3 and 4 in subsequent analyses, as well as those pictured in Figure 6.2.

THE EFFECTS OF SCHOOL RESTRUCTURING IN THE PRESENCE OF SCHOOL ORGANIZATION

The analyses in this section explore the questions raised in Ideas 2 and 3, which are of central concern in this book. Here we examine whether the restructuring effects on learning and its social distribution by students' SES (that is, the equity and effectiveness parameters) that were demonstrated in Chapter 4 for the first two years of high school were still in place during the last half of high school. If they were, we investigated whether the effects of restructuring were retained once more enduring organizational characteristics of schools were taken into account. Our analyses focused on four outcomes, measured early and late in high school: learning in mathematics and science and its social distribution in these two subjects.

Were Restructuring Effects Sustained?

Controlling for the student characteristics shown in Table 6.2, we estimated a set of school-effects analyses on Outcomes 1 to 4. Our analysis plan involved estimating restructuring effects on achievement gains early (between Grades 8 and 10) and late (between Grades 10 and 12) in high school. Taking into account the characteristics of students shown in Table 6.2 and described above, and the set of controls for school demographic composition and structure shown in Table 6.1 and described above, we estimated restructuring effects under two conditions. In the first condition, we evaluated whether restructuring effects on math and science learning were sustained in students' last 2 years of high schools (Idea 2). In the second condition, we estimated the restructuring effects after taking into account the several variables describing schools' social organization, academic organization, and the organization of instruction. A summary of the restructuring effects on early and late gains in achievement, without and with taking school organization into account, is presented in Figures 6.3 (mathematics) and 6.4 (science). Results shown in these figures are also presented in between-school effect-size units. These figures focus only on Outcomes 1 and 2.

FIGURE 6.3. Restructuring effects on achievement gains in mathematics, without and with taking school organization into account.

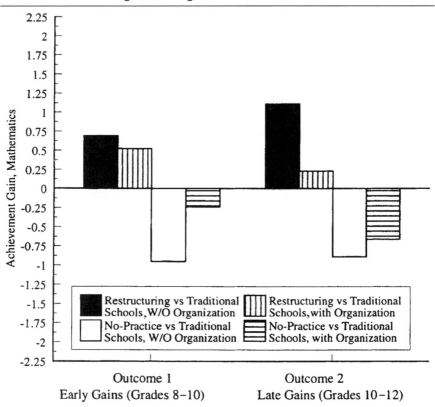

Legend:
- Restructuring vs Traditional Schools, W/O Organization
- Restructuring vs Traditional Schools, with Organization
- No-Practice vs Traditional Schools, W/O Organization
- No-Practice vs Traditional Schools, with Organization

Outcome 1
Early Gains (Grades 8–10)

Outcome 2
Late Gains (Grades 10–12)

FIGURE 6.4. Restructuring effects on achievement gains in science, without and with taking school organization into account.

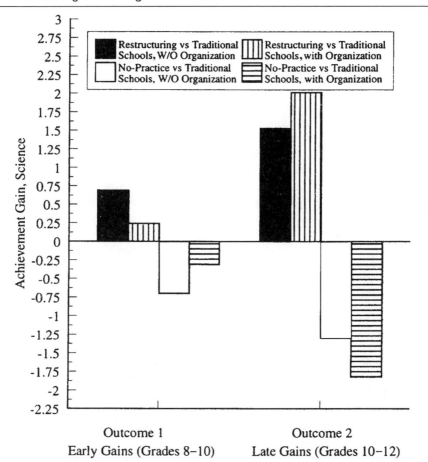

■ Restructuring vs Traditional Schools, W/O Organization	▥ Restructuring vs Traditional Schools, with Organization
☐ No-Practice vs Traditional Schools, W/O Organization	▤ No-Practice vs Traditional Schools, with Organization

Outcome 1
Early Gains (Grades 8–10)

Outcome 2
Late Gains (Grades 10–12)

For Outcomes 1 and 2 (the effectiveness parameters), students learned significantly more mathematics in restructuring practice schools than in traditional practice schools, both early and late in high school (the black bars in Figure 6.3). In fact, restructuring effects increased later in high school (the black bars). Students in schools with neither traditional nor restructuring practices were disadvantaged in learning mathematics compared with those in traditional practice schools (white bars), both early and late in high school. However, once the characteristics of schools' social, academic, and instructional organization were taken into account, the restructuring effects decreased dramatically (comparing the black and the vertically striped bars), especially late in high school. In general, the restructuring effects estimated in the presence of organizational factors were no longer statistically significant.

This pattern was quite similar for science learning (Figure 6.4) for Outcome 1 (early gain). Restructuring effects decreased to nonsignificance once organizational factors were taken into account. However, the same pattern did not hold for learning in science in the last 2 years of high school (Outcome 2). Here, restructuring effects increased, both in comparison with early gains and in the presence of organizational factors. However, once organizational factors were included in our full school-effects HLM models, the large restructuring effects were generally not statistically significant (because their standard errors were quite large).

The results displayed in Figures 6.3 and 6.4 provide information about Idea 2. That is, it appears that the restructuring effects were sustained, and even increased in magnitude, for learning between the first 2 and the last 2 years of high school. This held for both restructuring contrasts—restructuring practice schools showed larger effects on student learning in mathematics and science later than earlier in high school. Compared with traditional practice schools, students in schools without reform practices in place learned less later than earlier in high school in both subjects. However, in response to Idea 3, in general the restructuring contrasts were substantially reduced in magnitude and in statistical significance once other organizational characteristics of school were taken into account. An exception to this pattern was science learning later in high school. With that one exception, the results shown in Figures 6.3 and 6.4 provide a positive response to the questions posed under Idea 3: Organizational features of high school generally "explained away" the restructuring effects on learning, both early and late in high school.

Restructuring Effects on the Social Distribution of Learning

On the *equity parameters* (Outcomes 3 and 4) in Table 6.3 learning in science and math was more equitable among students in restructuring practice schools. Similar to the restructuring effects on the effectiveness parameters (Outcomes 1 and 2), restructuring effects (compared with traditional practice) increased later in high school. Effects of attending schools without reforms (also compared with traditional practice schools) suggest that learning in both subjects was both lower and more socially inequitable. Also similar to the restructuring effects on the effectiveness parameters, the effects declined in magnitude (typically they dropped below statistical significance) once features of the schools' social, academic, and instructional organization were accounted for. Because the pattern was so similar, we have not provided graphs of the equity parameters here.

The results shown in Table 6.3 confirm and expand the positive findings from Chapter 4 and provide a yet more positive answer to a question posed earlier in this chapter. We draw some general conclusions about how school restructuring influences learning in mathematics and science from these analyses. Quite simply, attending schools that are categorized as restructuring according to the definition laid out in this book has sustained, positive, and equitable effects on students' learning in science and mathematics. However, the fact that these effects decline when organizational properties of schools are introduced into the analyses suggests that we should take a closer look at the organizational effects on student learning and its equitable distribution.

A FOCUS ON SCHOOL ORGANIZATION

Technically, our analysis plan for investigating Idea 3 involved an attempt to "explain away" restructuring effects by taking into account characteristics of the schools' social, academic, and instructional organization in our HLM models. The results of these HLM organizational analyses are displayed in Table 6.3.[5] It is evident that organizational effects on the four outcomes (early and late achievement gains in science and mathematics in Panel I and the SES slopes on each of these gains in Panel II) were large, consistent, and logical. We organize our discussion here around the three types of school organization discussed earlier.

The results shown in Table 6.3 were adjusted for (1) student characteristics (those shown in Table 6.2), (2) school demographics (average school SES, minority enrollment, school sector), and (3) school structure (school size and the two restructuring contrasts). However, most of these effects have already been displayed and discussed. The restructuring effects, without and with taking school organization into account, were displayed in Figures 6.3 and 6.4. We note that the effects of *school size* followed the same pattern observed throughout this book—smaller schools were both more effective and more equitable in terms of learning in mathematics and science. This is striking, in that these HLM models contained many of the organizational measures that are often invoked as those that are typically associated with school size: school sector, school social organization, and academic organization.

Effects of School Social Organization

School social organization, which we captured in this analysis as collective responsibility for learning, was strongly and positively associated with both effectiveness and equity in learning in both subjects, with effect sizes in the moderate to large range.[6] Its effects, although consistently positive, differed

Table 6.3. Full Between-school Model for Early and Late Achievement Gains in Science and Math: Effects of School Organizational Factors

I. Outcomes Early in High School

	Dependent Variables[a]					
	Outcome 1 Early Gain, 8th–10th grade		Outcome 3 SES Slope on Gain, 8th–10th grade	
	Science	Math	Science	Math
Base Effect[b,c]	3.50***	6.92***	2.66*	1.01**
A. School Social Organization				
Collective responsibility for learning	.39*	.89**	-1.01*	-.59*
B. School Academic Organization				
Average number of math and science courses	.49*	.74*	-.76	-.95
Variability in math, science course taking	-.26	-.44	1.17*	.59*
Academic press	.35**	.67	-.83*	-.54
C. School Instructional Organization				
Authentic instructional practices in science and math	.42*	.50***	-.69	-.50
Variability in authentic instruction	-.29~	-.49~	1.11**	1.34**

120

II. Outcomes Late in High School

| | Dependent Variables[a] | | | |
| | Outcome 2 Late Gain, 10th–12th grade | | Outcome 4 SES Slope on Gain, 10th–12th grade | |
	Science	Math	Science	Math
Base Effect[b,c]	4.36***	2.73*	1.63	2.35*
A. School Social Organization				
Collective responsibility for learning	1.00*	.40*	-1.48**	-1.37**
B. School Academic Organization				
Average number of math and science courses	1.04*	.37***	-2.04~	-1.34~
Variability in math, science course taking	-.45	-.12	2.30*	1.88*
Academic press	.56*	.21	-1.15*	-.71*
C. School Instructional Organization				
Authentic instructional practices in science and math	1.66*	.36**	-3.27~	.43
Variability in authentic instruction	-.25	-.59~	3.08**	1.41**

[a] The numbering of these outcomes refers to designations in Figures 6.1 and 6.2.
[b] All models also include within-school adjustments for all variables shown in Table 6.2. They also include adjustment for the demographic charactistics of schools (average school SES, minority enrollment, school sector) and school structure (school size and the two restructuring contrasts).
[c] All effects are presented in a standardized effect-size metric, computed by dividing the HLM gamma coefficient for each outcome by the HLM adjusted school-level standard deviation (SD) of that outcome. These SDs are available in Lee, Smith, and Croninger (1997).
~$p \leq .10$; * $p \leq .05$; ** $p \leq .01$; *** $p \leq .001$

over time and subject. The effect of collective responsibility on science learning increased in magnitude from the beginning to the end of high school, but declined somewhat for mathematics learning between 10th and 12th grades. Effects on equity were large and increased over time in both subjects. These results support and expand those from Chapter 5: Schools with higher levels of collective responsibility are both more effective and more equitable, in terms of students' learning in mathematics and science over the 4 years of high school.

Effects of Academic Organization

The strongest organizational effects on both learning and its equitable distribution in science and mathematics were, not surprisingly, associated with schools' academic organization. We suggest that average levels of academic course taking in mathematics and science and the variability in course taking be considered together. We interpret these variables, as a pair, as indicators of a school that offers a narrow curriculum that is academic in content, one where most students take the same courses of this type (i.e., variability in course taking is low). Early in this chapter, in discussing this type of academic organization, we indicated that it is more typical in Catholic than in public schools. However, in Table 6.3 the effects were "net"; that is, they persisted even when school sector (public, Catholic, or elite private) was taken into account.

Academic organizational effects on learning and its equitable distribution were strong and consistent. That is, in such "core curriculum" schools, students both learned more, and learning was more equitably distributed by SES. Reflecting the pattern of effects for collective responsibility for learning, academic organizational effects were larger in mathematics than in science for learning and its equitable distribution early in high school (Outcomes 1 and 2), whereas the effects were somewhat larger in science than mathematics for achievement gain and social distribution by SES in the last 2 years of high school (Outcomes 3 and 4). The effects of yet another measure of academic organization, school academic press, followed the same general pattern as other measures in this group. Academic press was positively related to both early and late learning and was negatively associated with the SES/gain slopes, although effects were somewhat lower than for course taking.

Effects of the Organization of Instruction

Similar to academic course taking, we suggest that the level and distribution of authentic instruction in a school should be considered together. On average, in schools that are instructionally rich and incorporate active learning, and where this type of instruction is shared widely (i.e., the variability of authentic instruction is low), students learn more in science and mathematics both early and late in high school. Less variability in authentic instruction, which indicates that teachers in the same school share the same instructional approach, is also associated with gains that are more equitably distributed. A similar pattern, whereby effects in mathematics were stronger earlier and in science learning later, was evident for both authentic instruction and academic course taking.

For these variable pairs (academic course taking and authentic instruction), which measure how schools organize their curriculum and instruction, the pattern of effects is especially important. The school average of both measures was more strongly related to the effectiveness parameters (Outcomes 1 and 2, learning in these subjects), whereas the variability in these measures showed stronger association with equity parameters (Outcomes 3 and 4, the SES/learning slopes). That distributional measures were associated with distributional outcomes, and aggregate measures were related to aggregate outcomes, makes good sense but is also substantively important.

DRAWING IMPLICATIONS FOR OPTIMAL HIGH SCHOOL ORGANIZATION

The analyses presented in Chapter 4 and in this chapter, both of which investigated the influence of high school restructuring on students' learning, yield consistent conclusions.

The Peristence of Restructuring Effects

One important and obvious finding from our analysis is that resturucturing practices, as we identified them, really matter. Students learned more, and learning was more equitably distributed among students of different social backgrounds, in schools that adopted several restructuring practices. The restructuring categories we considered were meant to capture schools' willingness to adopt and sustain reforms that moved them away from bureaucracies and toward communities. Rather than disappearing after the early years of high school, when we might expect students to be most influenced by schools that are relatively new to them, restructuring effects on learning persisted or even increased somewhat in the later years of high school.

Nevertheless, we found that once other organizational properties of secondary schools were considered—how social relations, curriculum structure, and instruction were organized—the strength of the restructuring effects on learning faded. We conclude that these organizational properties of schools are more fundamental, and our empirical analyses suggest that they are more important qualities of schools, than the number of types of reform practices in which schools engage.

The Importance of Distributions

The outcomes that we have considered throughout this book incorporate the joint notions of effectiveness and equity, which we have used to define "good" schools. Although the general trends of effects for our academic and social organization measures showed favorable effects on both, the pattern was specific. For both the common curriculum and authentic instruction constructs, *levels* of course taking or authentic instruction in each school were associated with average learning, whereas the *pervasiveness* of such practices among school members was associated more with social equity in learning. Even when evaluated in the presence of a host of organizational features, small school size, although related to both effectiveness and equity, was most strongly associated with a more equitable distribution of learning. This pattern of association points out the importance of considering both *levels* and *distributions* as outcomes, when evaluating how characteristics of schools' organization influence student learning.

Revisiting Communal Organization

We return to the contrast of schools as bureaucracies and communities. Scholars agree about the dominance of the bureaucratic model in U.S. public secondary schools. Historically, there were valid reasons to structure schools in that way. Even recently, many have seen increased technological and human resources, coupled with modern management techniques, as the most appropriate means to foster student achievement. Until rather recently, the modern bureaucracy seemed to be the best way to provide equal educational opportunities to students disadvantaged by race, poverty, or immigrant status. Through expanded curricular offerings and specialized teachers' work, high schools aimed to become universal institutions that offered something for everyone. But such idealistic aims do not seem to have been realized. Our several studies of school restructuring described throughout this book give hints about this failure.

A New Type of Social Relations

Our results provide support for a substantially different type of school organization than that typified in the comprehensive high school. One aspect that should change is social relations. A different sort of social interaction than is typical in bureaucratic high schools should predominate: less hierarchy, less specialization, more cooperation. We found that teachers in "good" schools believe that they can (or should) succeed with all of their students. Rather than laying the cause of academic problems on the students and their families (that is, outside the schools and outside themselves), such teachers take responsibility for correcting them. The measure surely taps an important aspect of social relations. As McLaughlin (1994) commented, high schools should aim to become "personalized school environments, settings where teachers and students can come to know one another, and where students feel acknowledged and respected as individuals" (p. 11). Although the findings in Chapter 5 supported this same conclusion, our results here are even stronger. That is, the effect persists in the presence of other organizational features of the schools (as well as their restructuring status).

A Certain Type of Curriculum and Instruction

Although the communal perspective is more concerned with affective than cognitive dimensions of schooling, our findings suggest that good schools also have strong academic structures. Rather than the comprehensive high school that offers a broad range of courses at many different levels, rather than students' being free to select courses according to their "personal tastes," our evidence supports the value of a narrow academic curriculum, with a strong orgnizational push for all students to take these courses and master their content. In terms of how the courses should be taught, we have evidence that instruction should be authentic, and that this type of teaching should be pervasive rather than restricted to classrooms where teachers happen to prefer teaching this way.

Accumulating evidence from our several studies suggests that school organization really matters, and that the optimal organizational form for high schools is more communal than bureaucratic. Although convinced that this vision of the American high school would improve student learning and also its equitable distribution, we are far from sanguine about the best way to accomplish what surely involves a major organizational shift. School restructuring as a "reform movement" is difficult to conceptualize. Much of the term's appeal lies in its vagueness, so that people may "see" in it whatever they wish to see (Newmann, 1993). Although our results may clear up some of the vagueness, making the direction for change clearer, they also suggest that more fundamental features of how American secondary schools are organized may be more important—and probably even more difficult—both to implement and to sustain.

CHAPTER 7

A Focus on One Structural Feature: School Size

A defining characteristic of any school is the number of students that it is responsible for educating. Particularly in a high school, enrollment size has important implications for how the school is organized, the curriculum that it offers, and how school members interact with one another. In this chapter we consider how this important feature of a high school's structure—the number of students who attend—influences learning in two core school subjects: mathematics and reading comprehension.

All of the multivariate analyses described so far in this book have taken school size into account. Besides the major findings from these analyses, we have documented two consistent findings about size: (1) Students generally do better in smaller schools, and (2) achievement is generally less determined by students' family background in smaller schools. However, in the research reported so far we have not concentrated on school size as a major element of school restructuring or school organization. Rather, we included size in our analyses mainly to equalize schools on this dimension, so that the effects of the many facets of school restructuring and organization that we have considered would be estimated regardless of school size.

In Chapter 3 we investigated restructuring in middle-grade schools. There we used the number of 8th graders in each school as a proxy for school size. In Chapters 4, 5, and 6, where we explored restructuring effects for the same students across their high school years, again we included school size as a control—this time measured with total school enrollment. In Chapters 4 and 5 we considered how several elements of school restructuring and organization influenced student learning in the first 2 years of high school. Chapter 6 explored how the structure and organization of secondary schools influenced students' learning in mathematics and science across the 4 high school years. The results of the analyses in all those chapters led us to a general conclusion that "smaller is better."

In all these investigations, however, school size has been considered as a linear effect. That is, rather than using actual enrollments, we adjusted the variable so that its relationship with the outcome would be simplified to a straight line. This decision was motivated by statistical concerns. Neither the variable measuring high school size nor its counterpart in middle-grade schools, 8th-grade size, is normally distributed. Because there are considerably more small than large high schools (and more small than large 8th grades), the variables that measure school size are negatively skewed. Though there are many small high schools in the United States, most high school students attend large schools. However, the analysis techniques that we used require normally distributed variables. Therefore, for statistical purposes we had to transform the variable measuring school size to make it more normally distributed.[1]

The result of using a variable that was transformed in this way is that we have been unable, in the analyses discussed thus far, to answer some important substantive questions about the effects of high school size. The tradition for research on this subject (including our analyses in Chapters 3 to 6) couches the size question as, Is bigger better than smaller? However, in this chapter we organize our analyses around more practical ideas and questions, ones with more direct policy implications:

• *Idea 1 focuses on size and effectiveness.* We ask, Is there an ideal size for a high school, defined in terms of maximizing student learning? If so, what is it?

• *Idea 2 focuses on size and equity.* Here we ask, Does this ideal school size, defined in terms of maximal learning, also support an equitable social distribution of learning within the same school?

• *Idea 3 explores whether school size is a function of who goes there.* We ask, Does the ideal size change, depending on the types of students enrolled in the high school?

The purpose of this chapter is to explore these ideas and answer these questions. As in previous chapters we focus on changes in student achievement as the major outcome for our investigations. Before turning our analyses to address the questions listed above, however, we take a short detour to provide a brief summary of research and writings on this topic.

CONSIDERING SCHOOL SIZE

There are two streams of research on enrollment size, an important ecological feature of any educational organization. Most studies examine the issue in secondary rather than elementary schools. One strand, sociological in nature, explores how size influences other organizational properties. As schools grow, it becomes more and more difficult to keep track of what fellow staff members are doing through informal contacts. As a result, schools typically become more bureaucratic. Consequences flow from such changes. As there are more students with similar needs, instructional programs to meet those needs become more specialized. Human relationships become more formal. Another research stream, with an economic bent, focuses on the savings that might result from an expanded scale. This work highlights the potential for increased efficiency through reduced redundancy and increased resource strength as schools get bigger. The latter arguments have motivated the school consolidation movement.

Conclusions from the two streams go in opposite directions. Although the studies with an organizational focus generally favor smaller schools, the economic research suggests benefits from increased size. Because the economic stream is not very relevant here, we discuss it no further. The organizational research on school size also divides into two branches: Studies focus on either schools' academic or their social organization.

Size and the Specialization Argument

Research documents a relationship between organizational size and program specialization. In principle, large schools have more students with similar needs. Thus, they are better able to create specialized programs to address such needs (again, the efficiency argument). In contrast, small schools must focus their resources on core programs, with marginal students (at either end of a distribution of ability or interest) either excluded from programs or absorbed into programs that may not meet their needs very well (Monk, 1987; Monk & Haller, 1993). Despite the logic of the specialization argument, research on tracking suggests that extensive differentiation in curricular offerings and students' academic experiences has debilitating consequences (Gamoran, 1989; Lucas, 1999; Oakes, 1985). Increasing size invites curriculum specialization, resulting in differentiation of academic experiences and social stratification of outcomes (Lee & Bryk, 1989; Lee, Bryk, & Smith, 1993).

Research on the communal aspects of learning challenges the value of specialized curriculum. This perspective has motivated empirical work on curriculum effects that links differences in students' academic experiences to stratification in academic outcomes by social background (Garet & DeLaney, 1988; Lee & Bryk, 1988, 1989; Lee & Smith, 1993, 1995). How schools alter their offerings with a change in size differs by sector. Catholic schools add academic courses as they grow, while public schools typically add courses in personal development and other nonacademic areas (Bryk, Lee, & Holland, 1993).

Size and the Communitarian Argument

Sociological theory would suggest that human interactions become more formal as organizations grow (Weber, 1947). Organizational growth generates more hierarchical structures, as connections between individuals become more formal and less personal. These structures inhibit communal ties within schools (Bryk & Driscoll, 1988). The theory has been confirmed in research identifying organizational characteristics of effective schools. In school climate studies, for example, size operates as an ecological feature of the social structure, part of a physical environment influencing social interactions (Barker & Gump, 1964; Bryk & Driscoll, 1988; Garbarino, 1980). Some recent field-based studies investigate what happens when high schools are broken into smaller units (Lee, Ready, & Johnson, 1999; Mohr, 2000; Oxley, 1994, 1997). These authors' arguments rest on the premise that large schools have impersonal social climates that inhibit learning and hamper the development of community among students and between students and staff.

This line of research concludes that students benefit in several ways from attending smaller schools (Ayers et al., 2000; Clinchy, 2000; Lee, 2000). The more constrained curriculum in many small high schools is typically composed of academic courses, so that almost all students follow the same course of study regardless of their interests, abilities, or social background. This constraint results in both higher average achievement and achievement that is more equitably distributed (Lee & Bryk, 1988, 1989). Social relations are also more positive in smaller schools. The preponderance of sociological evidence about high schools supports a "smaller is better" conclusion.

School Reform and School Size

Currently, there is much reform activity targeted at making schools smaller. Garbarino's (1980) essay, suggesting the particular importance of high school size for marginal students, is typical of arguments that underlie these reform efforts. Echoing Barker and Gump's (1964) seminal study, Garbarino described "a threshold effect," whereby benefits of increases in size over about 500 students were minimal (although he presented no evidence to support this number). Zane (1994) echoed teachers' laments when one urban district's high schools-within-schools increased in size from 200 to 400 students. Relatively small high school size was considered acceptable even by James Bryant Conant, the acknowledged father of the comprehensive high school. According to Conant (1959), a high school with a graduating class of 100 should be sufficiently large to implement his recommended curriculum. John Goodlad (1984) indicated that he "would not want to face the challenge of justifying a senior high of more than 500 to 600 students" (p. 310). Although the

Coalition for Essential Schools has made no specific recommendations about high school size, founder Theodore Sizer (1984) listed "keep[ing] the structure simple and flexible" among the five "imperatives for better schools" (p. 214).

Contemporary reform efforts to create more personalized learning by reducing school size are also supported by foundations. For example, in the last decade some influential organizations have made major efforts to reform secondary education. A major recommendation of an influential report for reforming middle schools was "to create small communities for learning" (Carnegie Council on Adolescent Development, 1989, p. 9). The first of six themes of another report aimed at high school reform suggested that "schools must break into units of no more than 600 students so that teachers and students can get to know each other" (NASSP, 1996, p. 5).

REFOCUSING THE QUESTION OF SCHOOL SIZE

Although one argument made in writings about school size recommends larger schools as a move toward economic efficiency, such studies focused mostly on school consolidation in rural areas. Most writing within the contemporary policy area aimed at high school reform recommends that secondary schools should be smaller than they are (Ayers et al., 2000; Clinchy, 2000; NASSP, 1996). Although these writings advocate smallness, there is some logic to support a concern that high schools could become too small to serve their students well. Unless the school's population is quite homogeneous (in ability and aspirations), it is difficult to imagine that a very small high school could offer a set of courses sufficient to meet the academic needs of a diverse student body. Although our analyses in previous chapters have generally supported smaller school size, here we move beyond the issue of whether high schools should be big or small. Rather, here we try to identify an optimal size for a high school. By our definition, "optimal" is defined on two dimensions: (1) how much students learn over their 4 years of high school in mathematics and reading comprehension, and (2) how equitable learning in those two subjects is distributed by students' background characteristics.

The schools and students used for the analyses in this chapter were identical to the samples used in Chapter 6 (where we also examined achievement growth over the 4 years of high school). We studied 9,812 12th graders in 789 public, Catholic, and elite private high schools. The large majority of the schools are public. All of the students remained in the same high schools between 10th and 12th grade.

Departing somewhat from the logic we laid out in Chapter 6, we chose to evaluate the effects of school size on learning in mathematics and reading. Our indicator of learning is growth in achievement (or gain) in those subjects from the end of middle school (8th grade) to the end of high school (12th grade). We chose these subjects because skill in these areas is generally agreed to be very important for students' future success. We also thought that it was a good idea to select subjects whose content was quite distinct. It is possible that school size could influence these two subjects quite differently.

Relating School Size and Achievement Gains

Our major independent variable was school enrollment size. Rather than the logarithmically transformed measure of school size used in other chapters, here we were interested in actual enrollments. We decided on a strategy of using categories to represent school size. In order to decide on which categories to use, we pursued a set of sensitivity analyses for both learning and its equitable distribution in each subject.[2] The analyses generated a set of residualized outcomes, or school averages of achievement gains after adjusting for student- and school-level covariates. We plotted these outcomes against school size. Figure 7.1 displays a scatterplot of the residualized measure of mathematics learning, adjusted for several characteristics of students and schools, again high school enrollment size. Because the scatterplot for residualized learning in reading looked very similar, we have not included it.

It is evident from Figure 7.1 that residualized mathematics learning varies by school size. The peak for this graph suggests an optimal size range. Schools whose enrollments range between 500 and 1,000 students appear to be favored in mathematics learning. In schools smaller than 500, learning appears to drop. More dramatically, learning is consistently lower in larger high schools. Although this plot (and its counterpart for learning in reading) suggests that smaller schools are favored, it is also evident that the effects of size on learning are not linear. To accommodate potentially nonlinear effects, we divided the continuous measure of school size into a set of eight categories in groups of 300: less than 300 students, 300 to 600 students, 601 to 900 students, 901 to 1,200 students, 1,201 to 1,500 students, 1,501 to 1,800 students, 1,801 to 2,100 students, and over 2,100 students.

Controlling for Other School and Student Characteristics

We know from other research that several additional characteristics of students and schools influence learning. In order to eliminate the possibility of alternative explanations for our findings about school size, we needed to take into account several other factors. Gender, socioeconomic status (SES), minority status, and ability as students entered high school represent the characteristics of students that we included in the analyses.[3] We also controlled

for several school characteristics: school average SES, school minority concentration, and school sector (Catholic schools and elite private schools were each contrasted with public schools). These controls are the same set of student and school characteristics that we have included in the analyses in other chapters. As before, readers may find the details of construction of all variables in Appendix A.

Analysis Strategy and Presentation

Also consistent with the analyses described in Chapters 3 through 6 we have used hierarchical linear modeling (HLM) to evaluate the effect of school size on student learning (Bryk & Raudenbush, 1992). This technique is appropriate for analyses that pose multilevel research questions and use nested data (here, students are nested in schools). More detail on the HLM technique is provided in Appendix B.

As explained earlier, not only were we interested in identifying the ideal size of a high school for maximizing learning (Idea 1), but we also wanted to identify the ideal size for the equitable distribution of learning (Idea 2). A third idea focused on whether the "ideal" school size was different, depending on the type of students attending the school. Each of the questions generated by these ideas was explored with HLM. We chose to present results in this chapter almost entirely in graphic form, except for descriptions of students and schools in the several size categories. Readers interested in the numerical details from which the graphs were constructed are referred to Lee and Smith (1997).

Students, Schools, and Enrollment Size

What kinds of students attended schools in the eight enrollment-size groupings into which we divided our sample of almost 9,000 students and 800 schools? Were other school characteristics associated with size? Table 7.1 presents the characteristics of students and schools in each size category. The median-size high school enrolled about 1,200 students. Because the original National Educational Longitudinal Study of 1988 (NELS:88) sampling strategy called for drawing equal numbers of students in each NELS:88 school (regardless of size), both student and school sample sizes were reasonably well distributed across our groups, even though larger high schools actually enrolled more students.

In general, observed learning gains were largest in moderate-size to smaller high schools (though not the smallest ones). However, schools of these sizes also enrolled somewhat more able and more advantaged students. School factors varied more by size than did student characteristics. Average SES was

Table 7.1. Characteristics of Students and Schools for Eight Categories of High School Size

School Size	Below 300	300– 600	601– 900	901– 1,200	1,201– 1,500	1,501– 1,800	1,801– 2,100	Over 2,100
Student Sample	912	830	1,667	1,645	1,319	1,205	1,263	971
School Sample	75	67	148	139	83	70	101	106
I. Variables Describing Students								
A. Outcomes								
Mathematics gain	8.91	12.13	15.69	13.44	12.20	11.61	10.18	7.84
Reading gain	4.54	6.28	7.61	6.46	5.05	4.60	4.34	3.45
B. Control Variables								
Ability, math[a]	.03	.17	.17	.18	.12	.18	.05	.11
Ability, reading[a]	.05	.21	.14	.19	.13	.21	.07	.15
Female (%)	52.8	51.5	47.9	49.9	52.7	52.4	52.9	50.4
Minority (%)	14.5	24.3	14.3	18.0	16.6	15.6	23.5	21.5
Social class (SES)	-.12	.07	.11	.05	.03	.08	-.04	-.06
II. Variables Describing Schools								
Average SES[b]	-.21	.09	.18	.08	.09	.18	-.15	-.32
High minority[c] (%)	20.3	26.9	16.3	21.2	15.8	14.5	26.1	33.3
Public (%)	95.0	92.5	75.5	81.2	90.8	89.4	92.8	95.9
Catholic (%)	2.5	4.5	10.9	12.2	6.6	6.6	0.9	3.1
Elite private (%)	2.5	3.0	13.6	6.6	2.6	4.0	6.3	1.0

[a] Students' average achievement at 8th grade in the three other subjects was used as a proxy measure of ability, $M = 0$, $SD = 1$.
[b] Variables were z-scored at $M = 0$, $SD = 1$ on this sample.
[c] Schools with more than 40% minority students (Black or Hispanic) were coded 1, others coded 0, due to non-normal distribution.

higher in the moderate-size schools, lower in the smallest schools, and lowest in the very largest schools. Minority students were also concentrated in the largest schools. The majority of schools in all size categories were public. However, the fact that private schools were more common in the moderately small categories may explain some other differences. The fact that student and school characteristics varied by school size, as shown in Table 7.1, suggested that we should take these characteristics into account when evaluating size effects on learning in multivariate analyses.

THE EFFECTS OF SCHOOL SIZE ON STUDENT LEARNING

This section presents, mostly through graphic displays, the results of our multivariate and multilevel analyses that aimed to address the ideas and questions about "ideal size" posed at the beginning of the chapter. Our purpose was to identify the optimal enrollment size for a high school, defined in terms of both effectiveness and equity. Moreover, we wanted to know if the ideal size of high schools varied depending on the types of students the school served.

Learning, or Effectiveness

Figure 7.2 displays the results of analyses that estimate the effects of school size on learning in mathematics and reading. Because effects are compared with the modal size category, 1,200–1,500 students, the size effects in this category are zero by definition. Consistent with the pattern of presentation of results in other chapters, we have presented effects in standard deviation (SD) units. We suggest that readers follow the lead of Rosenthal and Rosnow (1984) for substantive interpretation of effect sizes. That is, effects are "large" if they are .5 SD or more, "moderate" if .3.5 SD, and "small" if they fall in the .1 to .3 SD range. Effects smaller than .1 SD are trivial. Because our choice of contrasts here was rather arbitrary, we concentrate more on the relative magnitudes of school size effects than on either the absolute size or the statistical significance of group differences.

School size showed a similar pattern of effects for learning in both reading and mathematics. However, size appears to influence learning in mathematics (dark bars) more than reading (light bars). Results here are clear and consistent: Students in moderate-size schools (particularly in the 600–900 range) learned most. Although achievement gains were lower in the smallest schools (under 300 students), learning in both subjects was lowest in the largest schools (over 2,100 students). Readers should remember that these results were adjusted for students' social background, their ability as they came into high school, school social composition, and sector. Even though the 600–900 size category contained somewhat more private schools than other categories, school sector was taken into account when these effects were estimated. Thus, between the beginning and end of high school, students learned most in neither the smallest nor the largest high schools. Rather, learning in mathematics and reading comprehension was highest in moderately small high schools, those that enrolled between 600 and 900 students. We conclude that this size high school is most effective, with "effectiveness" measured in terms of average learning in these two core academic subjects.

Figure 7.2. Effects of high school size on achievement gains in mathematics and reading.

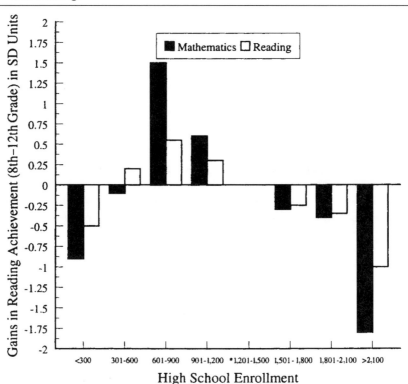

*Note: The size group of 1,201–1,500 students was used as the comparison group; thus by definition effects for that size group are zero.

The Social Distribution of Learning, or Equity

Readers may recall from other chapters that we have used a distributional outcome as a measure of social equity in learning. Similar to the results reported in Chapters 3 through 6, here we considered the relationship between students' socioeconomic status and achievement gains in reading and math within each school as an indicator of equity, or what we have called the social distribution of learning. By this definition, schools that are more equitable have a smaller relationship between SES and learning. In the same HLM analytic models in which we measured the size effects on average learning that were displayed in Figure 7.2, we also estimated size effects on the relationship between SES and learning in these two subjects. Following from our definition, we judge a more equitable social distribution of learning as a more modest relationship of SES to achievement gain in these subjects. Therefore, in the schools in the size categories that showed negative relationships to these outcomes (that is, where the bars go down instead of up), learning was distributed more equitably. Results of these analyses are shown in Figure 7.3. As before, comparisons were with schools enrolling 1,200–1,500 students. Thus, again, the effects for that size group would be zero by definition.

Although Figure 7.2 showed size effects on average learning (or effectiveness) that were larger for mathematics than for reading, size effects on the equitable distribution of learning were considerably larger in reading than in math. The pattern was otherwise similar here, in that learning was most equitably distributed in smaller schools and least equitably distributed in large

Figure 7.3. Effects of high school size on the relationship between SES and achievement gains in mathematics and reading.

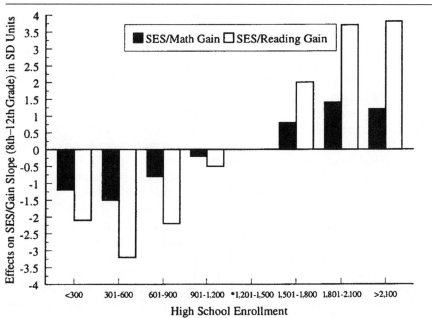

*Note: The size group of 1,201–1,500 students was used as the comparison group; thus by definition effects for that size group are zero.

schools. Reading learning was most equitably distributed by students' SES in schools that enrolled 300 to 600 students and most inequitably distributed schools that enrolled over 1,800 students. A similar pattern occurred for the distribution of mathematics learning by SES. Learning in mathematics was most equitably distributed in very small schools (enrolling 600 or fewer students). As with reading, larger schools were more inequitable.

Summarizing our findings so far, we conclude that high schools that enroll between 600 and 900 students are most effective, measured in terms of average learning in mathematics and reading. However, it is even smaller schools (enrolling fewer than 600 students) that are more equitable in terms of the social distribution of learning. Although size effects on effectiveness are larger in mathematics, size influences equity more strongly in reading comprehension. In all cases, our analyses favored schools that are smaller than most high schools in the United States. Our results definitely indicate that schools that enroll fewer than 1,000 students are both more effective and more equitable.

Size, Learning, and School Social Composition

Besides identifying the ideal high school size in terms of both effectiveness and equity, we also wanted to know whether the effects of school size on learning were consistent among schools that enrolled different types of students. We identified schools by their social compositions. In particular, in one set of analyses we focused on schools enrolling students of various social class levels; in another, we identified schools enrolling differing proportions of minority students. In these analyses, we have presented our results as actual point-score achievement gains between 8th and 12th grade in the two subjects, rather than in SD units. Figure 7.4 displays the results of our analyses that compared students in high-SES and low-SES schools for gains in mathematics achievement.[4]

We draw three conclusions from the results in Figure 7.4. The first is important, although not surprising. Even after taking into account many other characteristics of students and schools, we see that students learned considerably more mathematics over the course of high school in high-SES (light bars) than in low-SES schools (dark bars). The second conclusion is that the optimal school size was identical in low- and high-SES schools: between 600 and 900 students. The third conclusion is perhaps the most striking. School size seemed to make more difference in schools enrolling low-SES students than in those that enrolled high-SES students. Though the learning differences between low- and high-SES schools in the 600–900 size range were about 2 points on a 40–point test, learning differences between low- and high-SES schools that were very small (fewer than 300 students) were larger—about 3.5 points. Most striking were the learning differences in the largest schools: about 5 points between low- and high-SES schools. The results shown

Figure 7.4. Average gains in mathematics achievement by high school size in low-SES and high-SES high schools.

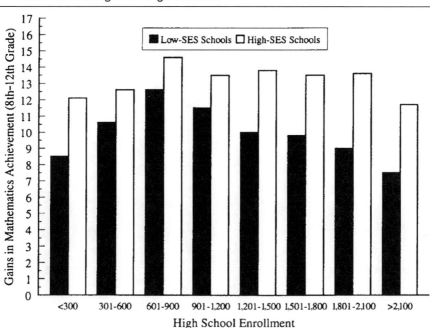

in Table 7.1 indicate that school average SES in both very large and very small schools was considerably lower than for schools in the middle size ranges. Thus, there were large numbers of socially disadvantaged students attending schools of a size where learning was lowest.

The results of our investigation of whether size is more salient in schools enrolling different proportions of minority students are displayed in Figures 7.5 and 7.6, which display achievement gains in mathematics and reading respectively.[5] In both subjects, the size-by-minority concentration interaction terms that we used to test for size differences by school composition were statistically significant. For learning in both mathematics and reading, the differentiation between schools with high- and low-minority enrollments was less striking than the contrasts by school average SES shown in Figure 7.4, although the learning differentials were not trivial in either venue. Also similar to the findings shown in Figure 7.4, the optimal school size in both subjects for both types of schools was in the middle size range.

These graphs also show some differences from our findings about school average SES. Focusing on the contrasts for math (Figure 7.5), somewhat larger

FIGURE 7.5. Average gains in mathematics achievement by school size in high schools with low-minority and high-minority enrollment.

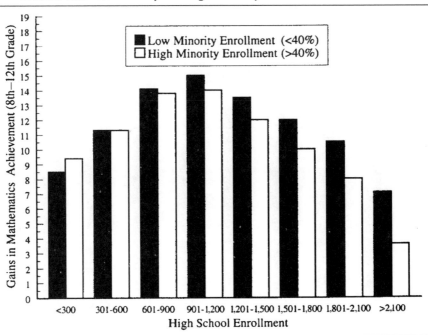

schools (enrolling between 900 and 1,200 students) showed slightly higher achievement gains for schools with both high- and low-minority enrollments. Also noteworthy is that, for gains in mathematics, students in very small schools (300 students or less) actually learned more in the schools that enrolled *more* than 40% minority students (although we saw in Table 7.1 that most very small schools enrolled very few minority students). Similar to our findings in Figures 7.3 and 7.4, very large schools were the most socially differentiating.

It is clear from these analyses that very large schools are problematic environments for learning, especially those that enroll large proportions of socially disadvantaged students. In general, the patterns are quite similar for learning in both mathematics and reading comprehension. As before, we see that students who attend high-minority schools enrolling over 1,800 students showed very few gains in achievement over the course of high school in these core subjects. Although the actual magnitude of the achievement gains in reading was smaller than in math, this difference was probably related to the relative length of the two tests (21 items on the reading test, 40 items on the mathematics test).

FIGURE 7.6. Average gains in reading achievement by school size in high schools with low-minority and high-minority enrollment.

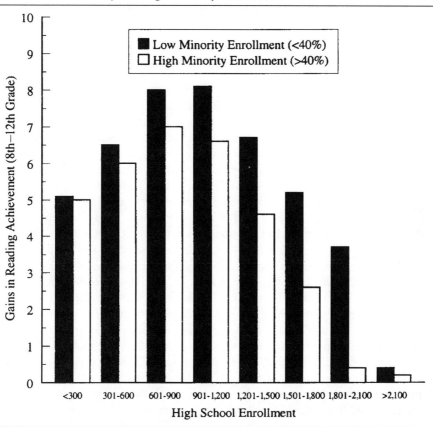

SOME POLICY RECOMMENDATIONS

Almost all of the analyses in this book have taken school size into account. However, in this chapter we have focused our attention on this structural feature of high schools, in terms of actual enrollment and how it influences students' learning in two core subjects. The size of a high school has a significant influence on average levels of learning (effectiveness) in the school and the social distribution of learning among students in the school (equity). Size is even more important to learning in schools that enroll substantial proportions of socially disadvantaged students. These findings lead us to offer some policy recommendations.

1. *High schools should be smaller than they are.* For several decades, large comprehensive high schools have been the norm in the United States. The economic arguments that favored school consolidation, ones that stressed the need for substantial numbers of students in order to offer a broad array of courses, have led the country in the wrong direction in designing its secondary schools. In general, the high schools that most students attend are too large. Our results are quite definitive in indicating the ideal size of a high school: 600 to 900 students. Although size effects differ somewhat for effectiveness and equity (we found even smaller schools more equitable), we feel confident in concluding that students learn more in smaller high schools.

2. *High schools can be too small.* Although we recommend making high schools smaller, there also seems to be a balance point. Schools must be large enough to offer a credible curriculum, but small enough that people can know one another well. Smaller schools are better able to function as communities. One issue motivating our work was to investigate the validity of policy calls for very small schools. In New York City, for example, many very small high schools have opened in the last decade. It might be logical that a school could function well with small size if the clientele were socially and academically homogeneous, the students' aspirations very similar, and the overall resource base rather high (for example, elite private schools). However, our results from analyses of almost 10,000 students in 800 U.S. high schools suggest that learning is limited in very small high schools (under 600 students) as well as in very large schools. Although the dual aims of effectiveness and equity do not converge on exactly the same school size, we feel confident in concluding in general that the ideal size high school enrolls at least 600 students.

3. *Ideal size is unrelated to the types of students who attend.* We were struck by the consistency of results across schools defined by differing social compositions. Regardless of whether we examined the full range of high schools in the United States, schools that enroll mostly high-SES or mostly low-SES students, or schools that enroll high or low proportions of minority students, the ideal size remains in the range of 600 to 900 students. Thus, we believe our finding here to answer the question, Which size high school works best, and for whom? is sturdy.

4. *Size is more important in some schools than others.* Although high school size is a significant factor in determining learning for all students, this structural feature has particular salience in school settings where disadvantaged students are concentrated. Learning is particularly low in very large high schools. And we know that these are exactly the high schools where large numbers of economically and racially disadvantaged students are being educated. Thus, from the point of view of inducing more social equity in learning for students in secondary schools, it is especially important to consider reducing the size of the largest high schools.

HOW DO WE CHANGE HIGH SCHOOL SIZE?

It is much easier to make recommendations for the *direction* of change that for the *implementation* of change in the size of U.S. secondary schools. The most obvious way to make high schools smaller is probably also the most difficult: build more new and small schools. Though this strategy might be feasible in school districts where school populations are growing, public tax support for school construction is forthcoming, and new schools are being constructed, this description captures very few school districts. In the current fiscal environment, there is at best modest public support for investment in any type of social betterment. Therefore, it seems unlikely that the U.S. public would support a campaign to build many new small high schools. This is particularly problematic in the nation's large cities, where financial resources are in especially short supply.

A rational alternative, and one that is spreading fast, is to create several schools-within-schools in existing large high schools. We are mildly optimistic about this policy, even though there is little empirical research on this organizational option. However, we recommend caution about this policy on two dimensions. One caution has to do with the size of the new units. Our results suggest that especially small units will not be optimal, so schools should not try to form mini-schools that are too small.

A second caution has to do with using schools-within-schools to create a series of "specialty shops" (Powell et al., 1985) within a single school building. We suggest that schools-within-schools should not be used to differentiate students by ability, interest, behavior, or almost any other dimension that may—intentionally or not—map onto student background. We believe that selection into the schools-within-schools should be close to random. Thus, we are somewhat wary of the movement to create career academies within inner-city schools in Baltimore, Philadelphia, Chicago, and other large cities. Our own field-based research in five high schools divided into schools-within-schools has suggested that social stratification is a definite possibility with this reform (Ready, Lee, & LoGerfo, 2000). We worry that this kind of specialization runs the danger of introducing more social stratification in academic experiences and outcomes than already exists in U.S. secondary schools. Ideally, each subunit should reflect the demographic and academic diversity that exists in the school as a whole. With these caveats, we are optimistic that schools-within-schools will help create smaller high schools. We hope that each will enroll no fewer than 600 students.

PART IV

Implications from the Study

Is school restructuring a determinant of student achievement? Our answer is a qualified yes. We found that over the course of the 4 years of high school, students who attend schools that adopted reform practices that were consistent with the purposes of the school restructuring movement learned more than their counterparts in high schools with more traditional practices in place. Restructuring schools were, thus, more effective—students gained more in achievement in such schools. Equally important, restructuring schools were also more equitable environments—their students' achievement gain was less differentiated by family social class. However, we also found that above and beyond the restructuring practices in place, more enduring structural and organizational features of America's public and private high schools that were characterized as restructured were even more important in inducing this dual pattern of favorable outcomes in their students. In this last chapter, we discuss some larger implications of our findings about the usefulness of school restructuring to improve America's secondary schools.

CHAPTER 8

The Larger Meaning of School Restructuring for American High Schools

Although there are many ways to characterize "good high schools," in this book we have used only two criteria. "Good" schools are simultaneously effective and equitable for the students who attend them. By effective, we mean that students who attend good schools learn more. However, above and beyond effectiveness defined in terms of students' learning more, by our criteria good schools are also equitable environments. That is, students' learning is not strongly differentiated according to their social background. That our investigations used data from a large and nationally representative sample of U.S. high schools and their students, and because the investigations followed the same students for 4 years (from the time they entered high school until they graduated), we are in a good position to draw several conclusions about how high school restructuring may influence the academic development of students. The conclusions are organized around a series of questions.

WHAT IS "RESTRUCTURING" MEANT TO CHANGE ABOUT SCHOOLS?

Writers who helped to develop the concept of school restructuring have focused on the fact that restructuring is *more than reform*, that it is meant to bring about profound changes in such aspects of schools as their goals, their structures, and the roles of those who work in them (students as well as teachers and administrators). Restructuring is supposed to change how schools are governed, how the work of students and teachers is organized, and how "successful performance" is defined and measured.

For secondary schools, the restructuring movement challenges some very basic notions that have guided how high schools have functioned for more than a century. "Undoing" some or all of these features of high school structure is the aim of the school restructuring movement. For example, high school restructuring advocates favor longer school periods, whereas the usual high school day is divided into discrete and subject-specific periods of an hour or less. They advocate that teachers have more sustained contact with fewer students (perhaps over multiple years), whereas most high school teachers see maybe 150 students for an hour each day for a year, or even a semester. Restructuring advocates favor dismantling the tracking system, with classes and instruction organized heterogenously. They advocate that teachers work collaboratively rather than individually and autonomously—in interdisciplinary teams that meet together often to plan an integrated curriculum that breaks down the traditional barriers that exist between subjects and departments. This would suggest a move away from teacher autonomy and individualism, which are now hallmarks of secondary teaching. Under restructuring, such teams should serve smaller groups of students over more sustained periods of time.

Restructuring advocates also favor a more interactive or constructivist approach to instruction, very different from the typical lecture-notes-test model. In the new approach, knowledge would be socially constructed, students would engage in activities that foster higher-order thinking, and the activities and assignments in which students engage would be tied to the world beyond school and to their personal interests. For this type of instruction, the quality of work would be assessed through projects, portfolios, and tests where students would produce knowledge, rather than through the more common multiple-choice and short-answer tests where students are asked to reproduce knowledge imparted by teachers or texts. The restructuring movement also urges shifting the locus of decision making downward—from the district to the individual school site, from the principal to teachers, and even to students—to involve all school members in important decisions that affect them. Efforts to create new small schools or to divide large high schools into smaller units, including the development of schools-within-schools organized around themes meant to appeal to students' interests and career plans, are consistent with the school restructuring movement.

HOW IS CHOICE INVOLVED IN RESTRUCTURING?

The U.S. comprehensive high school includes a substantial number of choices, many of which surround choosing coursework. However, choice of school has not been a common element of the structure of public secondary education. Rather, most students attend the public high school serving their residential location. Although the restructuring movement has not been identified with or tied to the contemporary and very active movement favoring school choice, the two movements are not inconsistent. The fact is that many private secondary schools, both Catholic and elite private schools, are orga-

Figure 7.1. Distribution of residuals from mathematics achievement gains compared to high school enrollment.

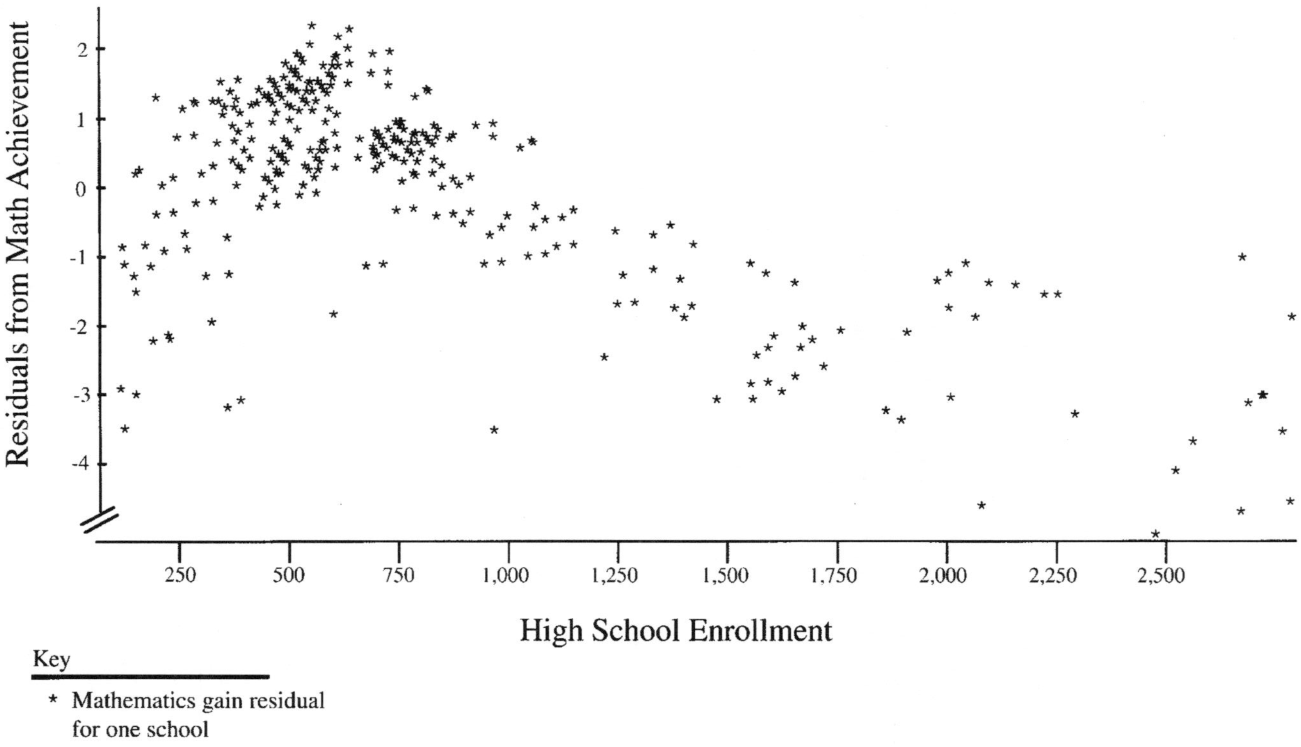

Key

* Mathematics gain residual
  for one school

132

nized in ways that reflect several aims of the restructuring movement. Private schools are usually smaller, they often have less tracking, and teachers often work collaboratively. The very fact that students and parents choose them suggests that there is some matching of interests between "sellers" and "clients." However, the private school model can be pushed only so far within the restructuring movement. Most private high schools are organized rather traditionally; they "sell" a traditional academic curriculum; and they focus almost entirely on preparing all their students for entry into, and success in, college. Although there is choice of whether to attend a private school (and to pay for the privilege), there are relatively few choices within them.

Most public high schools by definition have a much broader mission; they are required to enroll every student who presents him- or herself at the door; they cannot expel any but the most troublesome or academically unmotivated students; and they need to serve a broad range of students and families. To serve this broader mission, public high schools typically offer students a wide variety of choices about almost everything—what to study, at what level to study it, how hard to work, how deeply to engage in intellectual activity, which teachers to seek out, even whether to come to school regularly. Choice seems to be a fundamental American value that allows high schools to accomplish many social goals simultaneously—what Philip Cusick (1983) called "the egalitarian ideal." The public high school is a social institution that keeps most adolescents in school and off the street, provides a means for some students to prepare for advanced study at the university, provides training for students for whom secondary school is a terminal educational experience, and offers special services for adolescents who need them (for example, psychological counseling, learning English, special education, parenting and child care, college-level courses). In short, the American high school tries to provide something for everyone (Powell et al., 1985).

Within the public sector, perhaps a more productive use of choice involves high schools that have divided themselves into schools-within-schools. Most of these high schools are located in cities, and many of them enroll large proportions of disadvantaged students. These schools use choice (of small schools, often organized around career-based themes meant to attact students) as a major strategy for building commitment in schools (Lee et al., 1999). Among the 24 highly restructured schools that participated in the Center on Organization and Restructuring of Schools (CORS)–sponsored School Restructuring Study (SRS), some of the most successful were schools of choice or schools that were reconstituted after an earlier and publicly declared failing organizational structure had been dismantled (Newmann & Associates, 1996).

Although many features of educational choice introduce considerable stratification into American schools, the movement seems to be here to stay. Restructured schools try to make use of choice in new ways. Were schools to take care to avoid or ameliorate the stratification that frequently results from allowing choice, there might be positive consequences of allowing choice within educational settings. Such advantages would center around using choice to build students' commitment to the aims or purposes of education, without allowing students to inadvertently damage themselves with bad choices. Choice is now so embedded in the American educational system, as it is in the broader society, that it is difficult to take a doctrinaire stance against any form of it. The school restructuring movement surely involves choice as part of many of its features.

WHY MIGHT STUDENTS LEARN MORE
IN RESTRUCTURED SCHOOLS?

Several theories might help us understand why changes that take place in restructured schools lead to increased student learning. Throughout this book, we have invoked one explanation that centers on a theory about organizations: the contrast of schools as bureaucracies or as communities. Useful theories spell out possible mechanisms through which changes in the structure of secondary schools might translate into increased learning for all students. Three additional theories underlying the reform practices that are consistent with the restructuring movement seem useful in the context of secondary schools; they focus on relationships, epistemology, and empowerment.

More Sustained Human Interactions

A theory that focuses on the human dimensions of schooling would lay out a logical mechanism through which reforms that aim to change human interactions might induce higher achievement. The most obvious benefits are for students. As a result of being known better and having more positive relationships with their teachers, students would increase their commitment to, and engagement with, the educational process. Such increased commitment would increase students' motivation and effort. When students expend more effort on school assignments and activities, they learn more.

When teachers get to know their students better, they might see the teaching role in broader terms, rather than simply as "filling a large number of empty vessels." Much has been written about the alienating environment of high schools for most students, particularly for those who are unsuccessful in the conventional terms (performance) through which most schools define success—better grades and higher scores on standardized tests. When small groups of teachers and students see one another often, and over sustained periods of time, productive human interactions increase and commitment ensues.

Improving the human dimensions of schooling might also induce more commitment on the part of teachers, as they interact more with their colleagues rather than work in isolation behind closed classroom doors. Collaborative work by students might encourage them to know their peers—particularly those with whom they typically do not associate in social situations. Such restructuring practices as keeping students and teachers together in the same homeroom or advisory period for several years, interdisciplinary or grade-level teaching teams, creating schools-within-schools, and cooperative learning strategies would increase the human dimensions of schooling and, we argue, lead—directly or indirectly—to increased learning on the part of students.

Constructivist Teaching and Learning

One thrust of the restructuring movement focuses on changing the character of teaching and learning in response to a different conceptualization of knowledge. Here, the focus is on creating learning environments that encourage students to "use their minds well," as Sizer (1984) suggested. This view of teaching and learning would engage students in activities that encourage them to construct rather than reconstruct or reproduce knowledge, that characterize knowledge as process as well as content, and that engage students in long-range and complex projects that have meaning for them in the world beyond school.

Restructuring practices that foster this theory of knowledge would include students and teachers working together in indisciplinary teams, integrated projects drawing on their knowledge across several disciplines, independent studies where teachers and students individually negotiate projects that engage students deeply, project-based learning, and assessments that consider student work over a sustained period and on complex tasks. The processes to carry out such activites might involve block scheduling, flexible time schedules, or allowing students to learn in community or work settings (e.g., internships).

Downward Movement of Power

Another relevant theory centers on democratic governance. Similar to theories that focus on human interactions, this mechanism involves attempts to increase commitment and effort. School members (teachers and students) are more committed to their work when they are involved in major decisions that influence their lives in school. Included in this theory are the notions of site-based management and teacher autonomy. If schools are allowed to, say, manage their own budgets, they can allocate resources in areas they think are quite important, including activities and practices that are directly connected with student learning. This theory would support organizational autonomy at several levels. Not only should schools be freed up from the control of state or district-level policies and rules, but teachers should be given more responsibility over the school's core operations.

Democratic decision making is a central concept in the devolution of school power. Bringing parents into schools and involving them in some of the school's core activities would fit here. Involving students in educational decisions within the school that affect them directly would also be compatible with this theory. Allowing students to choose the programs with which they are associated, in schools-within-schools, would also belong within this theoretical framework, as would decentralized governance for each subunit with such schools. Virtually all restructuring advocates encourage a movement of power downward within the educational hierarchy. A devolution of power would also be easier in schools of choice and in smaller schools.

HOW IS SCHOOL ORGANIZATION RELATED TO RESTRUCTURING?

Important conclusions drawn from the empirical results described in this book are that school restructuring influences both how much students learn during their high school years and how achievement is distributed according to student background. High schools that have adopted reform practices consistent with the restructuring movement are "good" schools, according to these criteria. Is it really having these restructuring practices in place, however, that explains why these favorable outcomes accrue to students in these schools? The previous section laid our some theoretical mechanisms through which restructuring reforms might link to learning. However, the research findings described in Part III of the book suggest that there is actually more to the story. We showed that the high schools categorized as "restructuring practice schools" simultaneously possessed other organizational properties. When we took these organizational properties into account, the restructuring effects were "explained away."

There is a vast array of organizational properties on which high schools could be characterized. In our analyses, however, we focused on three broad categories: social organization, academic organization, and instructional organization. Although the analyses in Chapter 6 considered these three dimensions together, we discuss them separately here.

School Social Organization

We located our exploration of school social organization within two related notions: *schools as communities* (Bryk & Driscoll, 1988; Bryk et al., 1993) and *schoolwide professional community* (Louis et al., 1996). Although the professionalization of teachers' work is high on the contemporary school reform agenda, within the restructuring movement the focus on changing the nature of teachers' work aims instead to alter social interactions within the faculty: how teachers relate to and collaborate with one another, the norms and values they share, their influence on school policies outside their classrooms, and attitudes they share about their students' capacities to master skills and concepts.

The investigation described in Chapter 5 considered several of these dimensions: collaboration, control over school policy, and collective responsibility for learning. However, one aspect of school social organization—collective responsibility for student learning—was most important among those we considered. For individuals, rather than school social organization, this idea captured teachers' attitudes about their students' abilities and willingness to learn, whether teachers think they can "get through" to even the most difficult students, whether teachers change how they teach depending on whether their students are learning, and self-assessments of their efficacy in teaching. As an aggregate organizational property describing a school's staff, however, collective responsibility for learning assesses *the faculty's* focus on student learning and their willingness—as a group—to make sure that all students learn.

In good schools collective responsibility for learning is not only high, but such attitudes are also shared by the faculty. Not only do students learn more in schools where most teachers share these attitudes, but learning is also more equitably distributed. The explanation for this linkage seems obvious: When teachers work to make sure all their students are learning, when they change how they teach in order to make this happen, when they believe that all students deserve whatever efforts are needed to learn, students respond by learning more. Although the mechanism seems obvious, more troubling is the reality: Such attitudes are not common. Moreover, schools where collective reponsibility among teachers is low enroll students who are academically and socially less advantaged—exactly the schools where such "can do" attitudes are most important (because so many students are not learning).

How can schools change teachers' attitudes about their students' ability to learn and about the teachers' own abilities to be successful with all their students? We have no easy answer. Changing attitudes is not easily accomplished through training, professional development, or introducing reform practices. Rather, administrators who believe such attitudes are important may need to seek out new faculty with such attitudes. It is much easier for schools to adopt particular practices (although sustaining them may not be easy). Our results suggest that these two concepts are linked, but the causal order between school restructuring and collective responsibility is unclear.

That is, schools may engage in, and succeed with, particular reform practices *because* their teachers share these attitudes.

School Academic Organization

The characterization of this organizational feature was based both on our previous research comparing Catholic and public schools (e.g., Bryk et al., 1993; Lee & Bryk, 1988, 1989; Lee et al., 1993) and on research about tracking and the differentiated curriculum (e.g., Gamoran, 1987, 1989; Garet & Delany, 1988; Lucas, 1999; Oakes, 1985). Almost all research on the effects of tracking concludes that students in comprehensive high schools who follow a college preparatory curriculum learn more than those in the general and vocational tracks. A major explanation for why achievement in Catholic high schools is both higher and more equitably distributed than in public schools relates to differences in the two sectors' academic organization. Catholic high schools offer a narrow set of mostly academic courses, and almost all students take the same courses.

The typical public school curriculum is much broader, in terms of the *types* of courses available, the *difficulty level* of the courses, and the *effort* required to be successful in them. We have characterized school academic organization in three ways: the average number of academic courses in mathematics and science that students take throughout their high school careers (a proxy measure of curriculum structure), the homogeneity of students' course-taking patterns in these subjects, and how hard schools press their students academically. The mechanism by which these features of school academic organization translate into learning is straightforward. Students learn what they are taught in the courses they take. A more demanding curriculum, one that is followed by most students, and a press for all students to work hard and do well characterize good schools by our definition. We have evidence that this form of academic organization "works," in terms of both effectiveness and equity.

Why, then, are there so many high schools with academic organizations that don't look this way? How to implement and sustain this type of academic organization in U.S. public high schools is less straightforward than demonstrating its efficacy. Despite growing pressures to "tighten up" coursework and requirements for all students in the contemporary American comprehensive high school, we know that it continues to be organized in ways that cater to a wide range of student demands. Most teachers and administrators, and many parents, understand that demanding academic coursework and a press toward academics "pays off" for students. Although parents of high-achieving students, in particular, surely understand this well, they often argue that their children should not be in classes with less-motivated or less-able students. They fear that more heterogeneously organized classes would "dilute" the high-powered courses their children would otherwise enjoy. Pushing against pressures that the entire academic organization of a school be focused on demanding courses that all students take are countervailing pressures on schools to give students what they want. For many of today's American secondary school students, this involves less work and more relevancy. Many school people worry that pressing *all* students hard would alienate many and raise dropout rates.

School Instructional Organization

Beyond evidence about organizational features of high schools characterized by teachers' attitudes and courses offered, in "good" high schools, teaching should also be "authentic." Although we tailored our measures of authentic instruction to be consistent with the focus of CORS and the work of Fred Newmann and his colleagues (1996), our instructional measures are also consistent with much recent writing about teaching and learning. Other writers have variously called instruction of this form "interactive," "progressive," "student-centered," or "teaching for understanding." Our measures focused on instruction in mathematics and science, based on reports from both teachers and students about their 10th-grade classes in these disciplines. Instructional activities that are authentic involve the construction rather than reconstruction of knowledge, require more complex activities and projects, are connected to the world beyond school, use materials beyond texts, and have students working and discussing in groups rather than individually. Teachers spend less time lecturing; students themselves do science experiments rather than watch teacher demonstrations.

We characterized our measures of instruction as organizational features of schools. They captured not only whether, on average, a school's instruction in those subjects was more or less authentic, but also the degree to which all teachers of those subjects were teaching that way. Our findings suggest that in good schools, not only is instruction more authentic but also widespread; the majority of teachers engage in this type of instruction. The mechanism through which an organzational structure characterized by authentic instruction "translates" into higher and more equitably distributed achievement for students is also quite straightforward. Whereas the measures of academic organization focused mostly on the curriculum (which students take what courses), our instructional organization measures focused on how the curriculum was delivered to and engaged by students.

Even with clear evidence that when instruction was organized this way students learned more, influencing *how* teachers actually teach is perhaps even more difficult that changing *what* they teach. Most high school teachers work in isolation; they seldom work together. Moreover, they develop how they teach early in their careers, often drawing heavily on their own experiences as students (Lortie, 1975). Without strong support and leadership favoring a more authentic instructional approach, without professional development to strengthen such skills, and without an organizational press toward using this type of instruction, teachers without training in how to teach this way at the university invariably cling to "the old ways."

Organization Counts

Clearly, how schools are organized—which we defined in terms of their social relations, the curriculum they offer, and how that curriculum is delivered in the form of instruction—strongly influences how much all students learn. Although this book has presented much evidence about the effects of school restructuring on student achievement, we conclude that these more enduring features that define high schools are even more important. The features of school organization that we targeted, when considered in conjunction with school restructuring, had a more profound effect on student learning and its equitable distribution than did the reform practices that schools had in place. Thus, we are convinced that restructuring, although a promising means for raising student achievement, is not the main issue. Schools influence how much their students learn by how they organize themselves. It is, however, considerably easier for school administrators and teachers to implement individual practices—to hop on a well-publicized restructuring bandwagon—than to change more fundamental organizational features.

WHY DOES SCHOOL SIZE MAKE SUCH A DIFFERENCE?

We included, in virtually every analysis in this book, a measure of school size. It is usual in the type of research we have conducted to "control for" common demographic and structural features of schools. School size, like school sector, minority composition, and average SES, was included in this set of statistical controls. School size is also related to many other features of schools that we investigated. We know, for example, that Catholic and elite private high schools are generally smaller than public high schools. We also know that schools that enroll high proportions of disadvantaged students are typically larger than counterpart schools that enroll more-advantaged students. We also know from other research we have conducted that the organizational features we have found to be more favorable are also more common in smaller high schools. The fact that so many of these school elements are associated with one another, and with school size, is a major reason why we included school size in all our analyses.

However, even in our full analytic models, which took into account school demographic composition, sector, restructuring status, and several types of organizational structure, school size still had independent effects on student learning and its equitable distribution. In general, our analyses indicated that all students (but particularly disadvantaged students) learn more in smaller schools. Our more specific analyses of the effects of school size on student learning, in Chapter 7, suggest that students did better in smaller high schools—but not the smallest high schools.

Yet, as we mentioned in Chapter 7, school size is unlikely to be a direct causal factor for increasing learning. Moreover, the mechanism through which school size "translates" to student learning is surely quite complex, operating primarily though its influence on how schools are organized. More specifically, smaller school size is a facilitating factor for creating organizational features of schools that we have shown to be important determinants of learning. In discussing the organizational advantages of Catholic over public schools, Bryk, Lee, and Holland (1993) highlighted their smaller size:

> The coordination of work in larger schools typically imposes demands for more formal modes of communication and encourages increased work specialization and a greater bureaucratization of school life. In contrast, a smaller school size facilitates personalism and social intimacy, both of which are much harder to achieve in larger organizational contexts. (p. 299)

WHY ARE THERE SO FEW RESTRUCTURED HIGH SCHOOLS?

Many practices that we included in the "restructuring" categories introduced in Chapters 3 and 4 are hardly "cutting-edge." Yet, the proportion of high schools that reported practices such as using parent volunteers, focusing on cooperative learning, teaming their teachers across disciplines, offering mixed-ability classes in mathematics and science, providing teachers with common planning time, offering flexible time for classes, or keeping students in the same homeroom over several years was distressingly low (see Table 4.1).

The body of research evidence that such practices are effective in inducing positive development in students is growing. This includes evidence that transforming high schools into more humane places where students' experiences with adults and with one another are more personal increases student learning. However, not many American high schools are doing these things; even fewer are doing several of them. Our findings here indicate that the structure of most American high schools remains quite bureaucratic. In real terms, restructuring (as we would like to define it and not how we have measured it here) is quite unusual. The most obvious explanation for why there are not more schools (especially high schools) that are substantially restructured is that these practices are hard to implement and sustain. Although it is difficult to introduce and sustain reform practices in schools, moreover, it is even more difficult to change their organizations and structures in the directions we have discussed.

Much has been written about the difficulty of real reform in education. The movement to restructure schools may be an example of what Slavin (1989) described as the swing of a reform pendulum. Some school reforms become very popular before they are well studied in terms of how they influence students. By the time study results are well known, the reform is dropped and another (often quite different from the original) is embraced.

Stahl (1999) used the pendulum metaphor in his thoughtful essay about the "rise and fall" of the whole-language approach to teaching reading. It may be that restructuring, like whole language, has become politicized. That is, its advocates speak of the movement (and the need for it) in almost moral terms. Even more dangerous, according to Stahl, is that practitioners often look to researchers for dispassionate information. Often, they find instead political judgments. Some of the writings about school restructuring have that feel to them, in that they tend to "demonize" the old ways in their advocacy for the new. Decrying the fact that the debate about whole-language instruction in reading has become politicized, Stahl drew a larger lesson: "This is a danger with politicization of education: When one party has been found to fail, there is a tendency to swing to the other party. Politicization tends to eliminate a middle ground. It is precisely this middle ground that represents the best practices" (p. 20).

COULD RESTRUCTURING EFFECTS BE EVEN STRONGER?

Limitations of Survey Data to Capture This Phenomenon

Using survey data to investigate the effects of school restructuring has many strengths. The availability of longitudinal data on large and nationally representative samples of students, teachers, and schools has allowed us to use the longitudinal and multilevel statistical methods that are appropriate for the study of school effects. However, the use of survey data to explore such questions also has some limitations. Although survey methods are well suited to investigate the *occurrence* or *frequency* of organizational practices, they are not particularly good for studying their *implementation*. Although our data source, NELS:88, fortunately included reports from principals about whether the practices occurred in each high school, it included no information about the intensity and pervasiveness of, or support for, these practices.

For example, if a school reported that independent study was available or that it used interdisciplinary teaching teams, it is possible that these practices might actually have involved only a very small number of students and/or teachers in that school. Most teachers might actually have opposed these reforms, with only a small and self-selected group engaged in such activities. The fact that a particular reform practice was *available* in a high school would in no way assure that it was being taken *advantage of* or actually *involved* most of the school's students or teachers. We had no information about how often interdisciplinary teams actually met (or whether time was allotted for such activity in the school day), for example.

These are questions of participation and implementation—issues about which we had no information. Moreover, we didn't know whether the practices that in theory involved students (mixed-ability classes or independent study are examples) actually involved the few students in each school who were part of the NELS study. With an average of fewer than 15 students in each high school in our sample, unless the practice were almost universal (which is certainly possible), sampled students might not have actually experienced the programs reportedly offered by the school. From a statistical perspective, the inability to match practices to teachers and students introduces some degree of unreliability into our analyses.

Unreliable Measures of the Phenomena Under Study

The very constraints of using survey methods to study the phenomenon of school reform may underscore the substantive meaning we draw from our findings. In Chapter 4, we saw that high schools that engaged in as few as three practices classified as "restructuring" showed quite powerful effects on their students' learning and engagement, and the rather small proportion of American high schools that engaged in none of the practices had negative effects on their students. For that reason, the actual effects of restructuring we described probably represent lower bounds for the actual effects of school restructuring on student engagement and learning. If we had information on actual implementation of school restructuring, on which students were involved in the reform practices and for what length of time, the effects we showed here would probably be much larger.

The problems of using survey data for investigating the effects of school organization on student learning are similar. Because we did not design the data collection, we were limited to using the measures that others devised. We are fortunate that the organizational features we pursued—social organization, academic organization, and the organization of instruction—are important features of how secondary schools are structured. However, our focus on these organizational features in no way precludes the possibility of other important facets of school organization in influencing student learning and its equitable distribution.

The Nature of the Outcomes

The discussion above highlights the limitations of using survey data to measure restructuring or school organization, what are defined within quantitative research as "independent variables." We argue that if we had better measures of these constructs, and were able to link them more carefully to the students whom they influence, their effects might be larger. Similarly, a case could be made that the outcomes on which we have estimated the effects of school restructuring and organization are flawed. The achievement tests used in the NELS:88 study were short multiple-choice exams in which the students had no stake (neither they nor their teachers ever learned their scores on these tests). Because the tests were constructed to be administered to students with a broad range of competencies in a wide variety of high schools, there was little effort to tie them to specific curriculum content. For example, the 12th-grade tests in mathematics included no items that focused on calculus; indeed, the mathematics test focused on computation, algebra, and geometry—subjects usually encountered during (or even before) the first 2 years of high school. Moreover, the reading tests did not focus on literature; they focused on comprehension of short passages meant to be understandable and interesting to students regardless of the content of English courses. The same lack of connection to the curriculum was typical of the science and social studies tests.

Standardized, multiple-choice, timed tests such as these seldom probe higher-order thinking. Students are asked to reproduce rather than construct knowledge. Were the dependent variables used in this study more sensitive to detecting students' higher-order competencies that might be developed through more authentic instruction or higher-level coursework, perhaps the effects of school restructuring and school organization, defined as we have in this study, might be even larger. Our point here is that the outcome measures we used, which we drew from survey data, might not be sensitive to the independent variables that were the focus of our study. More information about how restructuring actually worked in a smaller number of highly restructured schools is available from Newmann and Associates (1996).

WHY ARE HIGH SCHOOLS SO DIFFICULT TO CHANGE?

Several fundamental organizational features that define secondary schools are challenged by the restructuring movement. It intends to change how students typically move through the school day and how they engage content, in a series of discrete and rather short periods. There are efforts to alter how high schools organize knowledge; typically subject matter is divided into departments, around which most teachers identify themselves. In most high schools, students are mapped into courses based on their tested abilities, stated interests, work histories, and future plans. Restructuring plans to change the pattern of how individual teachers typically work with "their" students, where they usually engage them in large groups, with a single teacher, for fixed amounts of time and behind closed doors. Traditional instruction in high schools locates knowledge and expertise in teachers and books, rather than as a socially constructed phenomenon that students develop for themselves. Most high schools maintain a rather formal division between the school, its parents, and the communities it serves—they desire support but not interference from these "outsiders." Power, in most high schools, is organized into a clear hierarchy, with decision making about school policy severely limited at lower levels of the hierarchy.

The organization of the comprehensive high school makes sense, given its original purpose. This structure was developed by progressive reformers as a means to avoid particularism and parochialism, and as the most efficient way for single schools to serve large numbers of students, with different interests and aims, within a single building (Tyack, 1974). This organizational structure still works quite efficiently, particularly in high schools that serve socially and academically heterogeneous clienteles and when the number of students to be served is quite large. It is not surprising that the structure of the high school, as a major social institution that operates with public funds, should be seen as an efficient means to prepare young people to enter a society that is itself organized hierarchically, around a capitalist structure (Bowles & Gintis, 1976).

Despite the efficiency with which these institutions have operated in terms of the aims they were designed for, almost everyone who writes about contemporary high schools speaks of the need to change them. As we have claimed throughout this book, the restructuring movement targets many entrenched features of high schools: tracking and curriculum differentiation, departmental organization, the way time is used, the way instruction is organized, even the meaning of knowledge and expertise. The very fact that restructuring calls for such fundamental change may be seen as quite threatening to those who have worked in high schools for decades—the problematic pendulum that Slavin (1989) and Stahl (1999) describe.

We suspect that very few would not agree that the outcomes we have focused on in this book—academic learning and its equitable distribution—are appropriate criteria for defining good schools. We have documented that restructuring practices and organizational or structural features of high schools that are consistent with the restructuring movement are associated with favorable outcomes for students. To make reforms consistent with restructuring really "take hold" in U.S. comprehensive high schools requires profound changes for many of their most fundamental and entrenched features.

How to accomplish such reforms is not the subject of this book, nor do we think that our research findings qualify us to make suggestions of this sort. Based on our study, however, we feel strongly that important changes in how U.S. high schools are organized are badly needed. Our evidence suggests the direction for these organizational changes.

Notes

CHAPTER 3

1. The information about restructuring practices was not part of the regular NELS:88 school questionnaire. Rather, the data were collected retrospectively through the *Hopkins Enhancement Survey of NELS:88 Middle-Grades Practices* (Epstein, McPartland, & MacIver, 1991).

2. Our measure of engagement is a factor-weighted sum of student reports of (1) how often they come to class without pencil and paper (reversed); (2) how often they come to class without books (reversed); (3) how often they come to class without homework (reversed); (4) how many hours/week they spend on homework; and (5) whether they ever feel bored in school (reversed). Exact details of the construction of this, and other variables used in this book, are found in Appendix A.

3. Our measure of at-risk behaviors is a factor-weighted sum of student reports of how often (1) they were sent to the office for misbehavior; (2) their parents received warnings about misbehavior in school; (3) they got into a fight with another student; (4) classmates see them as a troublemaker; (5) they skip or cut class; and (6) they come to class late. See Appendix A for more detail.

4. Readers may notice that coefficients with the same magnitude (effect of the restructuring on average engagement of .04 compared with the effect of heterogeneous grouping on engagement of .04) are sometimes statistically significant and sometimes not. The first is significant ($p \leq .01$) but the second is nonsignificant. Statistical significance is a ratio: A coefficient must be at least twice its standard error to be significant. Thus, although the two coefficients have the same magnitude, their standard errors (which we do not report in our tables) are of different sizes.

CHAPTER 4

1. The numbers in Table 4.1 are not raw probabilities for the 820 schools in the sample, but rather represent the probability that "an average high school" would engage in each practice. We computed these adjusted probabilities as follows. As the average number of practices in place in these schools was 12 (out of 30), we defined "the average high school" for this investigation as one that had adopted 11, 12, or 13 practices. We reestimated the frequency of each practice for these average high schools.

It is these frequencies, represented as proportions, that are displayed in Table 4.1. Compared with raw probabilities, the variable order is identical.

2. A fifth of the schools (20.2%) report more than four practices on this list, and only 6% report more than six (or half the practices) in place. No school engages in more than nine such practices. We do not suggest that adopting many reforms of this type simultaneously is necessarily good for students, only that it is rare.

3. As the distribution of the variable measuring total school enrollment is negatively skewed (i.e., there are a large number of small high schools), we used a logarithmic variable transformation for school size in multivariate analyses.

4. The first variable measured academic emphasis as the average number of math and science courses in each school taken by students in 9th and 10th grades (summed and aggregated). The second variable, a measure of course taking differentiation in schools, was constructed as the SD of the school-level aggregate of the academic emphasis variable.

5. Because the NELS items measuring engagement at 10th grade are different from 8th-grade measures, our engagement analyses were conducted as covariance models rather than simple gain-score outcomes.

6. The percentages of public, Catholic, and elite (NAIS) private schools listed on Table 4.2 were weighted, as were virtually all analyses presented in this book. The original NELS sampling design considerably oversampled private schools and students. However, in order to weight down this oversampled group, and weight up public schools (which were, as a result, undersampled), NELS supplied researchers with design weights. Because of the weighting, some group averages may not add up to the proportions of private schools in the overall sample.

7. In each analysis, we used a slightly different ability control. For the 10th-grade engagement outcome, we controlled for the 8th grade test composite. For the various gain-score outcomes, we constructed an ability control that includes the average of the other three 8th-grade tests. For example, for mathematics gain, our ability control was an average of the 8th-grade scores in reading, history, and science.

8. To investigate the SES/gain slope within each school as an outcome in between-school HLMs, we treated this variable differently from the other controls in the within-school models. Thus, SES was left "free" (i.e., it's variance was allowed to vary between schools), and it was centered around the mean in each school. The between-school variance of the other control variables was "fixed" to zero and they were grand-mean centered.

9. The numbers on these graphs were computed using the results from Tables 4.4 and 4.5, as follows. For mathematics achievement gain, we used the following equations:

$$y = 2.92 + -.21*[RESTR1] + ((.43 + .18)[SES]), \text{ or}$$
$$y = 2.92 + .49*[RESTR2] + ((.43 - .33)[SES])$$

where:

- 2.92 is the intercept for average mathematics gain;
- RESTR1 takes the value of 1 for no-reform practice schools and 0 for traditional practice schools;

- RESTR2 takes the value of 1 for restructuring practice schools and 0 for traditional practice schools;
- SES takes on the values of –1, 0, and 1 for students with low, medium, and high levels of socioeconomic status (SES);
- –.21 is the gamma coefficient for no-reform/traditional schools contrast (RESTR1) on average mathematics achievement gain;
- .49 is the gamma coefficient for restructuring/traditional schools contrast (RESTR2) on average mathematics achievement gain;
- .43 is the intercept for the SES/mathematics achievement gain slope;
- .18 is the gamma coefficient for the no-reform/traditional schools contrast on the SES/mathematics achievement gain slope; and
- –.33 is the gamma coefficient for the no-reform/traditional schools contrast on the SES/mathematics achievement gain slope.

We followed the same procedure to prepare the graphs for achievement gains in reading, history, and science, substituting the appropriate values for the intercepts and gamma coefficients for each outcome and each SES level. The pattern was similar for engagement; we have omitted these results only for the sake of brevity.

10. The graphs are simplified in another sense. Although the analyses take other characteristics of students that influence learning (shown in Table 4.3) or characteristics of schools that influence learning (Table 4.4) and its social distribution (Table 4.5) into account, such adjustments are not shown in these graphs. The numbers are computed for students and schools with values of 0 on other variables (e.g, schools of average size, average school SES, public schools, average academic emphasis, and the like).

CHAPTER 5

1. We compared the sample of 9,904 teachers in the 820 NELS high schools to a nationally representative sample of teachers from the Administrator and Teachers Study (ATS) of High School and Beyond (Moles, 1988). From these analyses, we determined that for high school teachers in these four subjects, the NELS and ATS teacher samples are demographically indistinguishable.

2. More detail about the construction of these composites, including the actual wording of items from which they were drawn, is found in Lee and Smith (1996). Reliability, as a measure of internal consistency measured on the teacher-level composites with Cronbach's alpha, are as follows: collective responsibility: .77; staff cooperation: .87; and teacher control: .76. These reliabilities are considered moderate to high.

3. The 12 NELS items on the teacher survey used to construct this measure are listed below, in the order of their factor weights. Each has a 5-level response set (strongly disagree to strongly agree):

- little I can do to ensure high achievement (reversed);
- I can get through to the most difficult student;
- different methods can affect a student's achievement;

- teachers make a difference in students' lives;
- it is a waste of time to do my best in teaching (reversed);
- teachers are responsible for keeping students from dropping out;
- students' attitudes reduce academic success (reversed);
- I work to create lessons that students will enjoy learning;
- students' success or failure is due to factors beyond me (reversed);
- students are incapable of learning the material (reversed);
- I change my approach if students aren't doing well; and
- student misbehavior interferes with my teaching (reversed).

4. Identical to Chapter 4, our ability controls included a composite measure of students' test scores in the subjects other than the subject being tested, converted to a z-score (M = 0, SD = 1). For example, for the analyses investigating learning in mathematics, the ability control includes students' scores on the eighth-grade tests in reading, social studies, and science.

5. The relationships between SES and achievement gains were as follows: mathematics: .19 SD; reading: .22 SD; history: .13 SD; and science: .15 SD. All are significant below the .01 probability level.

6. The numbers representing the heights of the bars in these graphs were computed using the HLM results displayed in Tables 5.2 and 5.3. For mathematics achievement gain, we used the following equation:

$$y = 2.97 + .33[COLLRESP] + ((.18 - .30[SES]) * COLLRESP))$$

where:

- COLLRESP took on the value of −1, 0, and +1 for schools with low, medium, and high levels of collective responsibility for learning;
- SES took on the values of −1, 0, and +1 for students with low, medium, and high level of SES;
- 2.97 and .33 were the intercept and the gamma coefficient for collective responsibility on average mathematics achievement gain; and
- .18 and −.30 were the intercept and the gamma coefficient for collective responsibility on the SES/mathematics achievement gain slope.

We followed the same procedure for computing bar heights representing achievement gains in reading, history, and science, substituting the appropriate values for the intercepts and gamma coefficients for each of those outcomes.

7. Unfortunately, NELS data were not designed to explore an association between teachers and students through the instructional process. Although we may link teachers to some of the students they teach, we have information neither on the classes the students were actually in nor on the instructional methods used in those classes. More important, data on student achievement were collected only at the end of 8th and 10th grades. Although the teachers are linked to students through their 10th-grade classes (in, say, mathematics), there is no measure of students' achievement status at the end of the 9th or beginning of the 10th grade (an appropriate pretest for measuring effects of instruction in 10th grade). Neither are the

tests designed for curriculum specificity (e.g., there are few geometry items on the mathematics test, and a 10th-grade mathematics class could well be geometry). Moreover, the numbers of students/class would be modest for a nested-classroom HLM model. In general, survey methods are not ideal for studying instruction.

CHAPTER 6

1. This decrease in sample was not due entirely to students who dropped out of high school between 10th and 12th grade. Some students may have transferred to other high schools (i.e., they left the sample but stayed in school); others may not have taken the tests in the 12th grade; still others may have been students in the small number of schools we dropped. The dropout rate between 10th and 12th grades is lower than 18%.

2. The numbers used to construct Figure 6.2 were calculated from within-school HLMs. In our three-level HLMs, these represent Level 2. In the within-school model, we treated SES as a random effect, and the variance of the SES/achievement slopes were centered around their respective school means. Other student-level controls (minority status, gender, ability) were treated as fixed effects and were centered around their respective sample means. We followed the same procedures in our analyses in Chapters 3, 4, and 5.

3. Two reasons motivated us to combine data about mathematics and science instruction. One was the sample: We wanted to include the entire sample of students. In both the base year and follow-ups, NELS collected data from two of each student's teachers—either English or social studies, and either mathematics or science. Thus, students did not have data from both science and math teachers, but rather from one or the other. The second reason concerned data quality. Including data from both students and teachers about instruction in their schools produced more reliable measures. The items were combined with Rasch scaling techniques.

4. This may be because the NELS math tests were "tailored." That is, at 10th grade, initially lower-scoring students were tested on a set of simpler math items than those with moderate or high scores at 8th grade. Such tailoring was introduced to make the tests more responsive to effects of the high school mathematics curriculum (which is typically tracked by ability), to avoid ceiling effects for the most able students, and to locate the discrimination parameter for the IRT scaling of the tests differentially by student ability. Although the NELS science tests were not tailored, more difficult items were introduced and simpler items dropped over the three testing periods (Ingels et al., 1994).

5. Although results on the four outcomes are presented in separate columns, it is important to note that the effects for gain and its social distribution by SES in Table 6.3 were estimated in single HLM models for each subject and time period. The model was, in fact, even more complex; it included the within-school controls shown in Table 6.2. As those effects did not change much, nor were they the focus of our analyses, we did not include them in Table 6.3.

6. Another measure of school social organization, staff cooperation, was statistically significant in an HLM model without the responsibility for learning mea-

sure. Once the latter variable was introduced, however, staff cooperation dropped to nonsignificance, so we deleted it from the model.

CHAPTER 7

1. Due to the negative skew, we performed a logarithmic transformation on the variable measuring high school size and on its middle-grade counterpart, the variable that measures the size of the 8th grade, used in the analyses in Chapters 3 through 6. This technique is quite common in quantitative social science research. Perhaps the most common logarithmic transformation is in research in economics, where almost any measure of earnings (or income) is negatively skewed. Obviously, there are more low-income than high-income people.

2. The multivariate sensitivity analyses used a multilevel residual technique. We saved the residuals from a two-level HLM model similar to that used in many other analyses in this book. Gain scores in both mathematics and reading between 8th and 12th grades were used as the outcomes, along with the SES/achievement gain for each analysis. We included the following variables as controls in our within-school models: SES, minority status, gender, and ability. The level-two controls included school average SES, minority composition, and school sector (Catholic and elite private schools contrasted with public schools). We saved the residuals from these analyses, which were measures of adjusted learning, and plotted them against the continuous version of the variable measuring school size. Lee and Smith (1997) provide more detail on these analyses.

3. Similar to the analyses of achievement gain in Chapters 4, 5, and 6, we controlled for students' ability as they entered high school by averaging students' test scores on achievement in the other school subjects measured at 8th grade. For example, for analyses that investigated achievement gains in mathematics, the ability control was the average of students' scores on the eighth-grade tests in reading, science, and social studies.

4. Low-SES schools were those whose average school SES was at least one SD below the sample average for school SES, and high-SES schools were at least one SD above the sample mean. We created a set of seven size-by-average SES interaction terms and included them in level two in the same HLM model that we used for the analyses in Figures 7.2. and 7.3. We also investigated a similar model for achievement gains in reading comprehension. As the interaction terms were not statistically significant (as a set) for that outcome, we do not present the results here.

5. To compute the size-by-minority concentration interactions, we followed a somewhat different procedure from the interactions of size with school-average SES. Here we used a two-piece linear model to capture large and small schools (Bryk & Raudenbush, 1992). Lee and Smith (1997) provide more detail about this procedure.

References

American Association for the Advancement of Science. (1984). *Equity and excellence: Compatible goals. An assessment of programs that facilitate increased access and achievement of females and minorities in K–12 mathematics and science education* (AAAS Publication 84–14). Washington, DC: Office of Opportunities and Science.

Ames, N.L., & Miller, E. (1994). *Changing middle schools: How to make schools work for young adolescents.* San Francisco, CA: Jossey-Bass.

Anderman, E.M., & Midgley, C. (1997). Changes in achievement goal orientations, perceived academic competence, and grades across the transition to middle-level schools. *Contemporary Educational Psychology, 22*(3), 269–298.

Anderson, C., & Barr, R. (1990). Modifying values and behaviors about tracking: A case study. In R. Page & L. Valli (Eds.), *Curriculum differentiation: Interpretative studies in U.S. secondary schools* (pp. 183–206). Albany: State University of New York Press.

Angus, D.L., & Mirel, J.E. (1999). *The failed promise of the American high school.* New York: Teachers College Press.

Ashton, P.T., & Webb, R.B. (1986). *Making a difference: Teachers' sense of efficacy and student achievement.* New York: Longman.

Ayres, L.P. (1909). *Laggards in our schools.* New York: Russell Sage Foundation.

Ayers, W., Klonsky, M., & Lyon, G. (Eds.). (2000). *A simple justice: The challenge of small schools.* New York: Teachers College Press.

Barker, R.G., & Gump, P.V. (1964). *Big school, small school: High school size and student behavior.* Stanford, CA: Stanford University Press.

Barry, B. (1995). School restructuring and teacher power: The case of Keels Elementary. In A. Lieberman (Ed.), *The work of restructuring schools: Building from the ground up* (pp. 111–135). New York: Teachers College Press.

Battistich, V., Solomon, D., Kim, D., Watson, M., & Schaps, E. (1995). Schools as communities, poverty levels of student populations, and students' attitudes, motives, and performance: A multilevel analysis. *American Educational Research Journal, 32*(3), 627–658.

Battistich, V., Solomon, D., Watson, M., & Schaps, E. (1997). Caring school communities. *Educational Psychologist, 32*(3), 137–151.

Berends, M., & King, M.B. (1994). A description of restructuring in nationally nominated schools: Legacy or the iron cage? *Educational Policy, 8*(1), 28–50.

Bidwell, C.E. (1965). The school as a formal organization. In J.G. March (Ed.), *Handbook of organizations* (pp. 972–1022). Chicago: Rand McNally.

Blyth, D.A., Hill, J.P., & Smyth, C. (1981). The influence of older adolescents: Do grade level arrangements make a difference in behaviors, attitudes, and experiences? *Journal of Early Adolescence, 1,* 85–110.

Blyth, D.A., & Karnes, E.L. (Eds.) (1981). *Philosophy, policies, and programs for early adolescent education: An annotated bibliography.* Westport, CT: Greenwood.

Bowles, S., & Gintis, H. (1976). *Schooling in capitalist America: Educational reform and the contradictions of economic life.* New York: Basic Books.

Boyer, E.L. (1983). *High school: A report on secondary education in America.* New York: Harper and Row.

Braddock, J.H., II. (1990). Tracking the middle grades: National patterns of grouping for instruction. *Phi Delta Kappan, 71*(6), 445–449.

Brattesani, K.A., Weinstein, R.S., & Marshall, H.H. (1984). Student perceptions of differential teacher treatment as moderators of teacher expectation effects. *Journal of Educational Psychology, 76*(2), 236–247.

Briggs, T.H. (1927). *The junior high school.* Boston, MA: Ginn and Co.

Brophy, J. (1986). *Socializing students' motivation to learn.* East Lansing: Michigan State University Press.

Brophy, J.E. (1983). Research on the self-fulfilling prophecy and teacher expectations. *Journal of Educational Psychology, 75,* 631–661.

Brown, R. (1993). *Measuring the progress of systemic educational reform.* Denver, CO: Education Commission of the States.

Brown, R. (1997). The learning organization: A model for educational change. *NAMTA Journal, 22*(1), 190–203.

Bryk, A.S. (1994). More good news that school organization matters. In *Issues in Restructuring Schools, 7,* Fall 1994:6–8. Madison: Center on Organization and Restructuring of Schools, University of Wisconsin.

Bryk, A.S., & Driscoll, M.E. (1988). *The school as community: Theoretical foundations, contextual influences, and consequences for students and teachers.* Madison: National Center on Effective Secondary Schools, University of Wisconsin.

Bryk, A.S., Easton, J.Q., Kerbow, D., Rollow, S.G., & Sebring, P.A. (1993). *A view from the elementary schools: Reform in Chicago.* Chicago, IL: Consortium on Chicago School Research, University of Chicago.

Bryk, A.S., Lee, V.E., & Holland, P.B. (1993). *Catholic schools and the common good.* Cambridge, MA: Harvard University Press.

Bryk, A.S., & Raudenbush, S.W. (1992). *Hierarchical linear models: Applications and data analysis methods.* Newbury Park, CA: Sage.

Burns, T., & Stalker, G.M. (1961). *The management of innovation.* London: Tavistock.

Carnegie Council on Adolescent Development. (1989). *Turning points: Preparing American youth for the 21st century.* Washington, DC: Author.

Carnegie Task Force on Teaching as a Profession. (1986). *A nation prepared: Teachers for the 21st century.* New York: Carnegie Forum on Education and the Economy.

Center on Organization and Restructuring of Schools. (1992, Fall). Estimating the extent of school restructuring. In *Brief to policymakers. Brief No. 4.* Madison, WI: Author.

Clinchy, E. (2000). *Creating new schools: How small schools are changing American education*. New York: Teachers College Press.

Cole, M., & Griffin, P. (Eds.) (1987). *Improving science and mathematics education for minorities: Contextual factors in education*. Madison: University of Wisconsin, Wisconsin Center for Educational Research.

Coleman, J., Campbell, E., Hobson, C., McPartland, J., Mood, A., Weinfeld, F., & York, R. (1966). *Equality of educational opportunity report*. Washington DC: U.S. Government Printing Office.

Conant, J.B. (1959). *The American high school today*. New York: McGraw-Hill.

Conant, J.B. (1960). *Recommendations for education in the junior high school years: A memorandum to school boards*. Princeton, NJ: Educational Testing Service.

Conley, D.T. (1993). *Roadmap to restructuring: Policies, practices, and the emerging visions of schooling*. Eugene: Eric Clearinghouse on Educational Management, University of Oregon.

Conway, J.A. (1984). The myth, mystery, and mastery of participative decision making in education. *Educational Administration Quarterly, 20*, 11–40.

Cooper, H.M., Findley, M., & Good, T. (1982). Relations between student achievement and various indexes of teacher expectations. *Journal of Educational Psychology, 74*(4), 577–579.

Cooper, H.M., & Tom, D.Y. (1984). Teacher expectation research: A review with implications for classroom instruction. *Elementary School Journal, 85*(1), 77–89.

Cooper, R. (1999). Urban school reform: Student responses to detracking in a racially mixed high school. *Journal of Education for Students Placed at Risk, 4*(3), 259–275.

Cuban, L. (1984). *How teachers taught: Constancy and change in American classrooms, 1890–1980*. New York: Longman.

Cuban, L. (1988). A fundamental puzzle of school reform. *Phi Delta Kappan, 69*(5), 341–344.

Cuban, L. (1990). Reforming again, again, and again. *Educational Researcher, 19*(1), 3–13.

Cusick, P.A. (1983). *The egalitarian ideal and the American high school*. New York: Longman.

Eccles, J. (1997). User-friendly science and mathematics: Can it interest girls and minorities in breaking through the middle school wall? In J. Eccles (Ed.), *Minorities and girls in school: Effects on achievement and performance* (pp. 65–104). Thousand Oaks, CA: Sage.

Eccles, J.S., Lord, S., & Midgley, D. (1991). What are we doing to early adolescents? The impact of educational contexts on early adolescents. *American Journal of Education, 99*(4), 521–542.

Edmonds, R. (1984). School effects and teacher effects. *Social Policy, 15*, 37–39.

Ellis, A.K., & Fouts, J.T. (1994). *Research on school restructuring*. Princeton, NJ: Eye on Education.

Elmore, R.F. (1990). On changing the structure of public schools. In R.F. Elmore (Ed.), *Restructuring schools: The next generation of education reform* (pp. 1–28). San Fransico: Jossey-Bass.

Elmore, R.F., & Associates. (1990). *Restructuring schools: The next generation of educational reform.* San Francisco: Jossey-Bass.

Elmore, R.F., Peterson, P.L., & McCarthey, S.J. (1996). *Restructuring in the classroom: Teaching, Learning, & School Organization.* San Francisco: Jossey-Bass.

Ennis, C.D. (1994). Urban secondary teachers' value orientations: Social goals for teaching. *Teaching and Teacher Education, 10*(1), 109–120.

Epstein, J.L. (1990). What matters in the middle grades—Grade span or practices? *Phi Delta Kappan, 7*(6), 438–444.

Epstein, J.L., McPartland, J.M., & MacIver, D.J. (1991). *Hopkins enhancement survey of NELS:88 middle grades practices. Codebook and data collection instruments.* Baltimore, MD: Johns Hopkins University Center for Research on Effective Schooling for Disadvantaged Students.

Esposito, C. (1999). Learning in urban blight: School climate and its effect on the school performance of urban, minority, low-income children. [Special issue, Beginning school ready to learn: Parental involvement and effective educational programs.] *School Psychology Review, 28*(3), 365–377.

Etzioni, A. (1975). *A comparative analysis of complex organizations.* New York: Free Press.

Fennimore, B.S. (2000). *Talk matters: Refocusing the language of public schooling.* New York: Teachers College Press.

Ferguson, R.F. (1998). Can schools narrow the Black-White test score gap? In R.F. Ferguson, *The Black-White test score gap* (pp. 318–374). Washington, DC: Brookings Institution.

Fink, D. (2000). *Good schools/real schools: Why school reform doesn't last.* New York: Teachers College Press.

Firestone, W.A., & Herriot, R.E. (1982). Prescriptions for effective elementary schools don't fit secondary schools. *Educational Leadership, 40*(3), 51–53.

Firestone, W.A., & Rosenblum, S. (1988). Building commitment in urban schools. *Educational Evaluation and Policy Analysis, 10,* 285–300.

Fox, W.F. (1981). Reviewing economics of size in education. *Journal of Education Finance, 6,* 273–296.

French, J.R.P., & Raven. B.H. (1968). Bases of social power. In D. Cartwright & A. Zander (Eds.), *Group dynamics: Research and theory,* (pp. 259–270). New York: Harper and Row.

Fullan, M.G., with Stiegelbauer, S. (1991). *The new meaning of educational change.* New York: Teachers College Press.

Gamoran, A. (1987). The stratification of high school learning opportunties. *Sociology of Education, 60,* 135–155.

Gamoran, A. (1989). Measuring curriculum differentiation. *American Journal of Education, 97,* 129–143.

Gamoran, A. (1997). Curriculum change as a reform strategy: Lessons from the United States and Scotland. *Teachers College Record, 98*(4), 608–628.

Garbarino, J. (1980). Some thoughts on school size and its effects on adolescent development. Journeys in achievement and engagement for early secondary school students. *Sociology of Education, 68*(4), 271–290.

Garet, M.S., & DeLany, B. (1988). Students, courses, and stratification. *Sociology of Education, 61*(2), 61–77.

Gill, S., & Reynolds, A.J. (1999). Educational expectations and school achievement of urban African American children. [Special issue, Schooling and high-risk populations: The Chicago Longitudinal Study.] *Journal of School Psychology, 37*(4), 403–424.

Gooding, R.Z., & Wagner, J.A., III. (1985). A meta-analytic review of the relationships between size and performance: The productivity and efficiency of organizations and their subunits. *Administrative Science Quarterly, 30*, 462–481.

Goodlad, J.I. (1984). *A place called school.* New York: McGraw Hill.

Greene, C.N., & Podsakoff, P.M. (1981). Effects of withdrawal of performance-contingent reward of supervisiory infuence and power. *Academy of Management Journal, 24*, 527–542.

Guiton, G. (1995). Opportunity to learn and conceptions of educational equality. *Educational Evaluation and Policy Analysis, 17*(3), pp. 323–336.

Guthrie, J. (1979). Organizational scale and school success. *Educational Evaluation and Policy Analysis, 1*(1), 17–27.

Haller, E.J., Monk, D.H., Spotted Bear, A., Griffith, J., & Moss, P. (1990). School size and program comprehensiveness: Evidence from High School and Beyond. *Educational Evaluation and Policy Analysis, 12*(2), 109–120.

Hallinan, M.T. (Ed.). (1995). *Restructuring schools: Promising practices and policies.* New York: Plenum.

Hanson, S. (1990). The college-preparatory curriculum across schools: Access to similar learning opportunities? In R. Page & L. Valli (Eds.), *Curriculum differentiation: Interpretative studies in U.S. secondary schools* (pp. 67–90). Albany: State University of New York Press.

Herriott, R.E., & Firestone, W.A. (1984). Two images of schools as organizations: A refinement and elaboration. *Educational Administration Quarterly, 20*, 41–57.

Hoffer, T.B. (1991, August). *The effects of ability grouping in middle school science and mathematics on student achievement.* Paper presented at the annual meeting of the American Sociological Association, Cincinnati, OH.

Imber, J., & Neidt, W.A. (1990). Teachers' participation in school decision making. In P. Reyes (Ed.), *Teachers and their workplace: Commitment, performance, and productivity* (pp. 67–85). Newbury Park, CA: Sage.

Imber, M., & Duke, D.L. (1985). Teacher participation in school decision making: A framework for research. *Journal of Educational Administration, 22*, 24–34.

Ingels, S.J., Abraham, S.Y., Spencer, B.D., & Frankel, M.R. (1989). *National Education Longitudinal Study of 1988. Base year: Student component data file user's manual* (NCES 90-464). Washington, DC: U.S. Department of Education, Office of Educational Research and Improvement.

Ingels, S.J., Dowd, K.W., Baldridge, J.D., Stripe, J.L., Bartot, V.H., & Frankel, M.R. (1994). *National Education Longitudinal Study of 1988. Second follow-up: Student component data file user's manual* (NCES 93-374). Washington, DC: U.S. Department of Education.

Ingels, S.J., Scott, L.A., Lindmark, J.T., Frankel, M.R., & Meyers, S.L. (1992). *National Education Longitudinal Study of 1988. First follow-up: Student component data file user's manual* (NCES 92-030). Washington, DC: U.S. Department of Education, Office of Educational Research and Improvement.

Ivie, S.D. (1998). Ausubel's learning theory: An approach to teaching higher order thinking skills. *High School Journal, 82*(1), 35–42.

Johnson, M.J., & Pajares, F. (1996). When shared decision making works: A 3-year longitudinal study. *American Educational Research Journal, 33*(3), 599–627.

Johnson, S.M. (1990). The primacy and potential of high school departments. In M.W. McLaughlin, J.E. Talbert, & N. Bascia (Eds.), *The contexts of teaching in secondary schools: Teachers' realities* (pp. 167–184). New York: Teachers College Press.

Kelchtermans, G., & Strittmatter, A. (1999). Beyond individual burnout: A perspective for improved schools. Guidelines for the prevention of burnout. In R.Vandenberghe & A.M. Huberman (Eds.), *Understanding and preventing teacher burnout: A sourcebook of international research and practice* (pp. 304–314). New York: Cambridge University Press.

Knapp, M.S., & Shields, P.M. (Eds.). (1990). *Better schooling for children of poverty: Alternatives to conventional wisdom (Vol. II)*. Washington DC: U.S. Department of Education, Office of Planning, Budget, and Evaluation.

Kordalewski, J. (2000). *How teachers and students negotiate learning*. New York: Teachers College Press.

Kozma, R.B., & Croninger, R.G. (1992). Technology and the fate of at-risk students. *Education and Urban Society, 24*, 440–454.

Kruse, S., & Louis, K.S. (1993, April). *An emerging framework for analyzing school based professional community*. Paper presented at the annual meeting of the American Educational Research Association, Atlanta, GA.

Kyle, R.M.J. (1993). *Transforming our schools: Lessons from the Jefferson County Public Schools/Gheen Professional Development Academy 1983–1991*. Louisville, KY: Jefferson County Public Schools.

LeCompte, M.D., & Dworkin, A.G. (1991). *Giving up on school: Student dropout and teacher burnout*. Newbury Park, CA: Corwin Press.

Lee, V.E. (2000). School size and the organization of secondary schools. In M.T. Hallinan (Ed.), *Handbook of the sociology of education* (pp. 327–344). New York: Kluwer/Plenum.

Lee, V.E., & Bryk, A.S. (1988). Curriculum tracking as mediating the social distribution of high school achievement. *Sociology of Education, 61*, 78–94.

Lee, V.E., & Bryk, A.S. (1989). A multilevel model of the social distribution of high school achievement. *Sociology of Education, 62*, 172–192.

Lee, V.E., Bryk, A.S., & Smith, J.B. (1993). The organization of effective secondary schools. In L. Darling-Hammond (Ed.), *Review of Research in Education, 19* (pp. 171–268). Washington, DC: AERA Publ.

Lee, V.E., Dedrick, R.F., & Smith, J.B. (1991). The effect of the social organization of schools on teachers' self-efficacy and satisfaction. *Sociology of Education, 64*, 190–208.

Lee, V.E., Ready, D.D, & Johnson, D.J. (1999, August). *High schools divided into schools-within-schools: Prevalence and design formats.* Paper presented at the annual meeting of the American Sociological Association, Chicago, IL.

Lee, V.E., & Smith, J.B. (1993). Effects of school resructuring on the achievement and engagement of middle-grade students. *Sociology of Education, 66*(3), 164–187.

Lee, V.E., & Smith, J.B. (1995). Effects of high school restructuring and size on early gains in achievement and engagement. *Sociology of Education, 68*(3), 241–270.

Lee, V.E., & Smith, J.B. (1996). Collective responsibility for learning and its effects on gains in achievement for early secondary school students. *American Journal of Education, 104*(2), 103–147.

Lee, V.E., & Smith, J.B. (1997). High school size: Which works best and for whom? *Educational Evaluation and Policy Analysis, 19*(3), 205–227.

Lee, V.E., & Smith, J.B. (1999). Social support and achievement for young adolescents in Chicago: The role of school academic press. *American Educational Research Journal, 36*(4), 907–945.

Lee, V.E., Smith, J.B., & Croninger, R.G. (1997). How high school organization influences the equitable distribution of learing in mathematics and science. *Sociology of Education, 70*, 128–150.

Leonard, L.J., & Leonard, P.E. (1999). Reculturing for collaboration and leadership. *Journal of Educational Research, 92*(4), 237–242.

Levine, D.U. (1988). Teaching thinking skills to at-risk students: Generalizations and speculations. In B.Z. Presseisen (Ed.), *At-risk students and thinking: Perspectives from research* (pp. 117–137). Washington, DC: National Education Association.

Lieberman, A. (1990). *Schools as collaborative cultures: Changing the future now.* New York: Falmer Press.

Lieberman, A. (1995). Restructuring schools: The dynamics of changing practice, structure, and culture. In A. Lieberman (Ed.), *The work of restructuring schools: Building from the ground up* (pp. 1–17). New York: Teachers College Press.

Little, J.W. (1982). Norms of collegiality and experimentation: Workplace conditions of school success. *American Educational Research Journal, 19*, 325–340.

Little, J.W. (1990). The persistence of privacy: Autonomy and initiative in teachers' professional relations. *Teachers College Record, 91*(4), 509–536.

Lortie, D.C. (1975). *Schoolteacher: A sociological study.* Chicago: University of Chicago Press.

Louis, K.S., Marks, H.M., & Kruse, S.D. (1996). Teachers' professional community in restructuring schools. *American Educational Research Journal, 33*(4), 757–798.

Lucas, S.R. (1999). *Tracking inequality: Stratification and mobility in American high schools.* New York: Teachers College Press.

MacIver, D.J., & Epstein, J.L. (1990). *How equal are opportunities for learning in disadvantaged and advantaged middle grades schools?* (Report no. 7). Baltimore, MD: Johns Hopkins University, Center for Research on Effective Schooling for Disadvantaged Students.

MacMullen, M.M. (1996). *Taking stock of a school reform effort: A research collection and analysis.* Providence, RI: Annenberg Institute for School Reform, Brown University.

Maehr, M.L., & Braskamp, L.A. (1986). *The motivation factor: A theory of personal investment*. Lexington, MA: Heath.

McCaslin, M., & Good, T.L. (1992). Compliant cognition: The misalliance of management and instructional goals in current school reform. *Educational Researcher, 21*, 4–17.

McLaughlin, M.W. (1994). Somebody knows my name. In *Issues in Restructuring Schools, 7*, (pp. 9–11). Madison: Center on Organization and Restructuring of Schools, University of Wisconsin.

McNeil, L. (1988). *Contradictions of control: School structure and school knowledge*. New York: Routledge and Kegan Paul.

Metz, M.H. (1993). Teachers' ultimate dependence on their students. In J.W. Little & M.W. McLaughlin (Eds.), *Teachers' work: Individuals, colleagues, and contexts* (pp. 104–136). New York: Teachers College Press.

Miller, L. (1999). Reframing teacher burnout in the context of school reform and teacher development in the United States. In R. Vandenberghe & M.A. Huberman (Eds.), *Understanding and preventing teacher burnout: A sourcebook of international research and practice* (pp. 139–156). New York: Cambridge University Press.

Mintzberg, H. (1983). *Power in and around the organization*. Englewood Cliffs, NJ: Prentice-Hall.

Mohr, N. (2000). Small schools are not miniature large schools: Potential pitfalls and implications for leadership. In W. Ayers, M. Klonsky, & G. Lyon (Eds.), *A simple justice: The challenge of small schools* (pp. 139–158). New York: Teachers College Press.

Mohrman, A.M., Jr., Cooke, R.A., & Mohrman, S.A. (1978). Participation in decision making: A multidimensional perspective. *Educational Administration Quarterly, 14*(1), 13–29.

Moles, O. (1988). *High school and beyond administrator and teacher survey (1984): Data file user's manual*. Washington, DC: Office of Educational Research and Improvement, U.S. Department of Education.

Monk, D., & Haller, E.J. (1993). Predictors of high school academic course offerings: The role of school size. *American Educational Research Journal, 30*, 3–21.

Monk, D.H. (1987). Secondary school size and curriculum comprehensiveness. *Economics of Education, 6*(2), 137–150.

Murphy, J., & Hallinger, P. (Eds.) (1993). *Restructuring schooling: Learning from ongoing efforts*. Newbury Park, CA: Corwin.

National Association of Secondary School Principals. (1996). *Breaking ranks: Changing an American institution*. Reston, VA: Author, in partnership with the Carnegie Foundation for the Advancement of Teaching.

National Commission on Excellence in Education. (1983). *A nation at risk: The imperative for educational reform*. Washington, DC: U.S. Government Printing Office.

Newmann, F.M. (1981). Reducing student alienation in high schools: Implications of theory. *Harvard Educational Review, 51*(4), 546–564.

Newmann, F.M. (1993). Beyond common sense in educational restructuring: The issues of content and linkage. *Educational Researcher, 22*(2), 4–13, 22.

Newmann, F.M., & Associates. (1996). *Authentic achievement: Restructuring schools for intellectual quality*. San Francisco: Jossey-Bass.

Newmann, F.M., Marks, H.M., & Gamoran, A. (1996). Authentic pedagogy and student performance. *American Journal of Education, 104*(4), 280–312.

Newmann, F.M., & Oliver, D.W. (1967). Education and community. *Harvard Educational Review, 37,* 61–106.

Newmann, F.M., Rutter, R.A., & Smith, M.S. (1989). Organizational factors that affect schools' sense of efficacy, community, and expectations. *Sociology of Education, 62,* 221–238.

Newmann, F.M., & Wehlage, G.G. (1995). *Successful school restructuring: A report to the public and educators*. Madison: Center on Organization and Restructuring of Schools, University of Wisconsin–Madison.

Oakes, J. (1985). *Keeping track: How schools structure inequality*. New Haven, CT: Yale University Press.

Oakes, J. (1993). Creating middle schools: Technical, normative, and political considerations. *Elementary School Journal, 33*(5), 461–480.

Oakes, J., Wells, A.S., Jones, M., & Datnow, A. (1997). Detracking: The social construction of ability, cultural politics, and resistance to reform. *Teachers College Record, 98*(3), 482–510.

Oliver, D.W. (1976). *Education and community*. Berkeley, CA: McCutchan.

Oxley, D. (1994). Organizing schools into smaller units: Alternatives to homogeneous grouping. *Phi Delta Kappan, 75,* 521–526.

Oxley, D. (1997). Theory and practice of school communities. *Educational Administration Quarterly, 33,* 624–643.

Perrow, C. (1967). A framework for the comparative analysis of organizations. *American Sociological Review, 32,* 427–452.

Phelan, P., Davidson, A.L., & Yu, H.C. (1998). *Negotiating family, peers, and school*. New York: Teachers College Press.

Plowman, T.S. (1998). The story of closely and loosely coupled organizations. *Journal of Higher Education Policy and Management, 20*(1), 13–18.

Powell, A.G., Farrar, E., & Cohen, D.K. (1985). *The shopping mall high school: Winners and losers in the educational marketplace*. Boston: Houghton Mifflin.

Purkey, S.C., & Smith, M.S. (1983). Effective schools: A review. *The Elementary School Journal, 83*(4), 427–452.

Quality Education for Minorities Project. (1990). *Education that works: An action plan for the education of minorities*. Cambridge, MA: MIT, Author.

Raudenbush, S.W. (1984). Magnitude of teacher expectancy effects on pupil IQ as a function of the credibility of expectancy induction: A synthesis of findings from 18 experiments. *Journal of Educational Psychology, 76*(1), 85–97.

Raudenbush, S.W., Rowan, B., & Cheong, F-Y. (1993). Higher-order instructional goals in secondary schools: Class, teacher, and school influences. *American Educational Research Journal, 30*(3), 523–553.

Ready, D.D., Lee, V.E., & LoGerfo, L.F. (2000, April). *Social and academic stratification in high schools divided into schools-within-schools*. Paper presented at the annual meeting of the American Educational Research Association, New Orleans, LA.

Rock, D.A., & Pollack, J.M. (1995). *Psychometric report for the NELS:88 base year through second follow-up* (NCES 95-382). Washington, DC: U.S. Department of Education, Office of Educational Research and Improvement.

Rogers, C. (1998). Teacher expectations: Implications for school improvement. In D. Child (Ed.), *Directions in educational psychology* (pp. 67–84). London, England: Whurr Publishers, Ltd.

Rosenholtz, S.J. (1987). Education reform strategies: Will they increase teacher commitment? *American Journal of Education, 95,* 534–562.

Rosenholtz, S.J. (1989). *Teachers' workplace: The social organization of schools.* New York: Longman.

Rosenthal, R., & Jacobson, L. (1968). *Pygmalion in the classroom.* New York: Holt, Rinehart and Winston.

Rosenthal, R., & Rosnow, R.L. (1984). *Essentials of behavioral research: Methods and data analysis.* New York: McGraw-Hill.

Roth, W.M., Masciotra, D., & Boyd, N. (1999). Becoming-in-the-classroom: A case study of teacher development through coteaching. *Teaching and Teacher Education, 15*(7), 771–784.

Rowan, B. (1990). Applying conceptions of teaching to organizational reform. In R.F. Elmore et al. (Eds.), *Restructuring schools: The next generation of educational reform* (pp. 31–58). San Francisco: Jossey-Bass.

Schwartz, S.H. (1999). A theory of cultural values and some implications for work. [Special issue, Values and work.] *Applied Psychology: An International Review, 48*(1), 23–47.

Sedlak, M.W., Wheeler, C.W., Pullin, D.C., & Cusick, P.A. (1986). *Selling students short: Classroom bargains and academic reform in the American classroom.* New York: Teachers College Press.

Shedd, J.B., & Bacharach, S.B. (1991). *Tangled hierarchies: Teachers as professionals and the management of schools.* San Francisco: Jossey-Bass.

Shouse, R.C., & Mussoline, L.J. (1999). High risk, low return: The achievement effects of restructuring in disadvantaged schools. *Social Psychology of Education, 3*(4), 245–259.

Simon, H.A. (1976). *Administrative behavior: A study of decision-making processes in administrative organizations* (3rd ed.). New York: Free Press.

Siskin, L.S. (1997). The challenge of leadership in comprehensive high schools: School vision and departmental divisions. *Educational Administrative Quarterly, 33,* 604–623.

Sizer, T.R. (1984). *Horace's compromise: The dilemma of the American high school.* Boston: Houghton Mifflin.

Sizer, T.R. (1992). *Horace's school: Redesigning the American high school.* Boston: Houghton Mifflin.

Sizer, T.R. (1996). *Horace's hope: What works for the American high school.* Boston: Houghton Mifflin.

Slavin, R.E. (1989). PET and the pendulum: Faddism in education and how to stop it. *Phi Delta Kappan, 70*(10), 752–758.

Stahl, S.A. (1999). Why innovations come and go (and mostly go): The case of whole language. *Educational Researcher, 28*(8), 13–22.

Terry, D.J., Hogg, M.A., & Duck, J.M. (1999). Group membership, social identity, and attitudes. In D. Abrams (Ed.), *Social identity and social cognition* (pp. 280–314). Malden, MA: Blackwell.

Tyack, D. (1974). *The one best system*. Cambridge, MA: Harvard University Press.

Tyack, D., & Cuban, L. (1995). *Tinkering toward utopia: A century of public school reform*. Cambridge, MA: Harvard University Press.

Waller, W. (1932). *Sociology of teaching*. New York: Russell and Russell.

Weber, M. (1947). *Theory of social and economic organization* (A.M. Henderson & Talcott Parsons, Trans.). New York: Macmillan.

Weinstein, R.S., Madison, S.M., & Kuklinski, M.R. (1995). Raising expectations in schooling: Obstacles and opportunities for change. *American Educational Research Journal*, 32(1), 121–159.

Westheimer, J. (1998). *Among school teachers: Community, autonomy, and ideology in teachers' work*. New York: Teachers College Press.

Wisconsin Center for Education Research. (1990). *Center on organization and restructuring of schools: Technical application*. Madison: University of Wisconsin.

Wyner, N.B. (1991). *Current perspectives on the culture of schools*. Cambridge, MA: Brookline Books.

Yukl, G.A. (1981). *Leadership in organizations*. Englewood Cliffs, NJ: Prentice-Hall.

Zane, N. (1994). When "discipline problems" recede: Democracy and intimacy in urban charters. In M. Fine (Ed.), *Chartering urban school reform: Reflections on public high schools in the midst of change* (pp. 122–135). New York: Teachers College Press.

APPENDIX A

Details of Construction of All Variables

The empirical analyses described in this book made use of data from the base year (1988), first follow-up (1990), and second follow-up of the National Educational Longitudinal Study of 1988 (NELS:88). Here we describe the composites we constructed, the names of the NELS variables in them, and some important psychometric properties of the composite variables we constructed. We have separated out the variables by the chapters in which they were introduced. If we used variables described earlier in the analyses for subsequent chapters (which was frequently the case), we have not described them again.

CHAPTER 3: VARIABLES

Dependent Measures

ACHIEVEMENT
+ BYTXCOMP—Composite of Reading test and Math test scores.
    Alpha: Reading Test = .84, Mathematics Test = .91

ACADEMIC ENGAGEMENT
Standardized Factor-score using principle components factor analysis:
    Eigenvalue = 2.06; Percent of Variance Explained = 41.2%; Alpha = .64.
+ BYS78A—how often come to class without pencil or paper (recoded to: 0 = usually . . . 3 = never)
+ BYS78B—how often come to class without books (recoded to: 0 = usually . . . 3 = never)
+ BYS78C—how often come to class without homework (recoded to: 0 = usually . . . 3 = never)
+ BYHOMEWK—how many hours per week student spends doing homework
+ BYS73—ever feel bored in school (recoded to: 0 = always . . . 3 = never)

AT-RISK BEHAVIORS
Standardized Factor-score using principle components factor analysis. Factor Eigenvalue = 2.75; Percent of Variance Explained = 39.3%; Alpha = .71. Components:
+ BYS55A—sent to office for misbehaving (coded: 0 = never; 1 = once or twice; 2 = more than twice)
+ BYS55E—parents received warning about my behavior in school (coded: 0 = never; 1 = once or twice; 2 = more than twice)
+ BYS55F—got into a fight with another student (coded: 0 = never; 1 = once or twice; 2 = more than twice)
+ BYS56E—students in class see me as a troublemaker (coded: 0 = never; 1 = somewhat; 2 = very much)
+ BYS75—how often miss school other than illness (recoded to: 0 = none; 1.5 = 1 or 2 days; 3.5 = 3 or 4 days; 7.5 = 5–10 days; 12 = more than 10 days)
+ BYS76—how often cut or skip class (coded: 0 = never; 1 = less then 1 a week; 2 = at least 1 a week; 3 = daily)
+ BYS77—how often come to class late (recoded to: 0 = none; 1.5 = 1 or 2 days; 3.5 = 3 or 4 days; 7.5 = 5–10 days; 12 = more than 10 days)

Measures of School Restructuring

RESTRUCTURING INDEX
A sum of 16 measures, composed of:
+ NOGRPCLS—SCHOOL HAS NO GROUPED ACADEMIC CLASSES
    (1 = yes; 0 = no)
    1 = 164 schools, 16.8%
We first summed the number of classes for which the principal stated homogeneous grouping was used for 8th graders. We then formed a dummy variable such that schools that had 0 total homogeneous classes were 1, others 0.
+ STNTGRP—SCHOOL HAS GT 40% SAMPLED STUDENTS IN NO GROUPED ACADEMIC CLASSES
    (1 = yes; 0 = no)
    1 = 106 schools, 10.6%
We first summed the number of subjects in which the student stated that he or she was not grouped (4 possible). We then formed a dummy variable such that students who had 4 total "not grouped" classes were 1, others 0. We then aggregated this measure to the school level, giving the percent of sampled students in each school who were respectively "not grouped" in all courses. Finally, we made a dummy coded variable, identifying schools that have 40% or more of the sampled students in nongrouped classes.

+ HES23H2—SCHOOL PRESENTLY HAS FLEXIBLE TIME
SCHEDULING
    (1 = yes; 0 = no)
    1 = 191 schools, 21.4%
This measure comes directly from the Hopkins School Enhancement Survey.
+ HES23S2—SCHOOL PRESENTLY HAS SCHOOLS-WITHIN-
SCHOOLS
    (1 = yes; 0 = no)
    1 = 122 schools, 13.8%
This measure comes directly from the Hopkins School Enhancement Survey.
+ TEAMTCH—8th GRADE USES TEAM-TEACHING
    (1 = yes; 0 = no)
    1 = 319 schools, 40.2%
This measure comes from 2 items in the Hopkins School Enhancement Survey,
one referring to interdepartmental team-teaching and the other to depart-
mental team-teaching. Schools that report either of these in use for 8th graders
were coded 1, other schools coded 0.
+ HES23K2—STUDENTS IN SCHOOL HAVE SAME HOMEROOM/
TEACHER ALL MIDDLE GRADE YEARS
    (1 = yes; 0 = no)
    1 = 217 schools, 24.2%
This measure comes directly from the Hopkins School Enhancement Survey.
There were no items referring to other types of teachers maintained for more
than 1 year.
+ HES23I2—SCHOOL PRESENTLY HAS SCHEDULED COMMON
PLANNING TIME FOR DEPARTMENT MEMBERS
    (1 = yes; 0 = no)
    1 = 323 schools, 36.3%
This measure comes directly from the Hopkins School Enhancement Survey.
+ HES23U2—SCHOOL PRESENTLY HAS A STAFF-DEVELOPMENT
PROGRAM
    (1 = yes; 0 = no)
    1 = 421 schools, 57.4%
This measure comes directly from the Hopkins School Enhancement Survey.
+ SEMIDEPT—SCHOOL IS NON- OR SEMI-DEPARTMENTALIZED
    (1 = yes; 0 = no)
    1 = 112 schools, 11.5%
This measure is recoded from three measures from the Hopkins School En-
hancement Survey. The first is a report from the principal on whether the
8th grade is predominantly deparmentalized (different teacher for each
class), self-contained (same teacher for all subjects), or semi-departmentalized (different teacher for some subjects). The second was a report from

the principal about whether the school had formal departments with their own chairs. The third measure taps the number of teachers the average student has (taking out schools that have team-teaching), such that students with 3 or fewer teachers per day were considered in semi-departmentalized schools for 8th graders. To be coded "1" on the final variable, schools had to be coded self-contained or semi-departmentalized on the first measure, have no formal departments from the second measure, and average 3 or fewer teachers on the third. The final measure thus compares non- or semi-departmentalized schools with those with more formalized departmental structures.

+ HES36A—BY POLICY, THIS SCHOOL DOES NOT RETAIN 8TH
   GRADERS
       (1 = yes; 0 = no)
       1 = 91 schools, 12.1%
This measure comes directly from the Hopkins School Enhancement Survey.

+ HES23G2—INTERDISCIPLINARY TEACHERS SHARE THE SAME
   STUDENTS
       (1 = yes; 0 = no)
       1 = 372 schools, 51.2%
This measure comes directly from the Hopkins School Enhancement Survey.

+ KPSMMATE—8TH GRADERS KEEP THE SAME CLASSMATES
   FOR ALL CLASSES
       (1= yes; 0 = no)
       1 = 176 schools, 18.1%
This measure comes from the Hopkins School Enhancement Survey, recoded from HES6C. Students who keep the same classmates for all classes are coded "1"; those who change for some or all classes are coded "0."

+ HES23M2—STUDENTS FROM DIFFERENT GRADE LEVELS ARE
   IN THE SAME CLASSROOM
       (1 = yes; 0 = no)
       1 = 330 schools, 36.8%
This measure comes directly from the Hopkins School Enhancement Survey.

+ HES23L2—8TH-GRADE CLASSES ARE ORGANIZED FOR COOP-
   ERATIVE LEARNING
       (1 = yes; 0 = no)
       1 = 225 schools, 30.9%
This measure comes directly from the Hopkins School Enhancement Survey.

+ HES23O2—8TH GRADERS HAVE EXPLORATORY CLASSES
       (1 = yes; 0 = no)
       1 = 449 schools, 50.1%
This measure comes directly from the Hopkins School Enhancement Survey.

+ SPCPROJ—8TH GRADERS DO SPECIAL PROJECTS AS REGULAR
   PART OF THEIR CURRICULUM

(1 = yes; 0 = no)
1 = 463 schools, 64.3%

This measure combines two items from the Hopkins School Enhancement Survey, measuring if the 8th graders regularly do special projects in English/Social Studies or in Math/Science. The recoding for this variable codes schools that have special projects in any subject as "1," other schools as "0."

The 16 indices are each dummy-coded variables. The operative theory here is that restructured schools have a higher portion of these indices. Thus, the mean for a school reflects the proportion of indices the school has. The variable "RSTRCTD" was made with the mean operator in SPSSX to accommodate missing data. The item alpha is .54, which is higher than the alpha computed for any single item deleted. On average, schools have roughly a quarter of these indices, ranging from 0 to 89%.

Submeasures of Restructuring (from the 16 items listed above)

REDUCED DEPARTMENTALIZATION
Mean of:
+ SEMIDEPT—SCHOOL IS SEMI-DEPARTMENTALIZED
+ LOTCHRS—8TH GRADERS HAVE FEWER THAN 5 TEACHERS A DAY

HETEROGENEOUS GROUPING
Standardized Factor-score using principle components factor analysis:
+ NOGRPCLS—SCHOOL HAS NO GROUPED ACADEMIC CLASSES (Principal's report)
+ STNTGRP—SCHOOL HAS GT 40% SAMPLED STUDENTS IN NO GROUPED ACADEMIC CLASS
+ KPSMMATE—8TH GRADERS KEEP THE SAME CLASSMATES FOR ALL CLASSES
Factor Eigenvalue = 1.62; Percent of Variance Explained = 54.2%; Alpha = .49

TEAM-TEACHING
Standardized Factor-score using principle components factor analysis:
+ HES23H2—SCHOOL HAS FLEXIBLE TIME SCHEDULING
+ TEAMTCH—8TH GRADE USES TEAM-TEACHING
+ HES23I2—SCHOOL HAS SCHEDULED COMMON PLANNING TIME FOR DEPARTMENT MEMBERS
+ HES23G2—INTERDISCIPLINARY TEACHERS SHARE THE SAME STUDENTS
Factor Eigenvalue = 1.65; Percent of Variance Explained = 55.0%; Alpha = .65

Controls for Student Background

SOCIOECONOMIC STATUS
+   BYSES—socioeconomic status composite

MINORITY STATUS
+   RACE—student race (recoded to: 0 = white or Asian; 1 = Black,
    Hispanic, or Native American)

GENDER
+   BYS12—student gender (recoded to: 0 = male; 1 = female)

ACADEMIC BACKGROUND
Average of:
+   BYGRADS—composite of self-reported grades for science, math,
    English, and social science
+   BYP44—parent report of whether student was ever held back (recoded
    to: 0 = yes; 1 = no)

Controls for School Demographics

AVERAGE SOCIOECONOMIC STATUS
+   BYSES—socioeconomic status (SES) composite, aggregated to the
    school level

MINORITY CONCENTRATION
+   RACE—student race (recoded to: 0 = white or Asian; 1 = Black,
    Hispanic, or Native American), aggregated to the school level, and
    recoded to a dichotomous variable (recoded to: 1 = 40% or more, 0 =
    less than 40% minority)

STANDARD DEVIATION OF ACHIEVEMENT
We aggregated the NELS:88 composite achievement measure BYTXCOMP
using the standard deviation operator in SPSSX to the school level. This process generated the standard deviation of achievement across all sampled students per school for each school.

SECTOR
Four levels of "school sector" were measured: public, Catholic, independent,
and other private schools from the G8CTRLP variable on the NELS:88 privileged data. We dropped schools and students attending other private schools,

but made dummy-coded measures of Catholic and independent schools, using public schools as the comparison group.

SIZE

We focused on the size of the 8th grade (G8ENROL), given on the NELS:88 privileged data file (the number of students in the 8th grade). As the distribution of this variable was positively skewed, we transformed the variable (natural logarithm) and restandardized it to mean (M) = 0 , SD = 1.

CHAPTER 4: ADDITIONAL VARIABLES

Dependent Measures

ACHIEVEMENT GAINS

+ F1TXMG—Mathematics IRT-estimated gain between 8th and 10th grade
+ F1TXRG—Reading IRT-estimated gain between 8th and 10th grade
+ F1TXHG—History IRT-estimated gain between 8th and 10th grade
+ F1TXSG—Science IRT-estimated gain between 8th and 10th grade

10TH-GRADE ACADEMIC ENGAGEMENT

Standardized factor-weighted composite (M = 0, SD = 1) of 8 items measuring student behaviors (related to their current courses). Composite created using principle components factor analysis. Item coding reflects students' assessment of the frequency with which they engage in each behavior, coded from 1 (never) to 5 (every day). Internal consistency (Cronbach's alpha) = .84. Factor eigenvalue = 3.76, percent of total variance in all items explained by the factor = 47.1. NELS student item components are:

+ F1S27A—OFTEN WORK HARD IN MATH CLASS
+ F1S27B—OFTEN WORK HARD IN ENGLISH CLASS
+ F1S27C—OFTEN WORK HARD IN HISTORY CLASS
+ F1S27D—OFTEN WORK HARD IN SCIENCE CLASS
+ F1S28A—OFTEN FEEL CHALLENGED IN MATH CLASS
+ F1S28B—OFTEN FEEL CHALLENGED IN ENGLISH CLASS
+ F1S28C—OFTEN FEEL CHALLENGED IN HISTORY CLASS
+ F1S28D—OFTEN FEEL CHALLENGED IN SCIENCE CLASS

Measures of School Restructuring

RESTRUCTURING MEASURES

Two dummy-coded items were created, using the variables in Table 4.1 and the method described in Lee and Smith (1995). Measures were drawn from items in the NELS first follow-up school file, where principals reported whether their schools engaged in each of a set of 30 school practices. Using those reports, we created two measures:

+ NO REFORM PRACTICES: Schools that engaged in no reform practices coded 1, schools classified as those with traditional reforms coded 0.
+ RESTRUCTURING PRACTICES: Schools that engaged in at least three practices listed at restructured in Table 1 were coded 1, schools classified as those with traditional reforms coded 0.

SCHOOL SIZE
+ F1C2 TOTAL ENROLLMENT AS OF OCTOBER 1989
  Principal's report of high school size (on NELS restricted school file) was transformed to its natural logarithm and standardized (M = 0, SD = 1).

Controls for Student Background

SOCIOECONOMIC STATUS
+ F1SES—socioeconomic status composite

MINORITY STATUS
+ F1RACE—student race (recoded to: 0 = white or Asian; 1 = black, Hispanic, or Native American)

GENDER
+ F1SEX Student gender (recoded to: 0 = male; 1 = female)

ACADEMIC CONTROLS
Analyses included different controls for each curriculum area. Controls were constructed as follows:
+ For math gain: Z-score of sum of BYTXRIRS, BYTXHIRS, BYTXSIRS
+ For reading gain: Z-score of sum of BYTXMIRS, BYTXHIRS, BYTXSIRS
+ For history gain: Z-score of sum of BYTXRIRS, BYTXMIRS, BYTXSIRS
+ For science gain: Z-score of sum of BYTXRIRS, BYTXHIRS, BYTXMIRS

ENGAGEMENT CONTROL
The same variable as the engagement outcome in Chapter 3.

Controls for School Demographics and Structure

AVERAGE SOCIOECONOMIC STATUS
+ AVSES—SES composite, aggregated to the school level

MINORITY CONCENTRATION
+ F1RACE—student race (recoded to: 0 = white or Asian; 1 = Black, Hispanic, or Native American), aggregated to the school level, and recoded to: 1 = 40% or more, 0 = less than 40% minority

ACADEMIC EMPHASIS
Summed 10th graders' reports of course taking in academic courses in mathematics and science:
+ F1S22C—HOW MUCH COURSEWORK IN ALGEBRA I
+ F1S22D—HOW MUCH COURSEWORK IN GEOMETRY
+ F1S22E—HOW MUCH COURSEWORK IN ALGEBRA II
+ F1S22F—HOW MUCH COURSEWORK IN TRIGONOMETRY
+ F1S22G—HOW MUCH COURSEWORK IN PRE-CALCULUS
+ F1S22H—HOW MUCH COURSEWORK IN CALCULUS
+ F1S23C—HOW MUCH COURSEWORK IN BIOLOGY
+ F1S23E—HOW MUCH COURSEWORK IN CHEMISTRY
+ F1S22F—HOW MUCH COURSEWORK IN PHYSICS
Variable was then aggregated to the school level as a school mean, and standardized (M = 0 , SD = 1).

VARIABILITY IN COURSE TAKING
The sum of students' course taking (academic emphasis, described above) was aggregated to the school level, using the standard deviation operator in SPSSX. Variable was standardized (M = 0, SD = 1).

SECTOR
Created from G10CTRL2, the school control measure on the NELS first follow-up restricted school file. Public, Catholic, and NAIS schools were retained; other private schools were dropped. Created 2 dummy-coded variables:
+ CATHOLIC—coded 1 for Catholic, 0 for public, NAIS schools
+ NAIS—coded 1 for NAIS, 0 for public, Catholic schools

CHAPTER 5: ADDITIONAL VARIABLES

Dependent Measures

ACHIEVEMENT GAINS
Identical to those used in Chapter 4.

Measures of Professional Community

COLLECTIVE RESPONSIBILITY FOR LEARNING
Standardized factor-weighted composite (M = 0, SD = 1) was created from 12 items completed by teachers. Items (6–level) coded with "strongly agree" = 6, "strongly disagree" = 1. Constructed using principle components factor analysis. Factor eigenvalue = 3.39; percent of total variance in all items explained by factor = 28.4. At the teacher level, internal consistency (Cronbach's alpha) = .77. Factor was aggregated to the school level, and restandardized. NELS teacher-level item components (in order of factor weights) are:

+ F1T4_5E—LITTLE I CAN DO TO ENSURE HIGH ACHIEVEMENT (REV)
+ F1T4_5A—I CAN GET THROUGH TO THE MOST DIFFICULT STUDENT
+ F1T4_5D—DIFFERENT METHODS CAN AFFECT A STUDENT'S ACHIEVEMENT
+ F1T4_5F—TEACHERS MAKE A DIFFERENCE IN STUDENTS' LIVES
+ F1T4_2J—IT IS A WASTE OF TIME TO DO MY BEST AT TEACHING (REV)
+ F1T4_5B—TEACHERS RESPONSIBLE KEEP STUDENTS FROM DROPPING OUT
+ F1T4_2N—STUDENT ATTITUDES REDUCE ACADEMIC SUCCESS (REV)
+ F1T4_11F—WORK TO CREATE LESSONS STUDENTS WILL ENJOY LEARNING
+ F1T4_1D—STUDENTS' SUCCESS OR FAILURE DUE TO FACTORS BEYOND ME (REV)
+ F1T4_1I—STUDENTS INCAPABLE OF LEARNING THE MATERIAL (REV)
+ F1T4_5C—I CHANGE MY APPROACH IF STUDENTS AREN'T DOING WELL
+ F1T4_1E—STUDENT MISBEHAVIOR INTERFERES WITH MY TEACHING (REV)

VARIABILITY IN COLLECTIVE RESPONSIBILITY FOR LEARNING
Standard deviation of the factor described above, computed within each school.

AVERAGE TEACHER CONTROL
A standardized factor-weighted composite (M = 0, SD = 1) was created from 9 items completed by teachers. Items (6–level) coded "no control (or influ-

ence)" = 1, "complete control (or influence)" = 6. Composite formed using principle components factor analysis, with loadings ranging from .68 to .54. At the teacher level, internal consistency (Cronbach's alpha) = .76, eigenvalue = 3.12. Percent of total variance in all items explained by this factor = 34.6. Factor was aggregated to the school level, and restandardized. NELS teacher-level item components (in order of factor weights) are:

+ F1T2_17B—TEACHER'S CONTROL OVER CONTENT OF WHAT IS TAUGHT
+ F1T4_9D—DEGREE OF INFLUENCE OVER ESTABLISHING THE CURRICULUM
+ F1T2_17C—TEACHER'S CONTROL OVER TEACHING TECHNIQUES
+ F1T2_17E—TEACHER'S CONTROL OVER AMOUNT OF HOMEWORK ASSIGNED
+ F1T4_9C—DEGREE OF INFLUENCE OVER GROUPING STUDENTS BY ABILITY
+ F1T2_17A—TEACHER'S CONTROL OVER TEXTS AND MATERIALS USED
+ F1T2_17D—TEACHER'S CONTROL OVER DISCIPLINING STUDENTS
+ F1T4_9A—DEGREE OF INFLUENCE OVER DISCIPLINE POLICY
+ F1T4_9B—DEGREE OF INFLUENCE OVER IN-SERVICE PROGRAMS

AVERAGE STAFF COOPERATION
Standardized factor-weighted composite (M = 0, SD = 1) was created from 14 items completed by teachers. Items (6–level) coded with "strongly agree" = 6, "strongly disagree" = 1. Constructed using principle components factor analysis, with loadings ranging from .75 to .44. At the teacher level, internal consistency (Cronbach's alpha) = .87. Factor eigenvalue = 4.37; percent of total variance in all items explained by factor = 38.4. Factor was aggregated to the school level, and restandardized. NELS teacher-level item components (in order of factor weights) are:

+ F1T4_2M—PRINCIPAL CONSULTS STAFF BEFORE MAKING DECISIONS AFFECTING THEM
+ F1T4_1P—ADMINISTRATION KNOWS PROBLEMS FACED BY STAFF
+ F1T4_1B—CAN USUALLY COUNT ON STAFF MEMBERS TO HELP OUT
+ F1T4_2H—THIS SCHOOL SEEMS LIKE A BIG FAMILY
+ F1T4_2K—PRINCIPAL INTERESTED IN INNOVATION, NEW IDEAS
+ F1T4_2F—BROAD AGREEMENT AMONG FACULTY ABOUT SCHOOL MISSION

+ F1T4_2E—GREAT DEAL OF COOPERATIVE EFFORT AMONG STAFF
+ F1T4_1Q—I AM ENCOURAGED TO EXPERIMENT WITH MY TEACHING
+ F1T4_2I—PRINCIPAL LETS STAFF KNOW WHAT IS EXPECTED OF THEM
+ F1T4_2C—TEACHERS AT THIS SCHOOL ARE CONTINUALLY LEARNING
+ F1T4_1C—COLLEAGUES SHARE BELIEFS ABOUT THE SCHOOL'S MISSION
+ F1T4_1L—STAFF MEMBERS ARE RECOGNIZED FOR A JOB WELL DONE
+ F1T4_2Q—TEACHERS' UNION AND ADMINISTRATION WORK TOGETHER
+ F1T4_2P—FAMILIAR WITH CONTENT OF OTHER COURSES IN MY DEPARTMENT

Controls for Student Background

The same set of controls used in Chapter 4 (SES, minority status, gender, the academic controls, and 8th-grade engagement) was used here. An added control was:

CURRICULUM TRACK PLACEMENT
+ F1S20—Present high school program. Three categories created, measuring track placement in the college preparatory or academic program, the general program, or any of several vocational programs. Two dummy variables created, contrasting (1) academic track placement and (2) vocational track placement separately with placement in the general track.

Controls for School Demographics and Structure

The analyses in Chapter 5 included several of the same controls used in Chapter 4 (average school SES, minority concentration, school sector, and school size). In addition, we included the following controls at the school level:

AVERAGE ABILITY LEVEL
+ BYTXCOMP—STANDARDIZED TEST COMPOSITE (READING, MATH). Test-score composite for sample students as 8th graders, aggregated to the high-school level. On full student sample, composite

was standardized by NELS at M = 50, SD = 10. On this sample, the aggregated achievement scores have M = 51.78, SD = 5.43.

PERCENT OF STUDENTS IN ACADEMIC TRACK
+   F1C11B—PERCENT OF 10TH-GRADE STUDENTS IN COLLEGE PREPARATORY ACADEMIC PROGRAM. Principal's report on NELS restricted file (M = 44.55, SD = 28.66).

CHAPTER 6: ADDITIONAL VARIABLES

Dependent Measures

+   F22XMIRR—Mathematics IRT-estimated number right (12th grade)
+   F22XSIRR—Science IRT-estimated number right (12th grade)

Controls for Student Background

We used the same set of student background measures as in Chapters 4 and 5 (SES, minority status, gender, and engagement). We also included the following controls:

ACHIEVEMENT
+   Z-score of sum of BY2XRIRS, BY2XHIRS, BY2XMIRS (8th-grade measures)

COURSE TAKING IN MATHEMATICS AND SCIENCE EARLY IN HIGH SCHOOL
For modeling science gains between 8th and 10th grade (Outcomes 1 and 2), we summed 10th graders' self-reports of course taking in mathematics and science. Variables coded 0 = none; 1 = 0.5 to 1 year; 2 = 1.5 to 2 years. Thus, the sum represents numbers of semesters of mathematics and science coursework. For the HLM analyses, variable was z-scored (M = 0, SD = 1).
+   F1S22B—HOW MUCH COURSEWORK IN PRE-ALBEBRA
+   F1S22C—HOW MUCH COURSEWORK IN ALGEBRA I
+   F1S22D—HOW MUCH COURSEWORK IN GEOMETRY
+   F1S22E—HOW MUCH COURSEWORK IN ALGEBRA II
+   F1S22F—HOW MUCH COURSEWORK IN TRIGONOMETRY
+   F1S22G—HOW MUCH COURSEWORK IN PRE-CALCULUS
+   F1S22H—HOW MUCH COURSEWORK IN CALCULUS
+   F1S23B—HOW MUCH COURSEWORK IN PHYSICAL SCIENCE
+   F1S23C—HOW MUCH COURSEWORK IN BIOLOGY
+   F1S23E—HOW MUCH COURSEWORK IN CHEMISTRY

+ F1S22F—HOW MUCH COURSEWORK IN PRINCIPLES OF
  TECHNOLOGY
+ F1S23G—HOW MUCH COURSEWORK IN PHYSICS
+ F1S22H—HOW MUCH COURSEWORK IN OTHER SCIENCE

*COURSETAKING IN MATHEMATICS AND SCIENCE OVER 4 HIGH
SCHOOL YEARS*
For modeling gains between 10th and 12th grade (Outcomes 3 and 4), we
summed several variables, each of which measured the number of Carnegie
units (a year-long course) in several courses over high school from students'
transcripts. The summed variable was then aggregated to the school level as a
school mean. For HLM analyses, the aggregate was z-scored ($M = 0$, $SD = 1$).
+ F2RAL1_C—CARNEGIE UNITS IN ALGEBRA I
+ F2RAL2_C—CARNEGIE UNITS IN ALGEBRA II
+ F2RGEO_C—CARNEGIE UNITS IN GEOMETRY
+ F2RTRI_C—CARNEGIE UNITS IN TRIGONOMETRY
+ F2RPRE_C—CARNEGIE UNITS IN PRE-CALCULUS
+ F2RCAL_C—CARNEGIE UNITS IN CALCULUS
+ F2REAR_C—CARNEGIE UNITS IN EARTH SCIENCE
+ F2RBIO_C—CARNEGIE UNITS IN BIOLOGY
+ F2RCHE_C—CARNEGIE UNITS IN CHEMISTRY
+ F2RPHY_C—CARNEGIE UNITS IN PHYSICS
+ F2ROSC_C—CARNEGIE UNITS IN OTHER SCIENCE COURSES

Variables Measured on Schools

We included the same controls for school demography and structure used in
Chapters 4 and 5 (average school SES, minority concentration, sector, and size).
We also used the same school restructuring contrasts used in Chapter 4. In
addition, we used the following measures of school organization:

COLLECTIVE RESPONSIBILITY FOR LEARNING
This is identical to the measure we used in Chapter 5.

AVERAGE ACADEMIC COURSE TAKING IN MATH AND SCIENCE
Aggregated from student reports of course taking, described above and
z-scored ($M = 0$, $SD = 1$).

VARIABILITY IN MATHEMATICS, SCIENCE COURSE TAKING
Standard deviation of student course taking in each school, from transcripts.
Variable was standardized ($M = 0$, $SD = 1$).

ACADEMIC PRESS
Variables, from reports by school principals, were combined into a composite, formed with principal components factor analysis and z-scored ($M = 0$, $SD = 1$). Reliability (Cronbach's alpha) of .81.
+ F1C93G—STUDENT MORALE IS HIGH
+ F1C93D—TEACHERS PRESS STUDENTS TO ACHIEVE
+ F1C93F—TEACHER MORALE IS HIGH
+ F1C93B—STUDENTS PLACE HIGH PRIORITY ON LEARNING
+ F1C93E—STUDENTS ARE EXPECTED TO DO HOMEWORK

AUTHENTIC INSTRUCTION IN MATHEMATICS AND SCIENCE
Details on the Rasch modeling methods used to construct this measure are available from the authors. Items in the four categories listed below were drawn from teacher and student reports about instruction in each subject at first NELS follow-up.

SCIENCE ITEMS FROM STUDENTS

+ F1S29G—HOW OFTEN DESIGN AND CONDUCT OWN EXPERIMENTS, PROJECT
+ F1S29F—HOW OFTEN MAKE UP OWN SCIENTIFIC PROBLEM, ANALYTIC METHOD
+ F1S29B—HOW OFTEN CHOOSE OWN SCIENTIFIC PROBLEM TO STUDY
+ F1S29M—HOW OFTEN DISCUSS CAREER OPPORTUNITIES IN SCIENCE, TECHNOLOGY
+ F1S29D—HOW OFTEN WRITE REPORTS OF LAB OR PRACTICAL WORK
+ F1S29N—HOW OFTEN WATCH TEACHER DEMONSTRATE OR LEAD IN EXPERIMENT
+ F1S29E—HOW OFTEN USE BOOK OR WRITTEN INSTRUCTIONS TO DO EXPERIMENTS
+ F1S29C—HOW OFTEN COPY TEACHERS' NOTES FROM BLACKBOARD
+ F1S29L—HOW OFTEN LISTEN TO TEACHER LECTURE IN CLASS

MATHEMATICS ITEMS FROM STUDENTS

+ F1S32E—HOW OFTEN USE COMPUTERS
+ F1S32F—HOW OFTEN USE HANDS-ON MATERIALS OR MODELS

+ F1S32B—HOW OFTEN USE BOOKS OTHER THAN MATH TEXTBOOK
+ F1S32H—HOW OFTEN PARTICIPATE IN STUDENT-LED DIS-CUSSIONS
+ F1S32I—HOW OFTEN EXPLAIN MATH WORK ORALLY
+ F1S32G—HOW OFTEN USE CALCULATORS
+ F1S32D—HOW OFTEN DO STORY PROBLEMS OR PROBLEM-SOLVING ACTIVITIES
+ F1S32C—HOW OFTEN COPY TEACHERS' NOTES FROM BLACKBOARD
+ F1S32A—HOW OFTEN REVIEW YESTERDAY'S WORK

Mathematics Items from Teachers

+ F1T2_18H—HAVE STUDENTS GIVE ORAL REPORTS
+ F1T2_18E—HAVE STUDENT-LED WHOLE GROUP DISCUS-SIONS
+ F1T2_18F—HAVE STUDENTS WORK IN SMALL GROUPS
+ F1T2_18C—USE WHOLE-GROUP DISCUSSION
+ F1T2_18G—HAVE STUDENTS COMPLETE INDIVIDUAL AS-SIGNMENTS IN CLASS
+ F1T2_18D—HAVE STUDENTS RESPOND ORALLY TO QUES-TIONS

Science Items from Teachers

+ F1T2_18H—HAVE STUDENTS GIVE ORAL REPORTS
+ F1T2_18E—HAVE STUDENT-LED WHOLE GROUP DISCUS-SIONS
+ F1T2_18F—HAVE STUDENTS WORK IN SMALL GROUPS
+ F1T2_18C—USE WHOLE-GROUP DISCUSSION
+ F1T2_18G—HAVE STUDENTS COMPLETE INDIVIDUAL AS-SIGNMENTS IN CLASS
+ F1T2_18D—HAVE STUDENTS RESPOND ORALLY TO QUESTIONS

VARIABILITY IN AUTHENTIC INSTRUCTION
The standard deviation of the Rasch-constructed measure of authentic in-struction in each school. Variable was standardized (M = 0, SD = 1).

CHAPTER 7: ADDITIONAL VARIABLES

Dependent Measures

ACHIEVEMENT GAINS
Mathematics gain between 8th and 12th grades was constructed as a simple difference in scores between:
+ BY2XMIRR—Mathematics IRT-estimated number right (8th grade)
+ F22XMIRR—Mathematics IRT-estimated number right (12th grade)
Reading gain between 8th and 12th grades was constructed as a simple difference in scores between:
+ BY2XRIRR—Reading IRT-estimated number right (8th grade)
+ F22XRIRR—Reading IRT-estimated number right (12th grade)

School Size

SCHOOL SIZE
+ F1C2 TOTAL ENROLLMENT AS OF OCTOBER 1989
  Principal's report of high school size (on NELS restricted school file).
+ School size categories (300 and below, 301–600, 601–900; 901–1,200, 1,201–1,500, 1,501–1,800, 1,801–2,100, over 2,100) were constructed from F1C2.
+ Two piecewise size terms were computed as follows. First, enrollment was centered at 900 students (i.e., 900 was subtracted from each school's enrollment size). The first linear term, representing smaller schools, was continuous up to 0 and coded 0 thereafter. The second term, representing larger schools, was coded 0 for all schools smaller than 900 (the breakpoint) and continuous thereafter.

Controls for Student Background

SOCIOECONOMIC STATUS
+ F2SES1—socioeconomic status z-scored composite.

MINORITY STATUS
+ F2RACE1—student race (recoded to: 0 = white or Asian; 1 = black, Hispanic, or Native American).

GENDER
+ F2SEX—student gender (recoded to: 0 = male; 1 = female).

ACADEMIC CONTROLS

Analyses included different controls for the two curriculum areas. Controls were constructed as follows:

+ For math gain: z-score of sum of BYTXRIRS, BYTXHIRS, BYTXSIRS
+ For reading gain: z-score of sum of BYTXMIRS, BYTXHIRS, BYTXSIRS
+ BYS77—HOW OFTEN COME TO CLASS LATE (REVERSED)

Controls for School Demographics and Structure

Same controls for school demographic (average school SES, minority concentration, and school sector) used in Chapter 6.

APPENDIX B

A Brief Description of Some Hierarchical Linear Models

We recognize that not all readers of this book are familiar with the hierarchical linear modeling methodology, which we used extensively. For these readers, we provide a brief exposition of some simplified models that address research questions in Chapters 4 and 5. More detail on the methodology is provided by Bryk and Raudenbush (1992) in their now-classic text on this method and in the Lee and Smith articles (1995, 1996).

CHAPTER 4: STRUCTURE OF TYPICAL HLM

Within-school Models

A simple form of hierarchical linear models (HLM) used in Chapter 4 consists of two equations, a within- and a between-school model. Some of the parameters estimated in the within-school model become outcomes to be explained in between-school equations. One within-school model investigated the gain in mathematics achievement of student i in school j, Y_{ij}, as a function of student background characteristics, X_{ij}'s (the X-variables considered here were ability, engagement, SES, minority status, and gender), and random error, R_{ij}:

$$Y_{ij} = \beta_{j0} + \beta_{j1}X_{ij1} + \beta_{j2}X_{ij2} + \ldots + \beta_{jk}X_{ijk} + R_{ij}.$$

The β_{jk} regression coefficients are structural relations occurring within school j that indicate how achievement in each school is distributed across the measured student characteristics. In the HLM models investigated here, we were particularly interested in two β parameters:

β_{0j} = the average gain in mathematics for students in school j; and

β_{1j} = the relationship between SES and math gain in school j.

We refer to this as the SES-math learning slope.

While the other β parameters (i.e., distributional effects) were also estimated in our HLM analyses, we were not interested in modeling these parameters as functions of school characteristics. As such, the other within-school controls (ability, engagement, minority status, and gender) were *fixed* in our HLM models. This means that we "fixed" the between-school variability in these other β parameters to 0 (i.e., they did not vary randomly between schools). On the other hand, variance in β_{oj} and β_{1j} was "free" to vary between schools.

Between-school Models

In the second set of equations, we modeled the random-effects β parameters, adjusted for student characteristics, as functions of school-level characteristics (W-variables). We estimated a single between-school model for each outcome, estimating the effects of the three restructuring components on the outcomes (β_0 and β_1 for each outcome). For each model, we also adjusted for the potentially confounding effects of school structure and demographics. A typical between-school model is as follows:

$$\gamma_{jk} = \gamma_{0k} + \gamma_{1k}W_{1j} + \gamma_{2k}W_{2j} + \ldots + \gamma_{pk}W_{pj} + U_{jk}.$$

The parameters of interest here were the effects associated with the school restructuring variables, W_{1j}—the γ_{pk} coefficients. Since the error terms in this equation are complex, conventional linear model techniques cannot be used. However, recent developments in statistical theory and computation, available through the HLM software, make this estimation possible. Briefly, the total variance in each outcome is partitioned into two components: parameter and error variance. It is only effects on the *parameter variance* that are estimated in HLM. This is an important development, since it is only variability in the structural parameters, $Var(\beta_{jk})$, that can be explained by school factors. In general, previous efforts to estimate school effects with ordinary least squares regression have systematically underestimated school effects for this reason.

CHAPTER 5: STRUCTURE OF A TYPICAL HLM

Within-school Models

Similar to Chapter 4, one within-school model investigated the gain in mathematics achievement of student *i* in school *j*, Y_{ij}, as a function of student background characteristics, X_{ij}'s (the X-variables considered here were ability, engagement, SES, minority status, and gender), and random error, R_{ij}:

$$Y_{ij} + \beta_{j0} + \beta_{j1}X_{ij1} + \beta_{j2}X_{ij2} + \ldots + \beta_{jk}X_{ijk} + R_{ij}.$$

In the HLM models investigated in Chapters 4 and 5, we were particularly interested in two β parameters:

β_{0j} = the average gain in mathematics for students in school j; and
β_{1j} = the relationship between SES and math gain in school j.

We refer to this as the SES-math learning slope. The other within-school controls (ability, track placement, engagement, minority status, and gender) were *fixed* in our HLM models.

Between-school Models

In the second set of equations, we modeled the random-effect β parameters, adjusted for student characteristics, as functions of school-level characteristics (W-variables). We estimated a single between-school model for each outcome, estimating simultaneously the effects of the four measures of professional community. Because these are school-level variables, the W_{jk} parameters associated with these four measures of professional community are of interest. As before, we also adjusted for the potentially confounding effects of school structure and demographics.

Index

About the Authors

Valerie E. Lee is a Professor of Education at the University of Michigan and a Faculty Associate at the University's Institute for Social Research. She earned her bachelor's degree in chemistry from Stanford University in 1959 and worked as a chemist, as well as a teacher of mathematics and science in U.S. and international schools. She earned her master's (1981) and doctoral (1985) degrees from the Harvard Graduate School of Education, specializing in Administration, Planning, and Social Policy, and received a two-year fellowship at the Educational Testing Service. Lee is a co-author (with Anthony S. Bryk and Peter B. Holland) of *Catholic Schools and the Common Good* (Harvard University Press, 1993), which was awarded the 1994 Willard Waller Award from the American Sociological Association. Lee was a fellow at the Rockefeller Foundation's Bellagio (Italy) Study Center in 1993. Her many studies have used both qualitative and quantitative methods to investigate school organization, educational equity, and school-based social capital. These interests have motivated recent studies of high schools divided into schools-within-schools and the contextual elements of early childhood settings that are favorable to children living in poverty. She was a lead researcher at the Center for the Organization and Restructuring of Schools at the University of Wisconsin (1990–95) and is now associated with the Annenberg Study Project and the Consortium for Chicago School Research at the University of Chicago.

Julia B. Smith is an Associate Professor at Oakland Univerity in Rochester, Michigan. She received a B.A. in Education, an M.S. in Mathematics, and an Ed.D. in Education from the University of Michigan, where Valerie Lee was her thesis advisor and frequent research collaborator. A former high-school math teacher, she has also taught community college students, Ford auto workers, football players, and graduate students at the University of Rochester and Western Michigan University. Her studies of school reform have been published in *Sociology of Education*, *Educational Evaluation and Policy Analysis*, and the *Journal of Educational Research*, among others.

WE WILL
ALWAYS LIVE IN
BEVERLY HILLS

WE WILL ALWAYS LIVE IN
BEVERLY HILLS

Growing Up Crazy in Hollywood

NED WYNN

William Morrow and Company, Inc.
New York

This book is dedicated to the memory of Ed Wynn and Keenan Wynn and to my loving mother, Evie

Acknowledgments and thanks to Lisa Bankoff, Ben Benjamin, Casey Coleman, Donna Cook, Michael Georgiades, Phil Goldberg, Jath Hathaway, Lisa Henricksson, Bob Horrigan, Evie Johnson, Schuyler Johnson, Doug Tibbles, Steven Ujlaki, Jann Wenner, Tracy Wynn, and Adrian Zackheim.

Copyright © 1990 by Ned Wynn

Recognizing the importance of preserving what has been written, it is the policy of William Morrow and Company, Inc., and its imprints and affiliates to have the books it publishes printed on acid-free paper, and we exert our best efforts to that end.

Library of Congress Cataloging-in-Publication Data

Wynn, Ned.
    We will always live in Beverly Hills : growing up crazy in Hollywood / Ned Wynn.
        p.   cm.
    ISBN 0-688-08509-1
    1. Wynn, Keenan, 1916–1986. 2. Wynn, Ned. 3. Motion picture actors and actresses—United States—Biography. 4. Fathers and sons—United States—Biography. I. Title.
PN2287.W9W96 1990
791.43'028'092—dc20
[B]   90-37030
                                                                      CIP

Printed in the United States of America

First Edition

1 2 3 4 5 6 7 8 9 10

BOOK DESIGN BY MARSHA COHEN

If all my words were stars on silver strings
Or oceanic jewels, or from the well
Of my heart's blood, there are some things
Of which I could not tell, could never tell.

I could not tell how autumn sadness stirs
Sere memories and balked desires half knowing,
Or how the summer moon, behind old firs
Smiles secretly, triumphant and alone.

Or, how far mountains move majestically
In evening shadows when the embers die,
Or why night is still, or of the fire,
High tumult of the wild geese in the sky.

Or where dead leaves go, or the leaves that blow
Down drifting winds to other lands than these,
Of summer isles and silent snow
And dim disasters under sullen seas.

Least could I tell you what is in my mind,
Seeing your face on mist I half forget,
Half hope, remembering the wind
Stirring your hair of old regret.

—SHERRY ABBOTT
"Autumn"

It was 5:55 in the morning. I was standing in front of Westward Ho market on San Vicente Boulevard. I had dragged myself to the market because I needed a drink. Just a couple of nice cold beers to put out the fire in my stomach, and a little half-pint of tequila to still the rockslide in my head. That is all I needed. The market opened at six, and I was there five minutes early, just in case my watch was slow.

At six sharp a white-haired man got out of his car in the parking lot and joined me at the door to the market. He was wearing a bathrobe, was unshaven and bleary-eyed and needed a drink as much as I did. He looked me up and down. Even a smile hurt. I squinted at him. It was a real effort to speak. So I didn't.

The manager opened the door and we went inside. We both padded softly to the liquor shelves, pulled down our favorite medicines, paid, and left. On the way out the older man turned to me. "Give us a call, huh, son? We'd love to see you."

"Sure, Pop," I said. I watched my father return to his car. He waved. I waved. He drove off. I slipped back to my apartment as swiftly and smoothly as possible, holding the bottles gingerly, as if they were condor eggs. We both knew I wouldn't call.